Mary Norton of New Jersey

Mary Norton of New Jersey

Congressional Trailblazer

David L. Porter

FAIRLEIGH DICKINSON UNIVERSITY PRESS
Madison • Teaneck

Published by Fairleigh Dickinson University Press
Co-published with The Rowman & Littlefield Publishing Group, Inc.
4501 Forbes Boulevard, Suite 200, Lanham, Maryland 20706
www.rowman.com

10 Thornbury Road, Plymouth PL6 7PP, United Kingdom

British Library Cataloguing in Publication Information Available

Library of Congress Cataloging-in-Publication Data

Porter, David L., 1941–
Mary Norton of New Jersey, Congressional Trailblazer / David L. Porter.
pages cm.
Includes bibliographical references and index.
ISBN 978-1-61147-609-5 (cloth : alk. paper)—ISBN 978-1-61147-610-1 (ebook)
1. Norton, Mary (Mary Teresa), 1875–1959. 2. United States Congress. House—Biography. 3. Legis-lators—United States—Biography. 4. Legislators—New Jersey—Biography. 5. Women legislators—United States—Biography. 6. Women legislators—New Jersey—Biography. I. Title.
E748.N67P67 2013
328.73'092—dc23
[B]
2013009700

Printed in the United States of America

Contents

Acknowledgments

I am indebted to the late Mary Norton for writing her unpublished memoirs, which her niece, the late Marion McDonough Burke, kindly granted me permission to use. The memoirs, housed at the Archibald Stevens Alexander Library at Rutgers, State University of New Jersey, provided a good starting point for examining Norton's congressional career. Norton's insights on her roles as chairperson of the House District of Columbia Committee and House Labor Committee proved helpful, but her memoirs seldom analyze the broader time and culture in which she played a valuable part as a prominent political figure.

Burke, who knew Mary intimately, graciously shared her recollections about Mary at her Greenwich, Connecticut, home. During the 1930s, she served as assistant clerk of the House District of Columbia Committee and as clerk of the House Labor Committee. She gave me a much fuller understanding of Norton's life, recounting her family life, precongressional career, professional and personal relationships, and retirement years. Burke described how Norton overcame meager financial resources, limited education, and little prior political knowledge to quickly ascend the political ladder to the U.S. Congress. Norton's great determination to have a voice in civic affairs inspired other women to become involved in politics.

The staff of the Special Collections Department of the Alexander Library afforded me valuable assistance during my research on Norton's papers and photocopied Norton's memoirs for me. The Norton collection, though not very extensive, includes her correspondence, political writings, publications, speeches, voting records, personal biographical material, and scrapbooks.

The staff of the Franklin D. Roosevelt Library at Hyde Park, New York also provided me considerable assistance. The Franklin D. Roosevelt papers, the Eleanor Roosevelt papers, and the Lorena Hickok papers contain correspondence with Norton. The Robert Wagner papers at Georgetown University contained his U.S. Senate correspondence on labor issues. The Library of Congress in Washington, D. C., has several books, articles, and unpublished material mentioning Norton and labor issues. *Women in Congress, 1917 – 1990*, published by the Office of the Historian of the U.S. House of Representatives, shed light on Norton's atypical ascendancy to the U.S. Congress and her significant legislative role.

The works of other scholars enhanced my understanding of Norton, the historical role of women in the U. S. Congress, labor legislation, and Jersey City politics. Carmela Karnoutsos, Barbara Tomlinson, Maureen Rees, and Gary Mitchell provided insights on Norton's career of public service, while Marcy Kaptur and Hope Chamberlin adeptly illuminated her historical role as a pioneering congresswoman. Irving Bernstein furnished perspective on the labor movement, while Lisa Kutlin and J. S. Forsythe delineated her role on the Fair Labor Standards Act. James Patterson clarified the House battles between Norton's New Dealers and the conservative coalition. Karnoutsos, Mark Foster, Thomas Fleming, and Richard Connors gave varying reflections on Mayor Hague, while William Chafe and Alice Kessler-Harris elucidated the economic role of women.

I wish to thank Harry Keyishian of Fairleigh Dickinson University Press and Brooke Bures, Jane Mara, and Kelly Shefferly of the Rowman & Littlefield Group for their editorial assistance and am especially grateful to Dr. Kalman Goldstein of Fairleigh Dickinson University for critiquing the manuscript.

The William Penn University Library secured material on interlibrary loan and has several books and magazine and newspaper articles cited in the bibliography. The University of Iowa Library photocopied other articles.

Ari Hoogenboom fostered my interest in both American political history and the U.S. Congress. Dr. Fred Allen, Dr. Noel Stahle, and Dr. Michael Collins of William Penn University gave their encouragement at various stages.

The Eleanor Roosevelt Institute and William Penn University provided generous financial support to facilitate the research phase.

I am especially indebted to my son, Kevin, who helped with the electronic preparation of the manuscript.

My wife, Marilyn, encouraged me throughout the project, provided editorial help with her perceptive eye and especially gave invaluable assistance in the final stages.

Oskaloosa, Iowa
April 2013

Preface

Mary Norton, just the fifth female ever elected to the U.S. Congress, ranked among the more significant women in twentieth-century American politics. She represented Bayonne and Jersey City, New Jersey, for thirteen terms as a Democrat in the U.S. House of Representatives between 1925 and 1951,[1] serving longer in that chamber than any other woman up until that time. Her congressional career spanned the presidencies from Calvin Coolidge to Harry Truman and covered the post–World War I era, the Great Depression, World War II, the beginning of the Cold War, and major industrial advances. It paralleled both Mayor Frank Hague's tight Democratic Party control of Jersey City and President Franklin D. Roosevelt's dynamic national leadership.

Norton was an extraordinary pioneering congresswoman, about whom surprisingly little has been written. In 2010, the *Jersey Journal* wrote "Norton's story deserves to be told. She is a model of a woman well ahead of her time, who defied all the stereotypes of the time about the role of women in politics." Norton grew up a very conventional, devout Roman Catholic woman with just an eighth grade education. She organized and later headed the Queen's Daughters' Day Nursery in Jersey City, providing child care for 400 working-class women. Norton soon impressed Jersey City Mayor Hague when appealing for municipal financial support for the nursery.

Hague prodded Norton to enter Democratic Party politics. Norton rapidly ascended the political ladder after the adoption of the women's suffrage amendment at the city, county, state, and national levels. After organizing Jersey City women politically, she was the first New Jersey woman elected to the Hudson County Board of Freeholders or Supervisors.

In 1924, Hague persuaded Norton to run for the U.S. House of Representatives. Norton became the first Democratic Party congresswoman and the first of her gender elected to the House of Representatives from an eastern state or any urban center east of the Mississippi River. Norton's early legislative career was clouded by her connection with the Hague political machine, but she hoped to demonstrate her independence.

Norton combined traditionalism and reform, cutting a fresh path for women of ordinary means. She represented an eastern, urban, predominately Roman Catholic, working-class district. Her career linked

American urban politics with the big-city Democratic party machine, the labor movement, and the Roman Catholic Church's social reform movement. Although not a feminist, Norton was still an outsider to her Capitol Hill colleagues because of her gender and to the Washington elite because of her Roman Catholic, working-class background. Nevertheless, she gradually moved up in the congressional seniority system and demonstrated that women could master parliamentary skills and provide deft leadership.

Norton made legislative history, establishing numerous political precedents for women. She in 1931 became the first woman to chair a standing congressional committee, the House District of Columbia Committee. As the unofficial mayor of Washington, D.C., Norton helped enact long-needed political, economic, and social legislation for the citizens of the nation's capital.

Six years later, Norton became the first of her sex to chair a major congressional committee, the powerful House Labor Committee. She championed the cause of blue-collar workers and helped secure passage of Franklin D. Roosevelt's major New Deal labor legislation for economically disadvantaged Americans. Norton sought to improve working conditions for America's newly industrialized workers and to allow employees to bargain collectively for the value of their work. In the House she steered the stormy passage of the Fair Labor Standards Act of 1938, establishing a minimum hourly wage and maximum employment hours. Norton also battled to make the Fair Employment Practices Committee permanent, equalize employment opportunities for women, and encourage other women to enter politics.

Norton later chaired the Memorials Committee (1941–1942) and Administration Committee (1949–1951), making her the first female to head four House committees. As Administration Committee head, she arranged the 150th anniversary celebration of Washington, D.C., as the nation's capital and valiantly sought anti--poll tax legislation and congressional salary increases.

Norton also played significant party roles at both the state and national levels. Besides being the first woman to direct a state Democratic Party committee, she belonged to the Democratic National Committee. Norton attended seven National Democratic Party Conventions, becoming the first woman to cochair a platform committee and head a credentials committee.

This book tells Norton's compelling story as a congressional trailblazer and her quest to inspire other women of limited educational background and meager financial resources to participate in civic affairs and pursue political careers.

NOTES

1. Mary T. Norton's unpublished reminiscences, "Madam Congressman: The Memoirs of Mary T. Norton of New Jersey," are in the Mary T. Norton MSS, New Jersey Collection, Archibald Stevens Alexander Library, Rutgers, The State University of New Jersey, New Brunswick, NJ and the Lorena Hickok MSS, Franklin D. Roosevelt Library, Hyde Park, NY, and provide the fullest account of her career. For further illumination on Norton's life and legislative career, see Marcy Kaptur, *Women of Congress; A Twentieth Century Odyssey* (Washington, D.C.: Congressional Quarterly, 1996), pp. 33–51; Barbara J. Tomlinson, "Making Their Way: A Study of New Jersey Congresswomen, 1924–1994," (Ph.D. dissertation: Rutgers: The State University of New Jersey, 1996), pp. 26–44; Maureen Rees, "Mary Norton: A 'Grand Girl'," *The Journal of the Rutgers University Libraries* 47 (December 1985), pp. 59–75; Gary Mitchell, "Women Standing for Women: The Early Political Career of Mary T. Norton," *New Jersey History* 96 (Spring-Summer 1979), pp. 27–42; Hope Chamberlin, *A Minority of Members: Women in the U.S. Congress* (New York: Praeger Publishers, 1973), pp. 53–59; Carmela Ascolese Karnoutsos, "Mary Teresa Norton, 1875–1959," in Joan N. Burstyn, ed., *Past and Promise: Lives of New Jersey Women* (Syracuse, NY: Syracuse University Press, 1997), pp. 368-70; Joan Lovero, "Life of Mary Norton," Jersey City Public Library, Jersey City, NJ; and Angeline Bogucki, "Summary of the Legislative Career of Representative Mary T. Norton," Legislative Reference Service, Library of Congress, Washington, D.C., November 3, 1950. For brief biographical sketches, see "Mary T. Norton," *Current Biography* 5 (1944), pp. 500–503; John Whiteclay Chambers II, "Mary Teresa Hopkins Norton," *Dictionary of American Biography*, Supp. Six, 1956–1960 (New York: Charles Scribner's Sons, 1980), pp. 479–81; and Helen C. Camp, "Mary Teresa Hopkins Norton," *American National Biography* 16 (New York: Oxford University Press, 1999), pp. 529–30. For her pioneering role in Congress, see Phyllis J. Read and Bernard L. Witlieb, *The Book of Women's Firsts* (New York: Random House, 1992), pp. 316–17. Her obituaries appeared in the *New York Times*, August 3, 1959; *New York Herald-Tribune*, August 3, 1959; and *Washington Post*, August 3, 1959. See also Barbara Griffin letter to editor, *The Jersey Journal*, November 5, 2010; Featured House Publications, *Women in Congress, 1917–2006*, 108th Cong., 1st sess., H. Doc. 108–223, http://www.gpo.gov; Irwin Gertzog, *Congressional Women: Their Recruitment, Treatment and Behavior* (New York: Praeger Publishers, 1984), p. 58.

ONE

The Formative Years

Mary Norton served thirteen terms in the U.S. House of Representatives from 1925 to 1951, representing constituents from Jersey City and Bayonne, New Jersey. She and Mayor Frank Hague were Jersey City's two most prominent politicians of the second quarter of the twentieth century. Norton's political career in the U.S. Congress coincided with Hague's firm control of Jersey City and President Franklin Roosevelt's decisive national leadership during the economic depression and World War II.

Norton gained prominence as a national legislator championing the working class poor. Her early life as Mary Hopkins paralleled that of many of her working class constituents. Hopkins, typical of many Jersey City residents of the late nineteenth century, came from an Irish, Roman Catholic immigrant family of moderate socioeconomic circumstances. Her father, Thomas Hopkins, worked in road construction, while her mother, Maria Shea, was a governess. Thomas and Maria, staunch Roman Catholics, had immigrated to the United States from County Langford, Ireland, in the mid-nineteenth century and were naturalized citizens.[1]

Thomas, the eldest son of a prosperous farmer, grew up in Langford County and was expected to marry and settle down on the family property. "Father hated farming," Mary learned. When Thomas was just sixteen years old, a close friend received a letter from his brother in the United States with passage money. Thomas begged his parents to let him emigrate, but they considered him too young. In 1854, he borrowed $200 from a family safe and sailed from Liverpool, England, for New York City anyway. Thomas endured "a hard, rough trip" lasting over three months. He toiled as an itinerant farmer and railroad construction contractor, enabling him to return the $200 he had borrowed from his parents. He worked for and lived with his uncle, a prosperous contractor,

1

in New York City. Thomas, who was stocky with curly black hair, later operated his own construction business. Mary described him as "an optimist, fun-loving, with a great sense of humor" and "a magnificent storyteller" of Irish folklore.[2]

Maria came from the same Irish parish as Thomas. The oldest of eight children, she was born in County Langford, Ireland, when her mother was only nineteen years old. Maria studied to become a teacher but needed to work to support her family after her father's death in 1860. She heard that the United States was a land of opportunity and persuaded her mother to let her emigrate. Maria traveled to Liverpool, England, and sailed for the United States. On the harrowing three-month boat trip across the Atlantic Ocean, she battled typhoid fever, homesickness, and tempestuous seas, leaving her physically drained. "There were bad storms and times, she said, when she thought the ship would never reach land. That, combined with terrible homesickness, must have been some experience for a girl of 19." For several weeks, a New York City doctor treated Maria for typhoid fever at Castle Garden. Maria, a perceptive, discerning woman with dark hair and deep set blue eyes, worked as a governess for that doctor's four children for a decade. According to Mary, Maria "always had a deep, underlying faith in God, combined with rare courage—and ambition, too."[3]

Thomas in 1868 became reacquainted with Maria, who had been a childhood playmate in Ireland. He wanted to marry her then, but Maria delayed the wedding for two years until she no longer needed to support her family. Thomas and Maria wed in 1870 and lived near Brewster, New York, northeast of New York City. Four of their first five children died in infancy, with only James surviving.[4]

The Hopkins moved in the early 1870s to Jersey City, located along the eastern banks of the Hudson River near New York City. Mary Teresa, their oldest of three daughters and second oldest of four surviving children, was born in Jersey City on March 7, 1875. Mary was taller than most girls and acted very mature for her age. Older brother James played an integral part in Mary's life and treated her with kindness and patience. "As a child," Mary recalled, "I used to try to imitate him, and his approval meant everything to me." The family's limited financial resources "were reserved for James to be educated for the priesthood." James, who was tall, very athletic, and intelligent, graduated from college at age nineteen and earned a master's degree at Seton Hall University. He did not become a priest but instead taught at Dickinson High School in Jersey City, became principal there, and later served as superintendent of schools in Jersey City. Mary also had two younger sisters, Anne and Loretta. Anne, three years younger, was sweet, pretty, and popular, while Loretta, five years younger, was very determined and always knew what she wanted to do.[5]

Jersey City consisted mainly of immigrant factory workers, Roman Catholics who were neither progressive nor especially well educated.[6] Mary grew up in the Eleventh Ward in a small house that Thomas had purchased with a $1,000 down payment. The Hudson County Bank held a mortgage on the balance. The Hopkins used a gaslight and stoves to heat their home, which lacked central heating, electricity, or telephones. "Ours was a happy, comfortable home," Mary remembered. "Though we had few luxuries we had much love." Her family solidly backed the Democratic Party.[7]

Mary attended Jersey City parochial schools and attained very good grades. "She did not complete her elementary education in consideration of her family's financial situation." For most of her life, Mary claimed to have graduated from Jersey City High School in 1892. Marion McDonagh Burke, Mary's niece, recalled, "She always felt ashamed of that." Mary explained, "It seemed important to me for many years to conceal my lack of education," but admitted that "it now seems a silly deception." Thomas disapproved of Mary receiving more formal education, insisting, "It was right for a boy, but a girl should learn to be a good housekeeper, make her own clothes, get married, and be a good wife and mother." Burke recollected, Mary "later became a source of inspiration to those who dropped out of school."[8]

When Mary was fourteen years old in 1889, Maria took her to live with a cousin who worked for Western Union in New York City. Mary studied telegraphy for a year at Cooper Union Institute and corresponded extensively with a telegrapher from Lake George, New York. According to Burke, "Mary had a romantic relationship by telegraph with another telegrapher." In 1890, Mary worked as a telegraph operator in Mount Carmel, Pennsylvania, and resided with a mine owner's family. "How few parents of today," she asked, "would allow a 15 year old the complete freedom from parental authority I was to have for the next year?" Mary wrote, "I had an interesting, pleasant, and surely educational year in this small mining community and came home 20 pounds heavier and 20 years older in knowledge."[9] She learned how the miners lived, spoke, and thought, broadening her understanding of the challenging working conditions.

Maria died suddenly in 1892 when Mary was seventeen years old. "The shock was deadening," Mary recollected, "for she had always appeared to be in perfect health." Maria often had shared her hopes and dreams with her daughter, boosting Mary's self-confidence. "Her theory," Mary recollected, "was that, if you really wanted to do anything and put your heart into it, you could gain your objective. And she had complete faith in God and prayer." As the eldest daughter, Mary managed the Hopkins's household in Jersey City for the next four years and "assumed responsibilities for her younger sisters, Anne and Loretta." She especially enjoyed housekeeping and cooking.[10]

Thomas remarried in 1896, dramatically changing Mary's home life. Mary complained, "Home was different with a stepmother who was not in sympathy with three young girls who adored their Dad." She, Anne, and Loretta relocated to New York City, lived a few months on Charles Street in Greenwich Village and then moved to St. Nicholas Avenue and 145th Street. Thomas trusted them completely and paid their monthly rent. The Hopkins sisters brought some furniture from home and bought the remainder on credit. Mary revealed, "We had very little left of our cash capital. But we did have plenty of courage and sublime faith." The New York adventure taught the sisters, especially Mary, self-reliance and independence. "Being together, independent and free from a stepmother's criticisms," Mary acknowledged, "meant more to us than living in our father's home and having our bills paid." The sisters often invited friends to dinner, enjoyed bicycling, and loved the New York lifestyle, too. "My sisters and I," Mary added, "found life as independent young businesswomen pleasant and exhilarating. We went out a good deal, to the theater and concerts." [11]

The Hopkins sisters wanted to become career women and trained for clerical work at Packard Business College in 1896. In the late 1800s, women working outside the home were considered a relatively new phenomenon. Mary, Anne, and Loretta strongly desired to improve their economic situation as clerks. Mary worked six months as a stenographer for a bustle factory on Centre Street in New York. "I can still remember how hard it was to get that first stenographic job," she recollected. "I applied at several New York offices before being accepted." [12]

Mary's salary as a stenographer started at $9 a week and rose to $14 a week within six months. When Mary applied for the job, the bustle factory owner warned her, "The salary I pay—$9 a week—wouldn't buy your clothes!" Mary replied that she was not asking him to buy her clothes. The factory owner treated her kindly and considerately but insisted that she wear a bustle. Mary initially demurred. "As nature had taken care of me," she recalled, "I felt reluctant to add anything that was obviously unnecessary! However, when a very beautiful silk number was presented to me, I gave up and decided to wear it, rather than argue about it." The independence and assuredness she learned on that job provided excellent training for her public career. Norton remained "absolutely self-supporting" and described those years as ones of "so much happiness and freedom" and "the very best preparation and discipline." [13]

Mary's next employment came as a stenographer at the Remington Typewriter Company. Remington, which furnished stenographers and secretaries temporarily for business houses, sent her to the New York Central Railroad Company passenger agency to replace a secretary on vacation. The job required a stenographer with at least four years experience who could take dictation very quickly from the general passenger agent. Mary admitted to her new boss the first day that she had only six months experience, but the agency retained her anyway. "I never knew a man who could talk faster than he could," she said of the general passenger agent. An assistant passenger agent helped her note the dictation she missed. Mary relieved other vacationing stenographers for the next ten weeks. [14]

Mary later secured a secretarial position with a large corporation at 17 Battery Place in New York City. The company president did not want to hire her but needed immediate help because a male employee was ill. "I don't want any woman around here, upsetting my business." he declared. The male employees initially avoided Mary because the general manager had required them to wear suit coats, behave like gentlemen, and not smoke in her presence. After learning what had happened, Mary persuaded the general manager to rescind the order so that the male employees could dress more comfortably. She worked for that company for $25 a week until 1909. [15]

Various published accounts portray Mary as brown-eyed with black hair, friendly, charming, gracious, witty, uncompromising, confident, conscientious, intelligent, perceptive, persuasive, articulate, realistic, poised, tactful, and well organized. Mary possessed strong faith in God, a strong moral conscience, common sense, a logical mind, and self-confidence. Burke pictured Mary as "big physically, but non-athletic," "persistent," "dignified," and "warm and affectionate" beneath the surface. Above all, Mary "followed through on her ideas." The Democratic National Committee described her as having "a finely molded, handsome face with bright brown eyes, surmounted by an exquisitely groomed head of short, waving black hair." The committee also sketched Mary as a "poised, clear-thinking, straight-talking politician," whose "womanly gentleness transcends the sterner qualities." The *Ladies Home Journal* painted her as "an ample figure" as "wholesome as a windy city," having "the directed energy of a steel riveting machine" and "being steady as a mountain in her convictions." "Partisan as she is enthusiastic," the magazine observed, "Norton can no more hold a grudge than she can coo." [16]

Helen Meagher of the *Women's Voice* portrayed Mary as "a handsome woman" with a "keen perception" and "trim round figure" that suggested "more force of character than beauty." Journalist Duff Gilfond called her "non aristocratic," "a ballast to the gentlewoman's group," and a "scrapper" who "swats hard at the Republicans." "If her face appears a little hard at first," Gilfond noted, "there is relief in the pleasantness of her smile and the heartiness of her handshake." [17]

Mary, now thirty-four years old, left the business world on April 21, 1909, to marry Robert Francis Norton, a forty-five-year-old widower, longtime friend, and manager of a large Jersey City wholesale cooperage firm. His first wife had died, leaving two daughters, Mary and Katherine. Robert had returned to his parents' home where his mother brought up Mary and Katherine. His daughters continued to live with his mother following Robert's marriage. The couple experienced a happy marriage. Mary described Robert as "a real friend in encouraging and helping me to make my dreams come true" and "a most understanding and wonderful person." She confided, however, he was "not personally interested in politics," but "he was always a real help to me in my work. He had excellent judgment and gave me good, sound advice, valuable in helping me to make decisions. He never tried to influence me, but he would offer suggestions when he thought someone was trying to distort a situation."[18] Her memoirs, however, mention him relatively little.

The Nortons lived for six years in a six-room Jersey City apartment and resided for a decade in the small frame Jersey City house that her father had left. When Mary entered the U.S. Congress in 1925, they moved to an apartment on 2600 Boulevard. Mary bore only one child, Robert Francis, Jr., who died at just seven days old in September 1910. His tragic death devastated her and followed a pregnancy complicated by pneumonia and severe physical illness. To make matters worse, doctors told Mary that she could not bear any more children. Mary became bitterly resentful and went into seclusion for two years at home, disclosing, "The bottom dropped out of my world for a time." She lamented, "It was a shock from which I did not recover for a long time." But Mary eventually realized, "Something had to take the place of the children I could not have," and she devoted her life "to help other mothers, more fortunate than I was, and their children." Burke recalled, "Mary never really got over her child's death. After that, her nieces really became her children."[19]

The Roman Catholic Church gave Norton a renewed sense of purpose when she began working at a day care nursery. "To adjust to the fact that she could have no more children, she turned to public service and volunteer work." In 1912 Monsignor Patrick Edward Smyth, the pastor of St. Joseph's Roman Catholic Church in Jersey City, asked her to meet with other parish women to find a place to care daily for young children of working mothers. Norton helped the parish women establish a non-sectarian day care center in the church basement for around 100 children of working-class women. Day care centers then were rare, small, staffed with volunteers, and privately financed. Monsignor Smyth donated $2,000 to start the center. The parish women eventually rented a small house for $25 a month. Working mothers left their children there weekdays from 7 a.m. to 6 p.m. Norton did not take an active role for several months but then "turned from her baby's empty cradle," "resolutely forced herself to face the crowded cots in the Day Nursery," and "plunged into its activities feverishly." Upon becoming passionate about the facility, she recalled, "I gave my whole heart to the work, and in it I found the consolation and peace of mind I needed so much." Burke observed, "The Day Care Nursery experience really helped draw Mary out of her seclusion. She helped the poor there and got others to help them, too."[20]

The school grew so rapidly within a year that the church purchased a larger house for $7,500 and incorporated it in April 1913 as Queen's Daughters' Day Nursery Association of Jersey City. Besides being an excellent organizer, Norton served as the school's recording secretary from 1913 to 1915 and president from 1916 to 1928. "She knew of the concerns of the working women for their children and worked on their behalf for the nursery for fifteen years." Norton often visited the children's homes and talked with courageous, hardworking mothers, whose husbands earned very low incomes, frequently suffered from alcoholism, or occasionally had even died. Under her tutelage, the Queen's Daughters' Day Nursery expanded its membership rolls to 400 working-class women and enlarged its physical plant. The facility became a forerunner of early childhood care across the United States.[21]

During World War I, Norton also chaired St. Joseph's Red Cross unit in Jersey City and worked with the Red Cross Employment Center to improve the plight of parish working-class women. Monsignor Smyth asked her to organize a Red Cross workroom in the basement hall at St. Joseph's Church, telling her, "There are plenty of women who know how to sew and knit, but we are going to need someone to run this thing. I think you are the woman who can do it." Around 200 parish working-class women were enlisted to sew on 100 machines installed by the church.

By 1917, the Queen's Daughters' Day Nursery needed even more additional space. The American entrance into World War I in April 1917 had forced around one million women to work outside the home to replace the men in uniform. Norton found a second facility to care for children in the downtown section of Jersey City and paid $300 to bind the sale. She needed $3,000 as a down payment within 30 days and raised that amount in just one day by visiting executives from the Atlantic & Pacific Tea Company, Butler Brothers, the Dixon Crucible Company, and the Mueller Macaroni factory. "That was a big day!"[22] Norton beamed.

Many downtrodden Jersey City women needed help but were reluctant to ask for it at municipal centers or charitable institutions. "Sometimes," Norton observed, "they did not know where to go for assistance." The Queen's Daughters' Day Nursery set aside two rooms as temporary housing in those emergency cases. Mary Tan, a young Chinese girl, had moved to Englewood, New Jersey, as a nursemaid for an American family and had run away after the mother had died. Tan rode a bus to Jersey City after learning that the nursery provided shelter for homeless girls. The nursery let Tan use one of those emergency rooms and secured her a job as an assistant to the file clerk at the Atlantic & Pacific Tea Company. Tan resided at the nursery until Monsignor Smyth arranged for her to become a nun at Maryknoll Mission in New York. She later served as a missionary in her native China.[23]

The nursery also aided a 55-year-old grandmother, whose daughter and son-in-law had died during the terrible 1919 influenza epidemic and left five children. The grandmother cared for the two older children, while the three younger children stayed and ate at the nursery. Norton recalled, "Their grandmother came to me and begged me, with tears streaming down her face, not to let them be separated." The grandmother agreed to work at a pencil company to keep the three younger children together. Norton arranged for Jim Green, a large furniture-store owner, to pay the grandmother's rent and persuaded Dixon Crucible Company to hire her to fill boxes with pencils. Mary declared, "I have never known anyone more appreciative than that woman was."[24]

By 1920, Norton began building a formidable political base. Norton's role as a fundraiser for the nursery led her to numerous political contacts. To secure municipal funding for the nursery, Norton in 1918 visited the Poor Department of Jersey City and met its Democratic Mayor Frank Hague. Hague came from an Irish background and appreciated Norton's Irish heritage, tenaciousness, and political potential. He served a record eight consecutive terms as mayor of Jersey City from 1917 to 1947, operating one of the nation's largest and "most notorious Democratic party machines." For nearly three decades, Hague dominated the political life of Jersey City, Hudson County, and New Jersey and achieved huge electoral victories in northern and eastern New Jersey through "a mixture of patronage, programs for his labor constituency, and, at times, direct intimidation of his opponents."

From humble beginnings, Hague grew up in a working-class Jersey City neighborhood inhabited by poor, Irish, Roman Catholic immigrants. He joined the local Democratic Party, being appointed deputy sheriff in 1898, precinct leader in 1901, ward leader in 1906, and constable in 1908. Mayor H. Otto Wittpenn appointed the nineteen-year-old Hague custodian of City Hall in 1908. Hague was elected street and water commissioner in 1911 and broke with Wittpenn to join other progressive reformers. Jersey City's adoption of a commission form of government to replace the mayor-council system in 1913 expedited his political advancement. He became commissioner of public safety in 1916, heading the police and fire department. Hague controlled appointments to these two departments, building a base for a patronage system. The city commission unanimously elected Hague mayor in 1917.

As Jersey City mayor through 1947, Hague erected his powerful machine by realizing the needs of Jersey City's politically ignored groups. His organization "provided family oriented services that would not be forgotten on election day." These services included furnishing poorer residents with coal in winter and jobs when unemployed. Hague exercised his authority in numerous ways. He successfully challenged James

Nugent of Essex County for control of the state Democratic Party, ending the latter's domination and marking "the ascendancy of Hague as a force to be reckoned with in the national party." With Hague's backing, Edward Edwards defeated Nugent for the Democratic nomination for governor in 1919. Hudson County helped elect six governors, including Edwards, George Silzer, and A. Harry Moore, during the next three decades. Hague's influence as a political boss and as vice-chair of the Democratic National Committee helped Franklin D. Roosevelt win the 1932 presidential election. Under Hague, Jersey City became the first American city to introduce fluoridated water and built one of the era's largest urban hospitals.

Hague became a masterful politician as Jersey City and Hudson County boss. Norton called Hague "a remarkable executive," who had "changed Jersey City from what used to be a 'back-yard of New York' to an outstanding Metropolitan City." "Unlike other political bosses of his time who worked behind the scenes, he ran for office, testing his popularity with voters." Hague reorganized the Hudson County Democratic Party to "Jersey City's political advantage." Populous Hudson County built a formidable "hierarchical organization controlled, through rewards and punishments, by the mayor of Jersey City." Hague considered Hudson County politics a business operation. Hague divided Jersey City into wards and smaller districts where neighborhood leaders, both male and female, dispensed patronage in return for votes. Hague's political machine "could get out the vote," perfecting frequently used political strategies of canvassing, transporting voters to the polls, and telephoning potential voters. These strategies enabled Hague to round up the votes for his Democratic candidates in local, state, and national elections. Jersey City's large working-class population and Irish Catholics provided the core of Hague's political support. "Hague championed their causes and obtained federal funding that provided employment during the Depression." He fought labor unions as "synonymous with communism and anti-Americanism." Irish Catholics, the largest voting bloc in the city, viewed Hague as the vehicle for change.[25]

Hague amassed considerable wealth as Jersey City mayor, earning, according to historian Thomas Fleming, an estimated $500,000 to $1 million annually. He reportedly earned a $7,500 to $8,000 salary per year but had several residences and lived extravagantly. His revenue allegedly "came from paybacks from real estate deals in the city" and "a percentage of the city's gaming operation (numbers racket, card games and off-track betting)." Local patronage provided the remaining revenue, largely from "the three-percent salary kickback" assessed to city employees and "the mandatory thirty-percent return on salary raises." According to Jack Alexander, the revenue was used for "political purposes." The city payroll also was inflated with questionable job descriptions and very well-paid police and fire departments.[26]

Norton, meanwhile, urged Hague in 1918 to increase financial support for nursery school education. "I had never met the Mayor," she recollected, "so I naturally felt a bit nervous the day I called on him in his office at the City Hall." Norton told Hague, "Our nurseries are overcrowded. Our funds are depleted. Mothers come to us in dozens every day begging us to care for their little ones while they are at work in the factories. We cannot turn away these children." She pleaded with the mayor, "Surely you will help us to continue to give these children daytime guardians." Hague, profoundly moved by Norton's eloquent appeal, asked, "How is it that I've never heard of this nursery before?" Norton replied, "Perhaps, Mr. Mayor, you're interested mostly in the political news and don't read the rest of the paper. We've had plenty of publicity." [27]

Hague asked Norton and two nursery board members to present their case before the Board of Commissioners the next morning at City Hall. Norton, "nervous and unsure of herself," arrived at City Hall that morning and sat at the back of the Assembly Chamber. "It was only the second time I had ever been inside the City Hall," she indicated. Norton did not recall what she said to the mayor, but Hague encouraged her. Commissioner Moore asked Norton if the nursery had given any direct assistance to the World War I effort. Norton described how the nursery had outfitted the young son of a U.S. Army soldier "who had been playing truant because he was ashamed to go to school in his ragged clothes." Moore asked Norton how much money the nursery needed. "A hundred dollars a month would be a big help," [28] she replied. The Board voted unanimously to give her nursery $100 a month.

Norton's remarks about the small boy upset her older brother, James. The Jersey City evening newspapers printed bold, front-page headlines "CIVILIAN DEFENSE FALLS DOWN - MRS. NORTON DESCRIBES PLIGHT OF SON OF A SOLDIER." The headlines implied that the Jersey City unit of the Red Cross, whose financial drive James had headed, had failed to help the young boy. "He asked me," Norton recollected, "if I had taken leave of my senses. Did I realize what I had done to the Red Cross drive?" Norton, "completely bewildered," assured James, "The last thing in the world I'd have done deliberately was anything to hurt the Red Cross drive." The incident, she lamented, "spoiled my pleasure over getting the help for our nursery." [29]

Hague, who realized the potential power of the women's vote unleashed by the Nineteenth Amendment granting women's suffrage, wanted to expand his power base by placing women in important party positions. "Hague was determined to recruit women to the Democratic Party." The advent of women's suffrage meant more votes for the Hague machine if women focused their political energies on the Democratic Party organization. New Jersey had ratified the Nineteenth Amendment in February 1920. "Hague courted the feminine vote and made it a major prop of his local power," adding ladies' auxiliaries to his Jersey City Democratic ward clubs in the 1920s. As vice-chairman of the Democratic National Committee, he declared, "I want to be the first leader in the Democratic Party to help elect a woman to Congress."

In June 1920, Norton received a message to call Mayor Hague at City Hall. She erroneously figured that the Mayor's message involved the nursery. When Norton called back, Hague told her, "Women are going to vote for a President this year. Only one more state to ratify, and that will happen in August." Hague, who "pressed Norton to enter politics as his protégé," asked her if he could submit her name to represent the Hudson County women on the Democratic State Committee when the last state ratifies. "It's your duty to organize the women of Jersey City,"[30] Hague commanded.

Norton had impressed Hague with her "personality and civic interests," especially her work on raising funds for the day care center. Hague, who sought "a role model for women to garner their support for his administration and its anointed candidates," wanted Norton to help organize New Jersey women so that they would vote Democrat and participate actively in the party. Hague was worried about the impact that voting women might have on his political operations. "If she could translate that drive from her social work to the political organization of women in the Democratic Party, his future in Jersey City, Hudson County, and even the state, would be assured." Hague supported women's participation in politics because James Nugent, the primary obstacle to his control of the State Democratic Party organization, adamantly opposed women's suffrage. "I want to prepare now," Hague insisted. In 1953, Norton explained Hague's motivation: "Men in control of party machinery were fearful of what women might do—how they would react to national suffrage—some thought a woman's party might be the result. The smart politicians didn't want that to happen."

Norton, a devout Roman Catholic, had concentrated on the needs of hard-pressed urban families rather than expanding political rights for women. She believed that the Jersey City Roman Catholic working mothers were more interested in day care than politics and claimed that a majority of New Jersey suffragists were upper-middle-class Protestants. Although a social activist, Norton had not been involved in the women's suffrage movement. "She was not opposed to suffrage for women but at the time did not see politics as her sphere of interest." Norton initially rejected Hague's offer, countering that "a woman identified with the suffrage movement might better serve in that role." "The idea struck me as absurd," she thought, "and I was tempted to laugh, but didn't. I politely explained that I knew nothing about politics and would have to decline." Hague interjected, "Neither does any suffragist" and added, "No women knew anything about politics. They would have to learn." He mentioned what roles women could play in politics and urged Norton to try serving on the Democratic State Committee for one year. Hague, though, conceded that he "didn't know how to proceed with women in politics" and claimed that the state committee responsibilities "would not involve any work."[31]

Norton finally reluctantly agreed to serve for just one year without having substantial responsibilities, making her the first female on the Democratic State Committee. Hague appointed Norton because of her leadership skills and knowledge of child welfare work. "Her personality and civic interests attracted the Democratic leadership, particularly Boss Frank Hague." Norton recognized that she "had been a leader in social welfare during World War I, was well known in the District and had the confidence of large groups." She also accepted the post because Hague had agreed to have Jersey City lend money to the nurseries. "I felt under obligation," Norton explained, "for the response to my appeal for our nurseries. I had no thought of a career in politics."[32] In August 1920, Tennessee became the thirty-sixth state to ratify the Nineteenth Amendment, thus giving women the right to vote.

Norton held moderate views on women's rights. The woman suffragettes, led by Carrie Catt and Alice Paul, had wanted her to support an equal rights amendment, but she declined. Norton feared that "women might be forced to do things they might not want to do," such as serving in the armed forces, and claimed that women in industry already had some laws protecting them. "I had not been a suffragist," Norton explained, "not that I did not believe in the cause, but because I was occupied otherwise to give it much time." Norton praised the suffragettes as "the real heroines in the battle" and admired "the great courage, broad vision and tremendous energy of those women." She lauded the enfranchisement of women in 1920 as "the greatest single achievement of that period." A practical rather than theoretical feminist, she drew "women into a sisterhood without alarming men" and managed "to get her way in certain matters while giving every appearance of the most complete docility."[33]

In September 1920, Hague asked Norton to preside over a meeting at Dickinson High School to organize Jersey City women to participate in the presidential campaign of Democrat James Cox against Republican candidate Warren Harding. Norton, visibly irritated, fired back, "I would do no such thing. I knew nothing about politics and had never addressed a public meeting." Hague, though, already had distributed newspaper advertisements that Norton would preside over the meeting and insisted that "since I was a member of the State Committee from Hudson County it was my duty." The duo engaged in a heated exchange. Norton reminded Hague, "I had allowed him to use my name to represent Hudson County on the State Committee only because I felt it was a small repayment of my obligation to him." She had expected Hague to find a more qualified woman. Hague stressed that women now had the right to vote and told Norton, it was her "duty to preside at the first meeting to organize the women in Hudson County." Norton snapped, "To say that I was bewildered does not express just how I felt."[34] Hague, however, knew that it was safer to train a novice like Norton and persisted until she reluctantly consented. "Politics is a business," he maintained. "You are smart. You can go far." Norton recognized, "Abruptly I was thrown into the pool of public service, and I had to sink or swim."[35]

On her way home, Norton visited her brother, James, a principal at Dickinson High School, to seek advice. Hague, who tightly controlled all appointments and commanded all aspects of Jersey City government, had provided generous support for public education through his tax policies. Norton told James how Hague had trapped her and insisted that she lacked the assurance to speak in public. James, though, advised, "It would be good for me—that I had become too engrossed in the day nursery." He encouraged her, affirming, "You can handle it. I know you can." James told her that it would be no different than presiding at a nursery board meeting and assured her that "no woman in any audience would probably do the job any better than I would—that I'd undoubtedly had more experience than most of them." His words comforted her. Norton acknowledged, "I left his office feeling better and decided that perhaps it wouldn't be so dreadful as I had thought."[36]

Norton nervously awaited the Hudson County meeting at Dickinson High School. "I was so jittery all day that I could not even think straight," she admitted. Governor Edwards; Carrie Catt, women's suffrage leader; all New Jersey State Democratic Party leaders; and the 1920 Democratic Party candidates attended. When Norton walked to the platform with Edwards, the crowd gave a rousing ovation. Norton figured that the ovation was for Governor Edwards, but he insisted that she walk to the front of the platform. The cheering intensified. "I was bewildered," Norton explained, "for I did not think many people in that political audience knew me. Then I looked up into the gallery, and there, filling the place, smiling and waving, I saw my four hundred faithful members of the day nursery." Catt, the keynote speaker, reminded the audience about the long, difficult seventy-two-year struggle for suffrage by self-sacrificing women of great vision.[37] The memorable night launched Norton's political career.

In October 1920, Norton addressed her first political rally at St. Michael's Hall in the Second Ward of Jersey City. She vigorously defended the newly formed League of Nations and stressed how that international organization would help preserve international peace and security. When Norton returned to her seat, Charles O'Brien, the Democratic Party candidate for the Twelfth New Jersey Congressional District seat, interjected, "What in God's name are you trying to do to me? Don't you know the League of Nations is dead?" She retorted, "You ought to be ashamed of yourself for selfishly ignoring the issue that was so much more important than your election." O'Brien, who was elected to Congress, muttered, "And they gave women the vote!" Norton, though, never wavered in her support of the League of Nations. "Irish bitterness, growing out of the long struggle with the Crown," she realized, "undoubtedly colored the feeling of the Irish toward the League." She feared that the Irish hostility to international organization "would affect the outcome of the election in cities with large Irish-American populations. It posed a problem for Democrats in Jersey City."[38]

In the 1920 elections, Democrats and Republicans vied for the women's vote. "Women, contrary to the expectations of many on both sides of the suffrage debate, did not vote as a single, unified bloc. They split over party affiliation, key issues, and the vagaries of local politics. They also voted in far lower percentages than predicted." Furthermore, "their voting preferences tended to mirror those of the men in the families."

In November 1920, the Republicans fared better than the Democrats in New Jersey. Garden State voters elected the first two women, both Republicans, to the New Jersey General Assembly. Margaret Laird and Jennie Van Ness, women's suffrage leaders from Essex County, won those seats in the state legislature. Laird, a Newark nurse, had served as vice president of the Women's Political Union, chair of the Newark chapter of the National Woman Suffrage Association, and organizer of the Newark Women's Republican Club. Laird spent two terms in the assembly, where she helped establish the state's juvenile court law and supported legislation for equal salaries for women employed by the state government. Van Ness, a substitute teacher at East Orange High School, had joined the New Jersey Woman Suffrage Association in 1867 and had operated the association's citizenship schools educating women throughout the state in government and politics. She later became a regional director of the League of Women Voters and chaired a board to frame a state program on legislative issues. Van Ness served just one term in the assembly where she sponsored controversial legislation assessing severe penalties on the sale and manufacture of alcoholic beverages.

New Jersey Democratic women, meanwhile, organized more than forty political clubs by December 1921. In Hudson County, every ward formed its own club with both male and female leaders. Norton boasted, "We had the best organization anywhere in the United States at that time." Public resistance made organizing these political clubs difficult. One woman asked Norton's assistance in organizing a political club where few Democrats resided. A dozen women and fifteen men braved the intense summer heat to attend that organizational meeting. The men feared that the twelve women might interfere with their control of the election district and claimed that other women would be better suited to organize political clubs. Norton, however, insisted that the twelve women attendees were the most reliable for organizing clubs. "We elected the officers of the club from that group," she stressed, "much to the disgust of the men, who evidently wanted to control it." [39]

Audiences did not always respect Norton when she delivered speeches. Norton especially encountered stern resistance in one industrial district while planning an organizational meeting for women. Upon arriving at the meeting site, she found mostly men in attendance and asked where the women were. A man stood up at the back of the hall and shouted, "Our women are home, looking after their children—where you ought to be." Norton, reflecting upon her son's death, retorted, "How very, very fortunate they are to have children! That privilege has been denied me." She added, "If I had children, I'd certainly be at home with them now if they needed me. But since I haven't, I am here to talk to you about a new responsibility that has been given to women (voting)." The embarrassed meeting coordinator publicly apologized to Norton, invited her to return, and promised to encourage women to attend next time. Norton later returned there and formed one of the best women's organizations in New Jersey. [40]

Norton, vice chairman of the Hudson County Democratic Committee, was elected to the New Jersey Democratic Committee in 1921. She served as state vice chairman from 1921 through 1931 and as state chairman from 1932 to 1935. Mayor Hague and other party leaders, unbeknownst to Norton, had arranged her appointment as state chairman in 1932. Norton became the first woman from either major political party to direct a state party organization. "It caused quite a stir among the political writers," she recollected. The *Newark Ledger* editorialized, "Facing a critical campaign with the Senatorship and Governorship at stake and determination of whether New Jersey will remain in the Democratic column, what would be more logical than the selection of Mrs. Norton, leader and strategist?" Joseph Tumulty, who had been press secretary under President Woodrow Wilson, was impressed with her leadership skills and claimed, "Mary Norton has more common sense than most men I know." [41]

As state party chair, Norton designated federal patronage in New Jersey. "That task required a great deal of work," Burke recalled. "Mary received numerous job requests." Norton resigned as State Democratic Committee head in 1935 because of her husband's death and growing congressional responsibilities but served a second stint from 1940 to 1944. "We were all new in politics," she realized, "but we tried to do our job. Women throughout the state cooperated with us. We often became discouraged by lack of cooperation on the part of the men, but wherever women persevered they usually won, even against great odds." [42]

Norton, meanwhile, continued her political ascension, being rewarded as the Democratic Party candidate for the Hudson County Board of Freeholders in 1923. Freeholders functioned as county commissioners or supervisors. Mayor Hague prodded her to seek the freeholder position. "You'll like it," Hague promised. "You can run the poor farm and the orphans' home." "I was surprised and somewhat hesitant," Norton confessed. After consulting with her husband, Robert, she accepted Hague's invitation and was nominated for the post.

Norton, however, suffered a terrible personal tragedy after accepting the freeholder nomination. James Hopkins, her older brother, who had become superintendent of schools in Jersey City, became ill in the summer of 1923 and went to Saranac Lake, New York, to recuperate. After seemingly recovering, he died suddenly of a heart attack on August 17. "I wanted to get away from everyone and everything," Norton disclosed. "When my brother died I decided I could not go on with it and also that I would withdraw as a candidate and end my political career."[43]

Grief-stricken Norton revealed her intentions to Mayor Hague. "I'm surprised," Hague retorted. "I thought you had guts, but you are just like most people. You can't take it. And I was silly enough to think you would make a career in politics!" After staring momentarily, Hague asked her, "What do you think Jim would think of you now?" Norton became livid. "Never in my life did I feel more like striking a person than I did at that moment. I told him he was a brute, with a few adjectives thrown in. Finally, completely spent, I began to cry." Hague, suddenly realizing that he had hurt her feelings, explained that he had not meant what he said and did not want "to see my spirit broken." He knew that "I could make a career in politics" and "did not want me to lose my opportunity." Hague ultimately convinced Norton that she should run for the Hudson County Board of Freeholders because her brother would have expected her to do. She suddenly began to see the real Hague as "a kind, generous husband and father and the friend of countless little people who needed a friend." According to Burke, "Mary was loyal to Mayor Hague and never criticized him publicly." But she added, "He cramped Mary's style."[44]

Norton attended the 1923 State Democratic Convention and remained a candidate for the Hudson County Board of Freeholders. "The women," she recalled, "did everything possible to make that first convention a success." In November, county voters elected her as the first New Jersey woman freeholder. Norton served as a freeholder for over one year, learning how the political system worked. "I enjoyed my work as freeholder," she acknowledged, "probably as much as anything I have ever done. It offered many opportunities for real service and taught me the importance of county government." Norton's initial meeting with the Hudson County Board of Freeholders did not run smoothly, however. Although board members treated her politely, she admitted, "I do not think they looked upon a woman on the board too happily."[45]

As a freeholder, Norton recognized the needs of her Hudson County constituents at a time when the nation did not have social security, unemployment compensation, or child welfare and did what she could to rectify those problems. At just her second meeting, Norton asked the Board of Freeholders to authorize construction of a maternity hospital in Jersey City at Hudson County expense. "My experience in the day nursery," she observed, "had made me aware of the tragically high death rate among babies and mothers through lack of proper care during childbirth." Her proposal, though, initially met stern resistance. Board members replied that "it would be illegal to use county funds for such a purpose without having a special authorization bill passed by the state legislature." Norton responded, "Well, why not get a bill passed?"[46]

A few days later, Walter O'Mara, clerk of the Hudson County Board of Supervisors, asked Norton's husband, Robert, "Can't you talk Mary out of that crazy idea of a maternity hospital? It's just going to make trouble for her with the board." Robert let O'Mara know, however, that it would be difficult to dissuade her about building the hospital. Mayor Hague likewise believed that a maternity hospital would benefit Hudson County, but told Norton that she had made a mistake by proposing it at just her second meeting. He advised her to use "a gradualist approach to win over the members of the Board." Hague counseled, "Don't rush the idea. The men will have to come to it gradually. It's something new."[47]

At a Hudson County Board of Supervisors meeting in his City Hall office a few months later, Mayor Hague raised the maternity hospital issue. He affirmed that Hudson County needed a maternity hospital because of its large industrial population, significant percentage of middle and lower income families, and high rate of infant mortality. Hague's family situation spurred his advocacy of a hospital. "Frank Hague and his mother Margaret, who died in 1921, both suffered from poor health and could not afford medical care. As mayor, Hague was determined to construct a facility to provide quality free health care for the city's poor." Norton informed board colleagues that infant mortality in Hudson County alarmingly was 212 per 1,000 births. Her gradualist strategy, along with Hague's "behind-the-scenes support," ultimately convinced the board to approve her proposal for construction of the Margaret Hague Maternity Hospital at public expense. "Many obstacles had to be overcome," Norton recalled. "To bring my resolution to fruition was a long struggle." On February 28, 1924, Mrs. Catherine Finn, Hudson County's representative in the New Jersey state legislature, introduced legislation authorizing the use of $1.6 million county bond issue to build and operate the maternity hospital. The New Jersey state legislature approved Finn's measure for the medical facility.

Hague made the hospital, named after his mother, Margaret, one of his pet projects. According to Norton, the Jersey City mayor "had the advantage of a very devoted and high principled mother and has always, in his personal and political life, held almost a reverence for women." The Margaret Hague Maternity Hospital, a 10-story building located at Clifton Place and Fairmount Avenue in Jersey City, became the first such facility built with county funds for impoverished mothers from crowded

and unsanitary tenements and quickly became one of the best of its kind
in the nation. The first baby delivered there arrived on October 15, 1931.
It accommodated 400 mothers and babies and was noted for low infant
mortality. Over 130,000 babies were born there within the first twenty-
five years, with a mortality rate a mere 2.3 percent. Critics complained
that taxes were too high because the hospital entailed the expenditure of
large sums of money, but Norton countered, "The large majority of our
citizens approve his every act."[48]

Norton attended her first of seven National Democratic Party Conventions at Madison Square Garden in New York City from June through
August 1924. "I can close my eyes now," she wrote over two decades
later, "and feel the steaming heat of those three weeks and hear those
monotonous roll calls." Norton especially was deeply stirred when polio-
stricken Franklin D. Roosevelt nominated Governor Alfred E. Smith of
New York as the Democratic Party nominee for president in what she
termed "one of the greatest speeches I ever heard in any convention."
Mayor Hague also passionately supported Smith's presidential candida-
cy. The convention delegates, however, deadlocked between the more
urban Smith and the predominately rural William McAdoo for 102 bal-
lots. Dark-horse candidate John Davis of West Virginia, a Wall Street
lawyer, prevailed on the 103rd ballot after forty-six grueling days.[49] The
1924 Democratic Party convention helped set the stage for Norton's increased involvement in the national political arena.

NOTES

1. 1 Mary T. Norton, "Madam Congressman: The Memoirs of Mary T. Norton of
New Jersey," (Hereafter cited as Memoirs) Mary T. Norton MSS, New Jersey Collection, Archibald Stevens Alexander Library, Rutgers, The State University of New Jersey, pp. 1–5. I refer to her as Mary until her marriage and as Norton thereafter.

2. Norton, "Memoirs," p. 8.

3. Norton, "Memoirs," pp. 6–7.

4. Norton, "Memoirs," pp. 9–10.

5. Norton, "Memoirs," p. 11; Carmela Ascolese Karnoutsos, "Mary Teresa Norton," in Joan N. Burstyn, ed., *Past and Promise: Lives of New Jersey Women* (Syracuse,
NY: Syracuse University Press 1997), pp. 368--70.

6. Marcy Kaptur, *Women of Congress: A Twentieth Century Odyssey* (Washington,
D.C.: Congressional Quarterly, 1996), pp. 34–35.

7. Norton, "Memoirs," pp. 1, 10, 30.

8. Marion McDonagh Burke, Interview with Author, August 7, 1981; National
Women's History Museum, "Women Wielding Power: Pioneer Female State Legislators: New Jersey," http://www.nwhm.org; Karnoutsos, "Mary Teresa Norton"; Mary
T. Norton, "Handwritten Notes for Autobiography," Norton MSS, Box 5, Autobiographical file.

9. Norton, "Handwritten Notes," Norton MSS, Box 5, Autobiographical file; Burke
Interview with Author, Aug. 7, 1981; Barbara J. Tomlinson, "Making Their Way: A
Study of New Jersey Congresswomen, 1924–1994," (Ph.D. dissertation, Rutgers, The
State University of New Jersey, 1996), p. 28.

10. Norton, "Memoirs," pp. 13–15; Mary T. Norton to Frances Parkinson Keyes, January 23, 1931, Norton MSS, Box 1, General Correspondence, 1931–1936; Joan Lovero, "Life of Mary Norton," Jersey City Public Library, Jersey City, NJ, p. 3; Burke, Interview with Author, Aug. 7, 1981.

11. Burke, Interview with Author, Aug. 7, 1981; Norton, "Memoirs," pp. 15, 19.

12. Burke, Interview with Author, Aug. 7, 1981; Norton, "Memoirs," pp. 15, 19.

13. Norton, "Memoirs," p. 16; Norton to Keyes, Jan. 23, 1931.

14. Norton, "Memoirs," p. 17.

15. Norton, "Memoirs," p. 18.

16. Burke, Interview with Author, Aug. 7, 1981; Andrews to Kellogg, undated; Democratic National Committee, Press Release, New York City, August 31, 1928, Norton MSS, Box 4, Personal Biographical Material; Maxine Davis, "Five Democratic Women," *Ladies Home Journal* 50 (May 1933), p. 117.

17. Helen Meagher, "Notes of Interview with Mary T. Norton," *Women's Voice*, March 26, 1931, Norton MSS, Box 1, Gen. Corr., 1931–1936; "Mary Teresa Norton," *U.S. News* 9 (May 10, 1940), p. 37; Duff Gilfond, "Gentlewoman of the House," *American Mercury* 18 (October 1929), pp. 159–160.

18. Norton, "Memoirs," pp. 20–21; Norton to Keyes, Jan. 23, 1931.

19. Norton, "Memoirs," pp. 22–23; Meagher, "Interview," Mar. 26, 1933. Mary hereafter is referred to as Norton.

20. Karnoutsos, "Mary Teresa Norton"; Frances Parkinson Keyes, "Truly Democratic," *The Delineator* 122 (March 1933), p. 39; Norton, "Memoirs," pp. 23–24; Burke, Interview with Author, Aug. 7, 1981.

21. Hope Chamberlin, *A Minority of Members: Women in the U.S. Congress* (New York: Praeger Publishers, 1973), p. 54; Karnoutsos, "Mary Teresa Norton"; John Whiteclay Chambers II, "Mary Teresa Hopkins Norton," *Dictionary of American Biography*, Supp. Six, 1956–1960 (New York: Charles A. Scribner's Sons, 1980), p. 479; Meagher, "Interview," Mar. 26, 1931; Dem. Nat. Com., Press Release, Aug. 31, 1928; Burke, Interview with Author, Aug. 7, 1981.

22. Norton, "Memoirs," p. 24; Karnoutsos, "Mary Teresa Norton."

23. Norton, "Memoirs," pp. 30–32.

24. Norton, "Memoirs," pp. 33–34.

25. Kaptur, *Women of Congress*, pp. 35–37; Norton to Keyes, Jan. 23, 1931; Thomas Fleming, "I Am the Law," *American Heritage* XX (June 1969), pp. 32–35; Arthur T. Vanderbilt II, *Changing Law: A Biography of Arthur T. Vanderbilt* (New Brunswick, NJ: Rutgers University Press, 1976), p. 67; Richard J. Connors, *The Career of Jersey City Mayor Frank Hague* (Metuchen, NJ: Scarecrow Press, 1971), pp. 84–98; Featured House Publications, *Women in Congress, 1917–2006*, April 27, 2007, 108th Cong., 1st sess., H. Doc. 108–223, http://www.gpo.gov; Carmela Karnoutsos, "Frank Hague, 1876–1956," *Jersey City Past and Present Home Page*, New Jersey State Historical Commission, http://www.njcu.edu.

26. Featured House Publications, *Women in Congress 1917–2006*; Karnoutsos, "Frank Hague"; Fleming, "I Am the Law," pp. 39–40; Jack Alexander, "King Hanky-Panky of Jersey City," *The Saturday Evening Post* 26 (October 1940), p. 121.

27. Norton, "Memoirs," pp. 26–27.

28. Norton, "Memoirs," pp. 27–28.

29. Norton, "Memoirs," pp. 28–29.

30. Connors, *A Cycle of Power*, p. 85; Karnoutsos, "Mary Teresa Norton"; Norton, "Memoirs," p. 60; "Mary T. Norton," *Current Biography* 5 (1944), pp. 500–503. For the history and legacy of the women's suffrage movement in New Jersey, see Delight W. Dodyk, "Education and Agitation: The Woman Suffrage Movement in New Jersey," (Ph.D. dissertation: Rutgers, The State University of New Jersey, 1997); Sylvia Strauss, "The Passage of Woman Suffrage in New Jersey, 1911–1920," *New Jersey History* 111 (1993), pp. 18–39; and Felice Gordon, *After Winning: The Legacy of the New Jersey Suffragists, 1920–1947* (New Brunswick, NJ: Rutgers University Press, 1986).

31. *Washington Post*, August 3, 1959, p. B2; Karnoutsos, "Frank Hague"; Norton, "Memoirs," pp. 35–36; Kaptur, *Women of Congress*, p. 37; Helen C. Camp, "Mary Teresa Hopkins Norton," *American National Biography* 16 (New York: Oxford University Press, 1999), pp. 529–30; Mary T. Norton to Joseph F. McCaffery, June 18, 1953, Norton MSS, Box 1, Gen. Corr., 1944. For the historical status and role of women in New Jersey, see Carmela Ascolese Karnoutsos, *New Jersey Women: A History of Their Status, Roles, and Images* (Trenton, NJ: New Jersey Historical Commission, 1997).

32. Christine Wiltanger, "Remember the Ladies," The Official Jersey City Web Site http://www.cityofjerseycity.com; *Washington Post*, Aug. 3, 1959, p. 28; Norton to McCaffrey, June 18, 1953; Meagher, Interview, Mar. 26, 1931.

33. Mary T. Norton, Report, Women's World Fair, Chicago Coliseum, Chicago, IL, May 24, 1927, Norton MSS, Box 1, Gen. Corr. to 1930; Anderson to Kellogg, undated; Norton to Keyes, Jan. 23, 1931; Margot Gayle, "Battling Mary Retires," *Independent Woman* 29 (July 1950), p. 198. For role of Alice Paul, see Miriam Feyerherm, "Alice Paul: New Jersey's Quintessential Suffragist," *New Jersey History* 111 (1993), pp. 18–39.

34. Norton, "Handwritten Notes," Norton MSS, Box 5, Autobiographical File; Norton, "Memoirs," p. 37.

35. Norton, "Handwritten Notes," Norton MSS, Box 6, Autobiographical File; Meagher, "Interview," Mar. 26, 1931; Mary T. Norton Speech, Baltimore Press Club, Baltimore, MD, March 1, 1927, Norton MSS, Box 5, Speeches, 1927–1940.

36. Kaptur, *Women of Congress*, p. 38; Norton, "Memoirs," p. 38.

37. Norton, "Memoirs," p. 39.

38. Norton, "Memoirs," pp. 42-43, 98.

39. Featured House Publications, *Women in Congress, 1917–2006*; *New York Times*, December 1, 1968; *New York Times*, November 21, 1920; Gordon, *After Winning*, p. 36; Carmela Ascolese Karnoutsos, "Mary Teresa Norton, 1875–1959," in Joan N. Burstyn, ed., *Past and Promise: Lives of New Jersey Women* (Syracuse, NY: Syracuse University Press, 1997), pp. 202-3; Norton, "Memoirs," pp. 44–45.

40. Norton, "Memoirs," p. 46.

41. Norton, "Memoirs," pp. 47, 126; *Newark Ledger*, May 27, 1934; Burke, Interview with Author, Aug. 7, 1981; "Mary Teresa Norton," *U.S. News* 9 (May 10, 1940), p. 37; Phyllis J. Read and Bernard L. Witlieb, *The Book of Women's Firsts* (New York: Random House, 1992), p. 317.

42. Norton, "Memoirs," pp. 47, 126; Burke, Interview with Author, Aug. 7, 1981.

43. Norton, "Memoirs," pp. 48–49; National Women's History Museum, "Women Wielding Power."

44. Norton, "Memoirs," p. 49; Joan Lovero, "New Jersey City's Mary Norton Blazed a Path for Women in Washington," *Hudson County Magazine* (Spring 1991), p. 28; Burke, Interview with Author, Aug. 7, 1981.

45. Norton, "Memoirs," p. 50; Kaptur, *Women of Congress*, p. 39; Wiltanger, "Remember the Ladies."

46. Keyes, "Truly Democratic," p. 39; Norton, "Memoirs," pp. 51–52.

47. Norton, "Memoirs," p. 52; Karnoutsos, "Mary Teresa Norton."

48. Karnoutsos, "Frank Hague"; Karnoutsos, "Mary Teresa Norton"; Norton, "Memoirs," pp. 53-55; Norton to Keyes, Jan. 23, 1931; Meagher, "Interview," Mar. 26, 1931; Wiltanger, "Remember the Ladies"; Carmela Karnoutsos, "Margaret Hague Maternity Hospital," *Jersey City Past and Present Home Page*, New Jersey State Historical Commission, http://www/njcu.edu.

49. Lovero, "Life of Mary Norton," p. 8; Norton, "Memoirs," p. 56.

TWO

The Early Congressional Years

Norton resigned from the Hudson County Board of Freeholders in 1924 when powerful Jersey City Mayor Frank Hague handpicked her as the Democratic Party candidate for the U.S. House of Representatives from the Twelfth New Jersey Congressional District. Democrat Charles O'Brien, who had represented that district in Congress from 1921 to 1925, retired, leaving the seat vacant. Powerful city and county leaders, whose primary goal was the protection of their own patronage and position, ruled New Jersey. Women seeking political office needed to establish loyalty to the county party leaders and dominant party organization. Hague wanted a woman who would remain loyal, not a visionary who would assertively advocate change. When Norton told Hague that she did not "know anything about Congress," the mayor replied, "Neither do most congressmen." Marion McDonagh Burke, Norton's niece, recollected, "Hague helped Mary get elected." *Ladies Home Journal* wrote, "Originally no feminist, office came unsought and undesired, fruit of her fine welfare work."

Hague selected Norton based on what she had accomplished at the day nursery and especially as a Hudson County freeholder. Norton claimed that Hague nominated her because he wanted "the honor of sending the first woman of the Democratic Party to Congress." According to journalist Duff Gilfond, Hague selected Norton "to give respectability to politics. It was very clever on his part, for the immaculate Mrs. Norton is as ardent a regular as any of the ward politicians that Jersey City used to send and much more conscientious and personable." *Ladies Home Journal* claimed, "She never questions the ethics or the discipline of the political machine." Political reformers, however, portrayed the mayor as an arbitrary ruler desiring a loyal female officeholder subject to his control. "Frank Hague," Mary Dewson, head of the Women's Division of the Democratic National Committee, charged, "did not want any rival in his field and felt safer with the Congressman from Jersey City a woman."[1]

As of the mid-1920s, very few women had served in public affairs. Although some states had permitted females to vote before the 1920s, U.S. women did not gain full suffrage rights nationally until the ratification of the Nineteenth Amendment in 1920. Few women suffrage leaders had sought public office and even fewer had prevailed. The Democratic and Republican parties did not welcome women into their decision-making circles, name them to party positions, or recommend them for appointive positions in government. The parties usually did not nominate women for public office unless their candidate had virtually no chance of winning the general election.

Norton not only campaigned extensively in the Twelfth Congressional District, but she also addressed Democratic Party meetings throughout New Jersey. As vice chair of the Democratic State Committee, she organized women politically in most New Jersey counties. In November 1924, Norton was one of only 183 Democrats elected to serve in the U.S. House of Representatives in the Sixty-ninth Congress. The Democrats suffered large setbacks nationally. Republican Calvin Coolidge defeated Democrat John Davis in the presidential election by a landslide, while the Republicans gained three seats in the U.S. Senate for a 54 to 40 numerical advantage and 22 seats in the U.S. House of Representatives for a 247 to 183 numerical edge.

Norton, however, defeated Republican Douglas Story in the Twelfth Congressional District race, 44,815 to 26,368. Bayonne and Jersey City residents gave her a plurality of nearly 18,500 votes and more than 61 percent of the total vote, "an astonishing victory for the time, even in a Democratic stronghold." In the 1924 congressional elections, Norton benefited from the women's vote and Hague's skill as a master politician. She correctly assumed that "the women she had met throughout the community would come out to support her." Hague canvassed, provided transportation, and offered other incentives to recruit voters on Election Day. Oscar Auf der Heide from the Eleventh District was the only other Democrat elected from the twelve-member New Jersey delegation. "I cannot say that I derived much satisfaction from it at the time," Norton reflected. "I was too disappointed and heartsick over the rest of the picture." The official announcement about her victory came around midnight. "The telephone was kept busy," she recalled, "and a great many people came to my home to congratulate me and wish me luck. I finally got to bed at 4 a.m."

Norton fared better than the other five women candidates seeking House seats in 1924. The other ladies did not enjoy the decisive advantage of having support from a political machine like Hague's. The four other women Democrats aspiring House seats ran in predominantly Republican districts, while the lone Republican woman candidate competed in a Democratic-controlled Southern district.

Norton's election held considerable historical significance. No woman from the Democratic Party, an eastern state, or an urban center east of the Mississippi River had served in the U.S. Congress. Norton, the first member of her family to hold political office, became only the third woman elected to the U.S. Congress without being preceded by a deceased husband. Republicans Jeannette Rankin of Montana (1917–1919, 1941–1943), Alice Robertson of Oklahoma (1921–1923), Winnifred Huck of Illinois (1922–1923), Mae Ella Nolan of California (1923–1925), and Florence Prag Kahn of California (1925–1937) preceded Norton in Congress. Burke recalled, "Women were rare in Congress in the 1920s."[2]

Norton shared a few similarities with the other U.S. congresswomen of that era. They were all Caucasians. The first non-Caucasian candidate was not elected until 1968 when Democrat Shirley Chisholm of New York was elected to the House of Representatives. Norton, like Representatives Rankin, Edith Nourse Rogers of Massachusetts, and Ruth Hanna McCormick of Ohio, had worked either as lobbyists, activists, or political party officials. "Before coming to Congress, many participated as volunteers and organizers in civic organizations and social welfare endeavors typical of Progressive Era reformers. These activities included suffrage and electoral reforms, missionary and education work, public health, nursing, veterans' affairs issues, legal aid, and children." Norton had participated in nursery day care activities prior to entering the Congress.

Norton, however, did not fit the traditional stereotype for the pioneering women in the U.S. Congress. She was born in the 1870s, one or two decades before the majority of early congressional women. Norton was the first Roman Catholic woman elected to a predominantly Protestant Congress. She never received formal education beyond eighth grade. "The women pioneers were exceedingly well educated, partly because many came from well-to-do families that could afford private schooling and post-secondary education." Norton gained political power through the vaunted Hague machine. "The pioneer Congresswomen, with several notable exceptions, were from outside the party power structure." Norton was the first woman to have held political office before entering the U.S. Congress, having been a New Jersey county freeholder. Representatives Ruth Baker Pratt of New York and Kathryn O'Loughlin McCarthy of Kansas were the only other women from the period between 1917 and 1934 with previous electoral experience.

Other striking differences surfaced, too. Norton did not replace a deceased relative, and she served thirteen terms in Congress. The other ladies were "political confidantes and campaign surrogates for the Congressmen to whom they were married or otherwise related." Fourteen of the twenty lady congressmen from the era were wives or daughters of officeholders. They often completed just the congressional terms of their late husbands and did not seek another term. Norton chaired the Labor Committee, was the first of her sex to head a major committee, and led three other committees. Most other women served on "lower-tier panels" and "seldom rose to positions of responsibility."[3]

Norton's election to the House sparked considerable media interest. Around 8 a.m. the following morning, reporters and photographers started appearing at her Reservoir Avenue home. Forty metropolitan newspaper reporters heard her first press conference. Photographers snapped numerous pictures of the newly elected congresswoman. "I was posed at my desk, at a typewriter, at my piano—I was no pianist," Norton recalled. One photographer came while she was eating lunch and asked her to pose standing by a stove holding a frying pan. So few women had served in the U.S. Congress that he misunderstood her projected role. Norton informed him that she expected mainly to deal with legislation in Congress. She assured him, "I do not intend to do any cooking in Congress and thought that such a picture would be ridiculous." The photographer insisted on snapping that picture anyway. Norton complained, "It took days to get the smell out of my living room curtains" because the "flashlights were taken with powder in those days before smokeless bulbs." Numerous flowers and hundreds of telegrams also arrived. Norton's husband, Robert, "an ardent Democrat and a student of politics," encouraged her. "I don't know what kind of congresswoman my wife will make," he told reporters, "but I know I've lost a darned good cook." Burke likewise remembered, "Mary was a marvelous cook and made a great variety of chocolate cakes."[4]

Norton ironically did not begin congressional service until December 1925, over a year after her election. The lame duck Sixty-eighth Congress remained in session until March 4, 1925. Norton officially became the U.S. representative from the Twelfth New Jersey District that day, but Congress took a nine-month recess. Norton formally took the oath of office from Republican Speaker Nicholas Longworth of Ohio on December 7, 1925, nine months after her fiftieth birthday. Her husband, Robert, sisters Anne Hopkins and Loretta McDonagh, brother-in-law Joseph McDonagh, and close friends witnessed the swearing-in ceremonies from the galleries. Norton wore a black satin dress with lace collar and cuffs and a black hat trimmed with a bird of paradise. Dorothy Shumate of the *New York World* told her, "You know it's against the rules of the House to wear a hat." "I didn't know,"[5] Norton replied. Following the House ceremonies, Norton held a reception in her congressional office for Jersey City and Bayonne constituents who had traveled to Washington.

Norton and her sister, Anne, resided in a small apartment at the Wardman Park Hotel the first year and at the Mayflower Hotel from 1927 until 1933. They returned to the Wardman Park Hotel from 1933 to 1938 and rented an apartment at the Kennedy-Warren Hotel from 1939 through 1950. They frequently commuted by train to and from Jersey

City on weekends and summered until the mid-1930s at Allenhurst on the New Jersey shore.

Norton found her new congressional role a striking contrast to her previous experiences. "I was starting of a new career—a career more strenuous, exciting, and rewarding than I had ever dreamed of having—at an age when women of my mother's generation wrapped themselves in shawls and sat down by the fireside to await the end." She added, "I was deeply impressed, but I felt strange in those new surroundings, as if it were a dream, not a reality." Norton quickly realized her unique role on Capitol Hill "in what seemed almost entirely a man's world." Burke recalled, "Mary listened very carefully to what was going on," quickly adjusting to her new world.

Two Republican Party women also served in the Sixty-ninth Congress. Kahn of California was elected in November 1924 to replace her late husband, Julius, while Rogers of Massachusetts won a special election in June 1925 to replace her late husband, John. Norton remained the only Democratic woman in the U.S. Congress until Pearl Oldfield of Arkansas and Ruth Owen of Florida were elected in November 1928.[6]

Norton hoped to advance the political cause of women nationally. "I felt a very heavy responsibility and duty," she confessed, "not only to my own constituents but to the country as a whole. I believed that I was representing not only my own district, but all women at a time when we were pioneers in politics." Norton later acknowledged, "I never lost the feeling that I was still representing women everywhere" and predicted that historians would evaluate her legacy "in terms of the record of a woman" instead of "as a member of Congress."[7]

From the outset, House colleagues treated Norton civilly. The genial, unswerving Norton, who was cool, witty, and competent in debate, never requested special consideration because of her sex and preferred instead to be treated like any other representative. She, however, resisted forming a woman's bloc in the House and considered representing the Twelfth Congressional District in New Jersey as her primary responsibility. "It will probably take another generation," she predicted, "to make women realize their own power."[8]

Norton recollected being "filled with enthusiasm and some fear" on her first day in the House of Representatives and received a very cordial welcome. Members and newspaper reporters filled the room. Norton recalled, "I stood before the Elevated Marble rostrum over which the Speaker presides and was surrounded by members wishing me good luck for I was the first woman to be elected to Congress from the Democratic Party. It was a day of congratulations and much joy." "How does it feel to be a member of Congress?" a colleague asked. "Glad you made the grade." "Thank you. I'm glad too," she replied. "Should I call you Congresswoman?" the same member inquired. "No," she replied. "Mrs. Norton is all right. I'm more used to it." Democrat John Boylan of New York, remarked, "Glad to have you with us. If I can help you just say how and when." Norton added, "And he did help. He and so many others." Republican Speaker Nicholas Longworth of Ohio smiled and applauded Norton but wondered, "How did you get to be elected in this Republican year." Norton noticed "so many new faces—people I had never met before—all friendly and all wishing me luck." She realized, however, "I needed luck, and a lot of other things too." A daunting responsibility lay ahead of her. "I was coming here to take part in trying to solve the many problems that would mean so much to many Americans," Norton admitted. "I was frightened. Could I live up to all the things I said I would do if I were elected? Well, I knew I was going to try, but I was a bit dubious about how successful I would be."

On December 15, one week after taking the congressional oath, Norton participated in her first House debate on the income tax bill. To fulfill a campaign promise, she aspired to help poorer families by increasing personal tax exemptions. Democrat Charles Abernethy of North Carolina, seated next to Norton, told her that she would need to introduce an amendment to that effect and showed her how to fill out an amendment form. He added, "And you must speak to the amendment for five minutes."[9] Norton introduced an amendment, which would have raised tax exemptions from $3,500 to $5,000 for married persons and from $1,500 to $3,000 for single persons.

Although freshman members seldom addressed their colleagues in that era, Norton delivered her maiden five-minute speech passionately trumpeting her amendment. She argued, "The burden of Federal taxation should be lifted from the wage earners. This is not a partisan question; it is the business of the people, and we in Congress . . . should heed their call and respond with quick action." Norton urged Democrats and Republicans "to vote as a unit, not as a party, on this amendment which affects all constituents. In your campaign speeches you have often declared yourself as 'a friend of the working people!' Now is your chance to prove it."[10] She added, "I could think of no better Christmas present for the hardworking taxpayer than the relief offered in my amendment." Norton reminded colleagues that income taxes had tripled since 1914. When asked by a freshman colleague about delivering her maiden speech, she replied, "Nothing to it! I have been accustomed to public speaking in New Jersey, and besides, I felt so keenly on the subject of taxes that I could not possibly feel nervous." The Republican-controlled House rejected her amendment, however, teaching her that "amendments to tax bills not offered by the powerful House Ways and Means Committee usually lost."[11]

During the Sixty-ninth Congress, Norton consistently backed urban, Democratic Party, northeastern interests and introduced several unsuccessful bills. She acknowledged, "I was filled with enthusiasm and ambition," but "learned quickly that a member of the minority party rarely succeeds in getting a bill through." Her legislation would have created a board of industrial adjustments to mediate labor-management conflicts in the coal mining industry, permitted foreign-born wives and children of American citizens to enter the United States on a non-quota basis, allowed American women who married foreigners to retain their United States citizenship, improved compensation benefits for mothers who had lost sons in World War I, strengthened enforcement of the Narcotics Drug Act, and increased the annuity ceiling for Civil Service retirees from $1,000 to $1,200, but the fiscal-minded Republicans rebuffed her measures. Norton blamed the Coolidge administration for her legislative setbacks. General Herbert Lord, the director of the budget, resisted Norton's attempt to raise the annuity ceiling to $1,200, preferring to retain a $1,000 maximum annuity as consistent with President Coolidge's program of economy. "Since when," Norton asked, "did the executive branch of the Government eliminate the legislative?"

Bayonne and Jersey City constituents in 1926 resoundingly reelected Norton by the widest margin (43,000) of New Jersey's entire delegation. Norton trounced Republican Philip Grece of Jersey City, 54,082 to 11,034, winning 83 percent of the votes in the Twelfth Congressional District. She compiled the fourth highest vote total among the New Jersey delegation, trailing only Republicans Harold Hoffman, Randolph Perkins, and Charles Wolverton. The Hague machine, Irish, Roman Catholic workers, and women voters helped trigger the landslide. The Democrats gained one House seat in the New Jersey delegation. Paul Moore joined Norton and Auf der Heide.[12]

During the 1920s, the token congressional women received less favorable committee assignments and usually were denied leadership positions. Norton initially was appointed to the House District of Columbia Committee and Labor Committee. She especially enjoyed representing the vote-less residents of the nation's Capitol as the first woman to serve on the District of Columbia Committee, acting as "Washington's city council." Representatives normally considered membership on that committee a futile job. "Yet she accepted it," *Ladies Home Journal* observed, because "she felt no woman had the right to refuse such service." Norton's District of Columbia Committee assignment indeed took considerable time away from serving her own New Jersey constituents.

Norton performed her District of Columbia Committee assignment enthusiastically, drawing upon her social service and freeholder experiences in New Jersey to improve the lives of Washington, D.C., residents. Her first individual committee task entailed inspecting the District's public schools. To her dismay, Norton discovered "all of the schools were overcrowded" and many lacked "the ordinary conveniences to be found in small towns elsewhere in the country."[13] She published her inspection report, prodding a few District public schools to upgrade their building facilities.

Norton hoped to establish a Board of Public Welfare for the District of Columbia and supported legislation to aid District mothers by providing home care for dependent children. Republican Senator Arthur Capper of Kansas introduced a bill placing the workhouse, jail, reformatory, municipal hospital, tuberculosis hospital, home for the aged, and other institutions under one board. Norton opposed combining the administration of the welfare functions with the penal institutions, proposing instead legislation establishing separate boards to administer welfare and criminal justice. "I objected to having mothers of dependent children lumped with criminals," she declared. During floor debate, Norton contended that a single board should not decide cases both involving both poverty and crimes. She insisted, "We should have two separate boards, one for the unfortunates and one for the felons." [14]

A conference committee reconciled the differences between the Capper and Norton versions. Five House District of Columbia Committee members, including Norton, served on the conference committee. Speaker Longworth appointed Norton upon the recommendation of Committee Chairman Frederick Zihlman of Maryland, making her the first Congresswoman to serve on a conference committee. Conference committee members normally were chosen on seniority, but Zihlman selected Norton. Norton recollected, "He believed that because I had been active in welfare work long before I came to Congress, I probably knew more about the bill than any other member of the committee." Since Capper still preferred having all functions combined under one board, Norton suggested instead that a subcommittee be established to treat mothers with dependent children. Capper readily consented to the idea, and the Board of Public Welfare was established. Norton was delighted that "the mothers of dependent children (were) not thrown in with malefactors." [15]

Veterans' legislation likewise attracted Norton's attention. When Norton entered Congress, New Jersey did not have a veterans' hospital. New Jersey veterans often were housed at hospitals considerable distances from their home state. Norton lamented, "There were hundreds of New Jersey men in hospitals all over the country, far from home, making it very difficult for their families to visit them. I had promised in my campaign to try to correct this injustice if I were elected." She battled from 1925 to 1928 for federal funds for construction of a veterans' hospital in New Jersey. [16]

Norton joined the House World War Veterans Legislation Committee when a vacancy occurred in 1926 and served on it until 1933. Norton's World War I service as chairman of a large Red Cross unit may have influenced her appointment to that committee. Norton on January 28, 1926, asked General Frank Hines, administrator of the Veterans Bureau, to support a veterans' hospital for New Jersey. She lobbied for the facility before the Hospitalization Board of the Veterans Bureau but returned to her office rather discouraged. The Hospitalization Board clerk, however, telephoned Norton's secretary, "Tell your boss she made a good impression. It looks like New Jersey will be considered." Norton also persuaded New Jersey Senators Republican Walter Edge and Democrat Edward Edwards to support it.

Despite Norton's plea, General Hines on January 7, 1927, submitted his proposed hospital building program without recommending a facility for New Jersey. When the subcommittee questioned him about the omission at the hearings, he testified that the American Legion had made no recommendation for a New Jersey hospital at its June 1926 convention. The New Jersey American Legion had not endorsed her plan either. "When I needed support from the American Legion, it failed me," she complained. The House World War Veterans Legislation Committee, therefore, initially overlooked New Jersey when considering locations to build veterans' hospitals and instead approved a $3.5 million hospital for Coatesville, Pennsylvania, although the Keystone State already had two veterans' hospitals. Since a Pennsylvania Republican served on the committee, Norton charged, "This is the 'spoils system' at work." [17]

When General Hines testified before the House World War Veterans Legislation Committee, Norton reminded him that New Jersey did not have a veterans' hospital and needed the facility. Hines agreed that New Jersey deserved a veterans' hospital "because of the number of men who had served and the casualties suffered." If the committee agreed to divide the Pennsylvania allotment equally with New Jersey, Hines promised, "He would gladly recommend the change to the Hospitalization Board."

The World War Veterans Committee verbally approved Norton's motion to divide the $3.5 million appropriation equally between Pennsylvania and New Jersey. [18] Norton, though, learned a few days later that the committee minutes contained no written record of the agreement. A Newark, New Jersey, newspaper the next Sunday morning broke the story that Norton's motion was not mentioned in the final committee report to the House floor. "This was a terrible shock to me," Norton disclosed, "but was I glad I'd seen the paper!" The next day, she asked the committee chairman for a copy of the report. The evasive chairman referred her to the committee clerk. "I was furious," Norton admitted, "and he did not improve my state of mind by remarking in a patronizing tone, "When you have been in Congress longer, Mrs. Norton, you will not take things so seriously." She asked him to convene the committee, but he deemed this "impossible." Norton, meanwhile, obtained a copy of the committee report and learned that the Newark newspaper story was accurate. "My fury was mounting," she disclosed, "so I went to every member of the New Jersey delegation—all Republicans except Oscar Auf Der Heide of Union City and me—and asked them to meet in my office at 5 o'clock to discuss a matter of importance to our state." The entire New Jersey delegation attended and backed her cause. [19] The House World War Veterans Legislation Committee met the following morning. Norton concluded, "Obviously the chairman of the Veterans com. was impressed by the unity of the N.J. delegation on the matter." She reminded the committee members that her motion had been approved and omitted from the final report. A Pennsylvania Republican concurred that the committee indeed had adopted her motion. Norton's motion carried in committee a second time and appeared in the revised committee report. "Never have I won one (battle)," she claimed, "which gave me greater satisfaction. I hate to be thought a fool."[20]

Norton in February 1927 sponsored a measure to allocate $11 million for the erection of a veterans' hospital at Somerset, New Jersey, near New Brunswick. The Subcommittee on Hospitals recommended building a 600-bed hospital for Philadelphia and a 400-bed hospital for Somerset. The House World War Veterans Legislation Committee on February 11 adopted, 13 to 3, the subcommittee's recommendation for a New Jersey hospital and urged that Congress appropriate $11 million for the twin facilities. Norton urged the House to approve it. "New Jersey," she explained, "had a large veterans population in hospitals throughout the country and I felt that in view of the numbers we sent to war and the type of service they rendered we were entitled to seek a veterans' hospital within our own state lines." The House adopted Norton's bill on March 2, but she experienced "bitter disappointment" when a Senate filibuster blocked further action on her measure that session.

In January 1928, Norton again pleaded the New Jersey case during hearings of the Subcommittee on Hospitals. The subcommittee in March drafted legislation recommending veterans' hospitals for New Jersey, southern New England, and Kentucky, rejecting an amendment by Republican Robert Luce of Massachusetts, subcommittee chairman, to delete the latter two facilities. Luce resigned as subcommittee chair, being replaced by Republican Rogers of Massachusetts.

The veterans' hospital remained one of Norton's passions. "This hospital has been my ardent desire since I was first elected to Congress," Norton explained in a press release. "I know there are many veterans waiting to avail themselves of its privileges. They are deserving of the best treatment under the happiest of circumstances that we can give them." Norton's press release helped expedite congressional action. Norton also argued the case for the New Jersey hospital before her House colleagues on April 16. The House the same day approved her measure to establish the Somerset hospital 30 miles from Jersey City. The Senate concurred on May 22. President Coolidge signed the bill the next day. Norton boasted, "It was the first promise to my constituents that I was able to fulfill." The congressional action elated Norton, who remarked, "There are many veterans waiting to avail themselves of its privileges. They are deserving of the best treatment under the happiest circumstances that we can give them." The Veterans Hospital at Somerset was enlarged several times during Norton's tenure in the U.S. Congress.[21]

During the Coolidge era, Norton occasionally attended White House social functions. She described President Calvin Coolidge as "a man of simple tastes and, I believe, complete honesty. He did the routine things a President was supposed to do in those uncomplicated times." Norton observed, "President Coolidge certainly lived up to his reputation for never wasting words." Norton, however, found First Lady Grace Coolidge much more sociable and "a woman I always think of with a great deal of admiration and respect." Aside from visiting the White House, Norton seldom circulated the Washington social scene. According to Burke, "She did not socialize very much" and usually was "too tired when she got home."[22]

Norton, meanwhile, increasingly encouraged women to participate in politics. She claimed that women did not realize how much government affected their lives and confessed, "The more I sit and listen to the debates here, the more I realize the close relation between politics and details of everyday home life." Since government concerned human welfare, Norton urged women "to understand and work at politics as earnestly as they do at their Bridge games."[23] Women, she claimed, vastly underestimated their potential political clout. "I believe that women today hold the balance of power," Norton argued in 1931, "and if they use that power intelligently they could make a valuable contribution to their state and nation." Disappointed that American women voted less than men, she urged females to join a major political party and perhaps even seek political office. Norton lamented, "A large percentage of women are either too indifferent or too lazy" to learn about the candidates and vote. "We need organization more than anything else,"[24] she concluded.

Norton served as a delegate-at-large at the 1928 Democratic Party convention in Houston, Texas, wholeheartedly backing New York Governor Al Smith for the presidency. Smith was the first Roman Catholic nominated for the presidency on a major party ticket. "I was tremendously impressed myself by his record," Norton observed, "and had come to know him personally." They held similar views on municipal issues, birth control, and prohibition. In January 1927, Norton had written Smith, "I am most anxious to do everything within my power to promote your cause."[25] She seconded the nomination of Senator Joseph Robinson of Arkansas for vice president.

During the Fall 1928 presidential campaign, the prejudice against Smith's Roman Catholicism dismayed Norton. Norton denounced both the "disillusionment" and "bitterness" of the presidential race and admitted, "It was one of the few times in my life when I almost lost faith in people." The bigotry against Smith even alarmed Protestant voters. "Many of my Protestant friends," Norton added, "have told me since that the vitriolic and unjust attacks made on Governor Smith because of his religion were responsible for their voting for him."[26]

Smith asked Norton to chair the Democratic Women's National Speaker's Bureau based in New York. Norton recruited dynamic speakers across the nation and organized over 1,000 volunteers to campaign for Smith. Nellie Ross of Wyoming, the nation's first woman governor, Emma Guffey Miller of Pennsylvania, and Eleanor Roosevelt of New York also crusaded relentlessly for Smith. "The prejudice they encountered in some audiences," Norton claimed, "actually increased the enthusiasm of most of our speakers, and they did an excellent job."[27]

Norton, still vice chair of the New Jersey State Committee, organized the women's portion of the Smith campaign and delivered many speeches throughout the Garden State. "Our women," she recollected, "responded with enthusiasm, and we had meetings in every county — more than one in most of them." In September 1928, Hague and the state Democratic organization held a very large political rally for Smith at Sea Girt on the New Jersey shore. Over 250,000 Democrats heard Smith as the featured speaker. Democratic rallies at Newark, Jersey City, Camden, and Trenton also attracted huge crowds. The crowd size boosted Norton's optimism. "I was not experienced enough those days," she later admitted, "to realize that big crowds and cheering can be deceptive."

Norton exuded with confidence about the election. Three nights before the election, she told Hague, "He's (Smith's) going to win! The tide is turning!" Hague, however, countered, "I'd willingly give my political career to put him over, but he isn't going to make it. There's too much opposition, and we haven't broken it down." New Jersey Democrats ultimately failed to carry the predominantly Republican state for Smith. "We were bitterly disappointed," Norton explained, "more particularly because religious prejudice had much to do with our defeat."

Republican Herbert Hoover routed Smith by over six million votes in the final tally. The Democrats carried just eight states and suffered their worst Electoral College defeat since the Civil War. Norton attributed the Smith's defeat to his Roman Catholicism, his opposition to prohibition, and the nation's economic prosperity. Norton won reelection to a third congressional term from the Twelfth District, outpolling Republican Philip Grece again, 56,748 to 34,817, and receiving 62 percent of the total vote. The Hoover landslide reduced her margin of victory. Auf de Heide was the only other Democrat elected among the 12-member New Jersey delegation. Republican Fred Hartley Jr. unseated Moore by less than 400 votes in the Eighth District.[28]

Norton reflected on the national Democratic Party election woes in response to a January 1929 letter from Franklin D. Roosevelt, newly elected Governor of New York. Roosevelt, "who feared Hague," had asked Norton to evaluate the Democratic Party. Roosevelt wrote, "I am convinced that, had we kept our national organization going between elections we should have done better, and hope that steps will be taken to have this carried out during the next three years." Norton replied, "Had we been more positive in our party organization, the result might have been different." She lauded the Hudson County Democratic women for their effective organization in having women leaders stationed in every ward and in getting voters to the polls. These women canvassed and surveyed every household before each registration deadline, primary and Election Day and tracked the movements of people entering or leaving the ward.

Norton's letter assessed the 1928 campaign results. Norton observed, "The women were divided on the religious and prohibition issues" and claimed, "The religious issue caused the greatest trouble." The prevailing economic prosperity also benefited the Republicans. Norton urged that the Democratic State and National Committees coordinate better and function throughout the year, that the State Committee have active representation from every county, and that the County Committee meet monthly to discussing policy matters and hear speakers. "I am a Democrat who feels that we have gained much knowledge in the defeat of 1928," she affirmed, "and I see no reason for feeling the least bit discouraged. However, I do see much work to be done if we are to profit by mistakes of the past."

Norton also recommended the Democrats revamp the Speakers Bureau system. "We were obliged," she lamented, "to send women out who knew little about the political attitudes of the states they were sent into and who were far from practical. If every state had the necessary vision to train even a dozen speakers, we could have an interchange of trained women during a Presidential campaign and be prepared to furnish the proper type speaker and this with a minimum of expense." Norton concluded, "If you consider my suggestions have any merit, and you feel I can serve you and the Democratic Party, please be sure I shall consider such service a great honor. I owe the Party a big debt in that it has been my privilege to have been elected the first woman in Congress from the East, and I stand ready and willing to discharge that debt insofar as it lies in my power to do so." Roosevelt welcomed Norton's suggestions and acknowledged, "The problem of the women's vote is still not entirely solved by either party." [29]

Norton, meanwhile, clamored for repeal of the Eighteenth Amendment regarding prohibition. Congress in December 1917 had passed the Eighteenth Amendment, which banned the manufacture, sale, or transportation of alcoholic beverages within or into the United States. By January 1919, thirty-six states had ratified the amendment. The Volstead Act of October 1919 provided the means to enforce the amendment, establishing the legal definition of intoxicating liquors and setting penalties for producing it. The prohibition issue split the women in Congress. Rogers of Massachusetts, Owen of Florida, Oldfield of Arkansas, and McCormick of Illinois supported the Eighteenth Amendment, while Norton and

Pratt of New York opposed it. Norton's Roman Catholic constituents favored repeal of the Eighteenth Amendment.

Several factors, Norton argued, led to the failure of prohibition. "Prohibition did not prohibit," she claimed. Norton alleged that prohibition was very costly and difficult to enforce. "You could not live in a big metropolitan area, as I did," she stressed, "without becoming aware of the fact that prohibition did not work." Norton believed, "Few people regarded the purchase of liquor as a crime." Besides deploring the decline in national morality, she charged that prohibition had sparked the rise in organized crime. Norton contended that prohibition encouraged increased crime rates and underworld profits. Bootlegging, she warned, was "becoming a big, organized, powerful and highly profitable business." She also asserted that prohibition encouraged the bribery of public officials and the death, blinding, or paralyzing of numerous unsuspecting violators.[30]

Norton charged that the Anti-Saloon League and the Women's Christian Temperance Union promoted an Eighteenth Amendment the American public did not intend to obey. Prohibition, she contended, was "thrust down the throats of a war-absorbed nation by a well-organized lobby of fanatical reformers" and constituted perhaps "the most heartily despised law that has ever graced our Federal statute books." Norton criticized prohibition as "a veritable Frankenstein, thrown together in a moment of hysteria, by a group of ignoble experiments" and warned "it now threatens to throttle those responsible for its existence and those of us who stood by while the outrage was being perpetrated." Many Americans followed a double standard, she noticed, supporting prohibition publicly but drinking privately in their homes. "If we are not honest in our attitude toward the law," Norton asked, "how can we expect our children to have any respect for us? The example we are setting for them now is horrible."[31]

Numerous colleagues, Norton claimed, held hypocritical attitudes on the prohibition issue. Norton complained that some representatives "drank wet and voted dry." She believed, "These members felt ashamed of those votes, but they thought their districts would defeat them if they voted in Congress as their consciences dictated. Most of them came from districts that were supposed to be dry."[32]

In 1928, Norton introduced the first House resolution to repeal the Eighteenth Amendment. She remained "an outspoken wet in days when many politicians were silent." After the House adjourned one day, Norton walked to her office with a colleague and a *New York World* correspondent. The colleague told Norton why he and other representatives had voted against repeal, even though they personally drank. "Mrs. Norton," he asked, "why don't you introduce a bill to repeal the Eighteenth Amendment?" The colleague knew that New Jersey favored repeal and considered Norton "in the right position to introduce such a bill." Although cognizant that Congress was not yet ready to repeal prohibition, he added that because she "was a woman, it would receive much publicity" and that "it would start the ball rolling and might do some good."[33]

The Legislative Counsel prepared for Norton a resolution for a public referendum on the Eighteenth Amendment. Norton introduced the resolution "to the amazement—and the amusement—of my colleagues," but her action aroused national ridicule. "I had plenty of publicity, a great deal of it of the kind one does not enjoy," she admitted. "My mail was bad. Most of the letters were from women, who did not mince words in telling me what they thought of me." Jersey City and Bayonne constituents, along with other New Jersey residents, backed her amendment. "My own district . . . supported me and gave me credit for having courage," Norton remembered, "and I received encouragement from people all over my state." She joined a bipartisan women's group favoring repeal of the Eighteenth Amendment and spoke against prohibition to a largely hostile Bar Harbor, Maine, audience and a Women's Christian Temperance Union (WCTU) meeting in New Jersey. Others warned Norton not to address the WCTU, but she countered, "I have always felt that nothing should be embarrassing to discuss if you really believe in what you have to say." The WCTU ladies listened politely, but Norton conceded, "I doubt if we made any converts that day!"[34]

Congress in 1928 rejected Norton's repeal resolution. "Of course it got nowhere," Norton lamented. "I was a member of the minority party." Norton discerned most colleagues "wouldn't dare come right out openly and oppose the Eighteenth Amendment, no matter how they felt about it privately. I was learning that a cloak of sanctity grows up around some public issues." To Norton's chagrin, the Jones-Stalker Act of 1929 increased the penalties for violation of the prohibition amendment. Norton told colleagues, "We cannot legislative morals; the failure of prohibition demonstrates that this is true."[35]

Norton's campaign to end prohibition ultimately succeeded. "Opposition to Prohibition became politically more expedient in the early 1930s, when the focus of the debate shifted from morality to economics" during the Depression. In 1932, Norton led the House Democrats seeking repeal of the Eighteenth Amendment and called the "noble experiment" a mistake. At a lame-duck session in February 1933, Congress adopted and sent to the states the Twenty-First Amendment repealing the Eighteenth. Congress in March 1933 amended the Volstead Act to allow the manufacture, sale, and taxation of beer with 3.2 percent alcohol content. Roosevelt, who had been elected president in November 1932, declared the official end to prohibition when the required number of states passed the amendment in December 1933.[36]

Norton, an active member of St. Joseph's Roman Catholic Church in Jersey City, adamantly opposed birth control. Margaret Sanger, former president of the American Birth Control League, had persuaded Republican Frederick Gillett of Massachusetts in February 1931 to introduce a bill permitting the distribution of birth control literature or contraceptive information through the mail. During the Senate Judiciary Committee hearings in February, Norton and other prominent Roman Catholics testified against the Gillett measure. Norton called birth control unnatural and denied that sex education would help poor women or safeguard their health. "The advocates of birth control," she countered, "would have you believe that children are an affliction, a liability, enervating, and many other horrible things, when, as a matter of fact, they are the greatest gift of God." She added, "Nothing abnormal and contrary to the laws of nature will tend to safeguard the health of any woman."

Norton also refuted Sanger's contention that some women suffered from having too many children. Sanger's mother, Anne, had died during the birth of her eleventh child. Norton, who had lost her only child, explained that "the fine womanhood of America" considered "the pressure of a baby face against their own the highest form of earthly happiness." She told Judiciary Committee members stories about many women, including her own mother, who had large families. Norton's mother had lost three of her seven children. "These women I knew were neither enervated nor unhappy," Norton claimed, "and I reminded Mrs. Sanger that anything abnormal or contrary to the law of nature would not tend to safeguard the health of any woman."[37] She claimed that "dissemination of birth control literature would be unnecessary if men and women would practice self-control." Other prominent Roman Catholics likewise opposed the measure, which never reached the Senate floor. The Gillett bill died in the Senate Judiciary Committee when the Seventy-first Congress ended on March 4.[38]

The economic prosperity of the 1920s, meanwhile, abruptly halted with the stock market crash of October 1929. The Republicans took principal credit for the business boom, but bore primary responsibility for the economic collapse. The crash, following years of flagrant stock speculation and weak federal regulatory policies, sparked an economic depression throughout the nation. "Investor's mounting losses, sharply lower consumer spending, plummeting agricultural prices, and widespread runs on banks sent the economy into a three-year skid." By late 1930, Norton recollected, "People were desperate, their savings gone, homes lost, no jobs to be had. Bewildered and bitter, they tried to place the responsibility. They blamed Hoover, but they couldn't do anything about him" because the president did not face reelection until 1932.[39]

Norton attacked the Smoot-Hawley Act of 1930 for raising tariffs on agricultural products and select manufactured items to the highest levels in American history. She warned that the tariff measure would increase the cost of consumer goods, particularly women's clothes, cosmetics, and accessories. "Lipsticks, perfumes and the like once were luxuries," she observed, "Today, they are necessities."

The Democrats experienced a congressional resurgence in the November 1930 elections, gaining forty-nine seats in the House of Representatives, initially slicing the Republican majority to 218 to 216. The worsening economic depression triggered the Democratic comeback. Norton was easily reelected for a fourth term, polling 53,565 votes to just 16,715 for Douglas Story. She tallied nearly 76 percent of the vote, 14 percent higher than in 1928. The continued backing of the Hague machine and women, the deepening economic crisis, and Norton's legislative efforts to help her Irish, Roman Catholic, working-class constituents contributed to her decisive victory. The Republicans retained ten of the twelve New Jersey seats, with Democrat Auf der Heide keeping his seat. Four Republican representatives died between November 1930 and March 1931, however, giving the Democrats a 220 to 214 advantage and control of the House. Norton boasted, "I was no longer a member of the minority party when I went back to the 72nd Congress in March, 1931."[40]

Economic issues dominated the Democratic-controlled House in 1931 and 1932. Norton continued to serve on the House Labor Committee, championing the American worker. The Labor Committee had played a secondary role during the business-dominated, Republican-controlled 1920s but assumed much greater importance when the Depression worsened. "By the winter of 1932–1933, more than 5,500 banks had been shut down, nearly one in four Americans was unemployed, and the gross national product had declined by nearly a third." Norton deplored the collapse of financial institutions, widespread unemployment, housing dislocation, sagging agricultural prices, and massive suffering.

In 1932, Norton eagerly backed four bipartisan federal relief and recovery measures, including the Reconstruction Finance Corporation Act, the Emergency Relief and Construction Act, the Federal Home Loan Act, and the Glass-Steagall Banking Act. The Reconstruction Finance Corporation Act enabled the RFC to make over $2 billion in loans to banks, mutual saving banks, insurance companies, credit unions, railroads, and savings building, and loan associations. The Emergency Relief and Construction Act authorized the RFC to make up to $300 million in loans to state and local governments to assist them in providing relief to the unemployed and $1.5 billion in loans to state and local governments to employ people in building self-liquidating public works. The Federal Home Loan Act provided loans to home mortgage holders similar to those that the Federal Reserve System offered to banking and commercial interests. The Glass-Steagall Banking Act expanded bank credit through lending by district or regional Federal Reserve Banks to member banks.[41]

In 1932, Norton also became involved in the decade-long argument over the payment of a bonus to World War I veterans. After World War I, the American Legion had lobbied Congress to pay a bonus to veterans to help make up for the wages they lost when they left higher-paying jobs for military service. The Soldiers Bonus Act of 1924 had provided veterans a bonus of $1.25 for each day of overseas duty and $1 for each day of domestic service, payable in 1945. Many veterans lost their jobs, savings, homes or farms during the Depression and demanded immediate payments of the bonuses. The Bonus Expeditionary Force, comprising thousands of unemployed World War I veterans, marched on Washington, D.C., in the spring and summer of 1932 to collect bonuses for their wartime services and encamped at Anacostia Flats, near the Capitol. By a 211 to 175 margin, the House on June 15 approved a measure by Democrat Wright Patman of Texas to pay those bonuses immediately.

Norton favored granting pensions to widows and former widows of soldiers from previous wars, but opposed hastening the payment of cash bonuses to World War I veterans. Bonus payments, she feared, might bankrupt the U.S. treasury, arouse widespread public opposition, and diminish the prospects for other veterans' legislation. Norton contended, "To single out the veterans for special consideration at this time would be unfair." She warned, "Payment would harm the cause of the veterans bringing public sentiment against them" and pointed out, "There were no funds available in the U.S. treasury to pay the huge sums called for." She conceded, however, "It cost me some sleepless nights, for the welfare of the veterans of World War I was dear to my heart."

Norton came under intense pressure to support the immediate cash payments to veterans. Irate veterans from Norton's district crowded the lobby of the Capitol building the day of the congressional vote. Constituents sent her hundreds of letters championing the cash bonuses. Norton recalled, "Tough lobbyists were growling at her office door and the newspapers back home were ready to pounce on her." The shrewd legislator tried to deflect criticism "by reminding everybody how much she had done for veterans." She reflected, "I think they realized after I had talked to them a little while that I was doing the thing I thought best for them, and that I was really their friend."

When Mayor Hague phoned her long distance the day of the House vote, Norton bravely told him that she opposed the Patman bill. "You know the veterans control a big block of votes—not only their own, but their families'," Hague warned. "If you vote against the bonus, you will lose at least ten thousand votes—maybe more. But it's your problem. I haven't any suggestions to make as to what you should do." Norton later confided, "Had he requested me to vote for the bonus, I'd have found it hard to refuse, and I would have been very unhappy." Norton followed the dictates of her conscience. She explained, "My political dealings with him (Hague) have never been hampered in any way. When I began my political career, he told me my success or failure depended upon my own sense of values and never forget that I was the servant of my constituents; that they trusted and believed in my ability to serve them."[42] The Senate, though, decisively rejected the veterans' bonus bill.

Norton, meanwhile, won considerable recognition from the academic community for her public service. In June 1930, the College of St. Elizabeth in New Jersey awarded her its first honorary degree, a Doctor of Laws for her welfare and government work and invited her to be commencement speaker in 1931. She also earned honorary degrees from Rider College in Trenton, New Jersey, in 1937 and St. Bonaventure University in Olean, New York, in 1950. "Since I had never gone to college," she surmised, "these degrees probably meant more to me than they would have meant to women who had the privilege of a college education."[43] Norton soon faced more legislative challenges ahead as new chairman of the House District of Columbia Committee and as a member enacting crucial New Deal relief and recovery measures.

NOTES

1. Barbara J. Tomlinson, "Making Their Way: A Study of New Jersey Congresswomen, 1924–1994," (Ph.D. dissertation, Rutgers, The State University of New Jersey, 1996), p. 28; Featured House Publications, *Women in Congress: 1917–2006*, April 27, 2007, 108th Cong., 1st sess., H. Doc. 108–223, http://www.gpo.gov; National Women's History Museum, "Women Wielding Power: Pioneer Female State Legislators: New Jersey," http://www.nwhm.org; Marion McDonagh Burke, Interview with Author, August 7, 1981; Mary Norton to Joseph F. McCaffrey, June 19, 1953, Norton MSS, Box 1, General Correspondence, 1944; Barbara Griffin to Editor, *The Jersey Journal*, November 5, 2010; Duff Gilfond, "Gentlewoman of the House," *American Mercury* 18 (October 1929), p. 159; Maxine Davis, "Five Democratic Women," *Ladies Home Journal* 50 (May 1933), p. 22; William H. Chafe, *The American Woman: Her Changing Social, Economic, and Political Roles, 1920–1970* (New York: Oxford University Press, 1972), p. 38.

2. Ivy Maude Baker Priest and Eliza Jane Pratt, "Women Elected to Public Offices," http://www.maxizip.com; Mary T. Norton, "Madam Congressman: The Memoirs of Mary T. Norton of New Jersey," (Hereafter cited as "Memoirs") Mary T. Norton MSS, New Jersey Collection, Archibald Stevens Alexander Library, Rutgers, The State University of New Jersey, pp. 56–57; "Statistics of the Congressional and Presidential Election of November 4, 1924," (Washington, D.C.: U.S. Government Printing Office, 1925), p. 12; Carmela Ascolese Karnoutsos, "Mary Teresa Norton, 1875–1959," in Joan N. Burstyn, ed., *Past and Promise: Lives of New Jersey Women* (Syracuse, NY: Syracuse University Press, 1997), pp. 368–70; Carmela Karnoutsos, "Frank Hague, 1876–1956," *Jersey City Past and Present Home Page*, New Jersey State Historical Commission, http://www.njcu.edu; Marcy Kaptur, *Women of Congress; A Twentieth Century Odyssey* (Washington, D.C.: Congressional Quarterly, 1996), pp. 39, 50; Featured House Publications, *Women in Congress, 1917–2006*; Burke, Interview with Author, Aug. 7, 1981. For Norton's pioneering role in Congress, see Phyllis J. Read and Bernard L. Witlieb, *The Book of Women's Firsts* (New York: Random House, 1992), pp. 316–17.

3. Featured House Publications, *Women in Congress: 1917–2006*.

4. Norton, "Memoirs," pp. 57–58; Mary T. Norton to Frances Parkinson Keyes, January 23, 1931, Norton MSS, Box 1, Gen. Corr., 1931–1936; Margot Gayle, "Battling Mary Retires," *Independent Woman* 29 (July 1950), p. 198; Burke, Interview with Author, Aug. 7, 1981.

5. Norton, "Memoirs," p. 61.

6. Norton, "Memoirs," pp. 59–60.

7. Mary T. Norton, Speech, Baltimore Press Club, Baltimore, MD, March 1, 1927, Norton MSS, Box 5, Speeches, 1927–1940; Mary T. Norton to *Newark Star-Ledger*, January 1951, Norton MSS, Box 2, Gen. Corr., January-June 1951.

8. Gayle, "Battling Mary," p. 200; John Whiteclay Chambers II, "Mary Teresa Norton," *Dictionary of American Biography*, Supp. Six, 1956–1960 (New York: Charles Scribner's Sons, 1980), p. 480.

9. Mary T. Norton, "Handwritten Notes," Norton MSS, Box 4, Personal Biographical Material; Norton, "Memoirs," p. 63.

10. *Congressional Record*, Vol. 67, Pt. 1, p. 880; Angeline Bogucki, "Summary of the Legislative Career of Representative Mary T. Norton," Legislative Reference Service, Library of Congress, Washington, D.C., November 3, 1950, p. 1; Bamberger, "A Congresswoman from New Jersey," *The Charm* (March 1926), p. 27; Emily A. Geer, "A Study of the Activities of Women in Congress with Special Reference to the Congressional Careers of Margaret Chase Smith, Mary T. Norton, and Edith Nourse Rogers," (Masters thesis: Bowling Green State University, 1952), p. 136.

11. Norton, "Memoirs," pp. 63–64; *Congressional Record*, 67, Pt. 1, p. 880; Bamberger, "Congresswoman from New Jersey," p. 27.

12. Featured House Publications, *Women in Congress, 1917–2006*; Norton, "Memoirs," p. 66; *Congressional Record*, Vol. 67, Pt. 1, p. 12424; Bogucki, "Summary," p. 2; "Statistics of the Congressional Election of November 2, 1926," (Washington, D.C.: U.S. Government Printing Office, 1927), p. 12.

13. Tomlinson, "Making Their Way," p. 31; Norton, "Memoirs," p. 65; Maxine Davis, "Five Democratic Women," *Ladies Home Journal* 50 (May 1933), p. 22.

14. Norton, "Memoirs," p. 67.

15. Norton, "Memoirs," pp. 68–69; Featured House Publications, *Women in Congress, 1917–2006*.

16. Norton, "Memoirs," pp. 70–71; Mary T. Norton to Hubert McCauley, January 27, 1927, Norton MSS, Box 1, Gen. Corr. to 1930.

17. Norton, "Memoirs," pp. 70–71.

18. Norton, "Memoirs," pp. 71–72; Tomlinson, "Making Their Way," p. 31. Mary is referred to as Norton hereafter.

19. Norton, "Memoirs," pp. 72–73.

20. Norton, "Memoirs," pp. 73–74.

21. Karnoutsos, "Mary Teresa Norton"; Mary T. Norton, Press Release, Washington, D.C., April 28, 1928, Norton MSS, Box 1, Gen. Corr. to 1930; Helen Meagher, "Notes of Interview with Mary T. Norton," *Woman's Voice*, March 26, 1931, Norton MSS, Box 1, Gen. Corr., 1931–1936; "New Jersey Hospital Bill Chronology," Norton MSS, Box 3, Public Health items; Lucille Considine, Memorandum to Mr. Casey, February 21, 1944, Norton MSS, Box 4, Personal Biographical Material.

22. Norton, "Memoirs," pp. 76–78; Featured House Publications, *Women in Congress, 1917–2006*; Burke, Interview with Author, Aug. 7, 1981.

23. Bamberger, "Congresswoman from New Jersey," p. 27; Norton, Speech, Baltimore Press Club, March 1, 1927.

24. Meagher, "Interview," March 26, 1931; Mary T. Norton, "Why Should Women Be Interested in Government?" Radio Address, CBS, Washington, D.C., May 5, 1932, Norton MSS, Box 5, Speeches, The American Woman, 1932–51.

25. Norton, "Memoirs," p. 83; Mary T. Norton to Alfred E. Smith, January 11, 1927, Norton MSS, Box 1, Gen. Corr. to 1930.

26. Norton, "Memoirs," p. 82.

27. Norton, "Memoirs," p. 85.

28. Norton, "Memoirs," pp. 87–88; "Statistics of the Congressional and Presidential Election of November 6, 1928," (Washington, D.C.: U.S. Government Printing Office, 1929), p. 18.

29. Norton, "Memoirs," pp. 90–92; Franklin D. Roosevelt to Mary T. Norton, November 30, 1928, Norton MSS, Box 2, Corr., Franklin D. Roosevelt, 1928–1945; Mary T. Norton to Franklin D. Roosevelt, January 18, 1929, Norton MSS, Box 2, Corr., Franklin D. Roosevelt, 1928–1945; Franklin D. Roosevelt to Mary T. Norton, January 29, 1929, Norton MSS, Box 2, Corr., Franklin D. Roosevelt, 1928–1945.

30. Norton, "Memoirs," pp. 81–82; "Mary Teresa Norton," *U.S. News* 9 (May 10, 1940), p. 37; Featured House Publications, *Women in Congress, 1917–2006*.

31. Mary T. Norton, "Prohibition," *The Jeffersonian* (1932), pp. 4–5; Democratic National Committee, Press Release, New York City, August 31, 1928, Norton MSS, Box 4, Personal Correspondence, Personal Biographical Material.

32. *Washington Post*, August 3, 1959, p. B2; *New York Herald Tribune*, August 3, 1959, p. 8; Norton, "Memoirs," pp. 92–94; Burke, Interview, Aug. 7, 1981.

33. Norton, "Memoirs," pp. 94–95.

34. Norton, "Memoirs," pp. 95–97; Featured House Publications, *Women in Congress, 1917–2006*.

35. Norton, "Memoirs," p. 82; *Congressional Record*, Vol. 70, Pt. 5, p. 4644; Bogucki, "Summary."

36. Karnoutsos, "Mary Teresa Norton"; Geer, "Activities of Women in Congress," p. 137. For the forces behind the decline of prohibition, see David E. Kyvig, *Repealing National Prohibition* (Chicago, IL: University of Chicago Press, 1979).

37. "Mary T. Norton," *Current Biography* 5 (1944), p. 501; Norton, "Memoirs," p. 98; *Congressional Record*, Vol. 74, Pt. 5, p. 4958; Bogucki, "Summary," p. 4.

38. Congressional Research Service, *Women in Congress*, p. 62; *Congressional Record*, Vol. 74, Pt. 5, p. 4958; Mary T. Norton, "Should Legal Barriers Against Birth Control be Removed?" *Congressional Digest* 10 (April 1931), p. 106; Geer, "Activities of Women in Congress," p. 137; Kathleen A. Tobin, *The American Religious Debate over Birth Control, 1907–1937* (Jefferson, NC: McFarland & Company, 2001), pp. 179–81.

39. Norton, "Memoirs," pp. 98–99; Featured House Publications, *Women in Congress, 1917–2006*. See David M. Kennedy, *Freedom from Fear: The American People in Depression and War, 1929–1945* (New York: Oxford University Press, 1999) for an analysis of the Great Depression era.

40. Norton, "Memoirs," pp. 98–100; "Statistics of the Congressional Election of November 4, 1930," (Washington, D.C.: U.S. Government Printing Office, 1931), p. 15.

41. National Women's History Museum, "Women Wielding Power"; Featured House Publications, *Women in Congress, 1917–2006*; "Mary Teresa Norton," *U.S. News* 9 (May 10, 1940), p. 37; Bogucki, "Summary," p. 4. See also Jordan A. Schwartz, *The Interregnum of Despair: Hoover, Congress, and the Depression* (Urbana, IL: University of Illinois Press, 1970) and Kennedy, *Freedom from Fear*.

42. Norton, "Memoirs," pp. 116–118; Norton to Keyes, Jan. 23, 1931; Featured House Publications, *Women in Congress, 1917–2006*; Eleanor Andrews to Elenere Kellogg, undated, Norton MSS, Box 4, Personal Biographical Material.

43. Norton, "Memoirs," p. 99; Sister Mary Agnes to Mary T. Norton, June 20, 1930, Norton MSS, Box 1, Gen. Corr. to 1930.

THREE

The District of Columbia and New Deal Years

When the Democrats regained control of the U.S. House of Representatives upon the convening of the Seventy-second Congress in March 1931, Norton became chairman of the House District of Columbia Committee and the District's first and only "Lady Mayor." Only one other woman previously had headed a congressional committee. Republican Mae Ella Nolan of California had chaired the House Expenditures in the Post Office Committee from 1923 to 1925. Norton initially ranked second among Democratic District of Columbia Committee members in seniority. Christopher Sullivan of New York, the top-ranking Democratic committee member, normally would have become chairman of the nonprestigious committee because of his seniority but instead switched to the powerful House Ways and Means Committee.

Norton, who rose to the District of Columbia Committee helm in a surprisingly short amount of time, relished her new task. "It was also very unusual for any member to become chairman after only six years' service." The post brought little political recognition and was considered "the most thankless job in Washington," "one of the least favored in the House," and a "bottom-of-the-basement assignment given to congressional outsiders." "No member of Congress," Annabel Paxton wrote, "wants to be saddled with the appointment. It brings no credit from constituents. Taxpayers in Washington don't want fingers in their cherry pie." Norton, though, deemed the post a "high honor" and devoted considerable energy to the committee. "Fortunately I had been deeply interested in the committee," she explained, "and had enjoyed serving as a minority member."[1]

Norton headed the twenty-one-member District of Columbia Committee from 1931 to 1937, governing and handling finances for a city that had no internal municipal government and had disfranchised citizens. Her committee resembled a city council or Board of Alderman. All bills and petitions related to District management came across Norton's desk. Norton appointed several standing subcommittees, which examined legislation regarding the police, fire, public works, and other departments. Between 1931 and 1937, her committee averaged 250 measures monthly regarding taxation, schools, hospitals, police and fire protection, welfare, public works, and utilities for 900,000 Washington, D.C., residents.[2] "Ours was a hardworking, patriotic committee, fairly free from politics," Norton explained. "Service on the District Committee could not help us get votes in our own districts. It did and does add work for a member."[3] The House set aside two Mondays each month for presenting District bills. Most representatives, however, remained apathetic about District needs and legislation.

The chairmanship enabled Norton to treat welfare problems, an area in which she already had gained considerable experience, knowledge, and skill. "I could best serve my state and my country generally," Norton contended, "by concentrating on the work with which I was familiar." She conceded, "While this human element may not be as picturesque, nor attract the publicity that accompanies other lines of endeavor, to me it is far more important." At her first committee meeting as chairperson, Norton exhibited adept leadership and quickly won the respect of the twenty male colleagues. Gender prejudice, though, confronted her from the outset. Republican Frank Bowman of West Virginia lamented, "This is the first time in my life I have been controlled by a woman." "It's the first time," Norton countered, "I've had the privilege of presiding over a body of men, and I rather like the prospect." The New Jersey congresswoman, "adept at navigating toward power within the institution," showed "the surest way for women to attain power and influence in Congress was to work within the prescribed system to mitigate gender differences."[4]

On April 14, 1931, Norton planned to report 26 District bills from her committee to the House floor. Routine measures usually required little time or stirred no floor debate. She presented those bills first and saved the more controversial ones for last. Republican Fiorello LaGuardia of New York strongly opposed one contentious District measure but also planned to attend the Washington Senators season opening baseball game against the Philadelphia Athletics at Griffith Stadium. Norton realized that, "This might be a good time to bring up that bill." LaGuardia asked her if she intended to call up the controversial measure. "Certainly," Norton replied. "But I want to go to the ball game," LaGuardia retorted. "Go ahead. Go right along," Norton counseled. When LaGuardia refused to leave the House chamber, Norton interjected, "I'll put it way down at the bottom, and the chances are we won't get to it today." LaGuardia, however, wanted Norton to promise that she would not bring up the legislation. When Norton refused to make such a pledge,

LaGuardia returned to his seat. "As game time drew near," Norton noticed, "He began to squirm like a small boy, looking very unhappy." LaGuardia again pleaded with her not to consider the measure. Several other opponents of the bill also planned to attend the game. "I let him go back to his seat and worry a little longer," Norton recollected. "Then I laughingly announced to the House that I would not bring that bill up that day. I knew by that time that I would not reach it anyway." LaGuardia grinned, bolted quickly from his seat, and arrived at Griffith Stadium just in time to see President Herbert Hoover throw out the first pitch. The Athletics, winners of two consecutive World Series titles, defeated the Senators, 5 to 3.[5]

Norton plunged her District of Columbia Committee into an unprecedented flood of activity. She in 1933 received around 300 letters and met 50 to 275 visitors daily, figures "three times greater" than before becoming committee head. She favored giving Washington, D.C., residents home rule or self-government in local matters. During her first year as chairperson, the House adopted thirty-seven committee bills helping the District's residents. "Enactment of these laws in so short a period, establishes what is perhaps a record unprecedented in the history of local legislation."[6] These measures, however, often aroused animated exchanges during committee hearings and floor debate. The *Washington Post* and *Washington Star* published editorials lauding Norton's legislative accomplishments, political skills, and determination to overcome conservative resistance while improving the welfare of Washington, D.C., residents. "In view of the highly prejudiced opposition encountered in the House," the *Washington Post* wrote, "the District of Columbia received more competent attention from Congress during the last session than is usually the case" and added "it was only through the earnest and persistent championship of Chairman Norton that these laws are now on the statute books." In another editorial, the *Washington Post* commended her "tact, energy, and . . . leadership" in quickly helping enact measures establishing "a record unprecedented in the history of local legislation." Several of these bills, it added, "were literally hoary with age and had lingered about the committee-room for years awaiting passage."

The new laws brought major changes to the District within the first six months. Norton's committee changed the inequitable District licensing statutes. Trades and occupations requiring inspections at a cost to the District government had not paid taxes under a 1902 act, whereas other businesses, which operated at no expense to the local municipality, had been taxed. The new licensing law based taxes solely upon the cost of the inspections made by the various municipal departments concerned. Firearms legislation, which had been stalled for two decades, imposed stricter regulations over the sale and use of deadly weapons. The District Committee relieved unemployment by authorizing railroad extensions to Buzzard's Point, permitting the installation of pipelines for the Griffith

Consumers and Gulf Refining Companies, and authorizing construction of a power plant for the Potomac Electric Power Company and the new American Pharmaceutical building. Another measure required drivers involved in certain traffic violations or accidents to take out liability insurance before driving again. Norton's committee also permitted credit unions to operate in the District, benefiting residents needing a small loan but lacking the credit requirements of banking institutions.[7]

During Norton's seven-year tutelage, the District of Columbia Committee accomplished numerous economic and social reforms for Washingtonians. Norton, who advocated broadening the authority of the commissioners, administered the committee's affairs diligently. "My first major accomplishment as chairman," she recalled, "was securing passage of legislation merging the two street railway (car) companies." The comprehensive transportation measure had languished in the committee for three decades. "It had been bitterly opposed year after year," Norton lamented, "by certain interests." The merger legislation not only improved transit service in Washington, D.C, but kept street railway fares lower and created more jobs. "My only interest in the bill," she acknowledged, "was to get it out of the pigeon hole where it had been collecting dust for thirty years!"[8]

In 1933, Norton's office received numerous complaints about the District's outdated tuberculosis hospital. One Saturday morning, Norton visited that hospital unannounced and verified the complaints. "I had never seen any public hospital," she declared, "to compare with it in miserable equipment and lacking of everything you expect to find in a hospital. I was so shocked that the following Monday morning I addressed the House for twenty minutes, describing the hospital as I found it." Norton secured Public Works Administration funds, authorizing $1.5 million for construction of a new tuberculosis hospital for the District of Columbia. The House and Senate approved her amendment, leading to erection of the Glenn Dale Tuberculosis Hospital for Children. The *Washington Post* called the hospital, "a monument to her work." Norton also inspected the Children's Hospital and secured a PWA loan of $100,000 to make necessary repairs at the facility.

During the First New Deal in 1933 and 1934, the District of Columbia Committee authorized federal funding for the construction of a municipal building in the industrial section and secured loans to build a sewage disposal plant. It also sanctioned the clearance of dilapidated slum dwellings and enabled construction of modestly priced, sanitary houses. Norton's committee enacted unemployment compensation for District residents and approved the first pensions for Washingtonians over age 60 and blind residents. Other committee measures exempted certain patriotic and educational societies from taxation, created a parole board, financed education for veterans' orphans, and established a much-needed bird and game sanctuary for preserving wildlife. "None of these things,"

Norton affirmed, "would have been done, though, without the cooperation of my committee."[9]

In 1933, Norton introduced legislation to legalize the sale of alcoholic
beverages in Washington, D.C. The revenue from taxes on such sales, she
argued, would help the federal government finance relief programs. The
night after Congress enacted her measure, Norton found a package containing a sterling silver cocktail set from a luggage shop. The sender, a
lobbyist for the repeal of prohibition, promised to mail later "something
to be served in it." Norton promptly returned the package to the luggage
shop.

Norton's committee also clashed over establishing a racetrack in
Washington, D.C. "It had considerable support," Norton claimed, "and I
could see no reason why the District should not have a race track." When
the committee began considering the measure, one Washington woman
testified against building a District racetrack. Norton countered, "You all
go to Baltimore to the races. What's the difference? Why not have our
own race track and bring some of that money into the District." The
committee nearly had completed action when she discovered that "a race
track promoter had tried to bribe a member of my staff" and thus "immediately withdrew the bill."[10] Her committee likewise rejected attempts to
legalize gambling and strengthen enforcement against prostitution but
permitted boxing in Washington, D.C., for the first time since 1880.

The House also debated an appropriations measure slashing federal
financing for the District of Columbia. House rules mandated that appropriations bills must not include any legislative items, but representatives
seldom invoked the rule unless a member raised a point of order against
the legislative item. In such cases, the committee chairman was required
to sustain a point of order. Norton collaborated with Democrat Loring
Black of New York to stymie the appropriations measure. "We made a
point of order against every single item of legislation in that bill," she
said, "and there were a great many of them. We took turns at it, solemnly
voicing our objection each time a legislative item came along." Appropriations Committee chairman James Buchanan of Texas sustained each
point of order. House colleagues knew what Norton and Black were doing, but could not thwart their strategy. The House consequently rewrote
the bill, but Norton and Black still could not secure increased funding for
Washington, D.C. Norton declared, however, "We were successful in
calling attention to the discrimination against the District."[11]

Political reforms for Washingtonians, however, proved elusive. Norton, who championed home rule (self-government) for the District of
Columbia, viewed its residents as "democracy's stepchildren." She favored permitting Washington inhabitants to vote in presidential elections
and send delegates to national political conventions. Since residents of
the nation's capitol were denied the full rights of other American citizens,
Norton insisted that they be given greater voice in their own affairs.

Despite introducing or cosponsoring such measures annually, she lacked the committee or House floor votes to secure for District residents either home rule or the right to vote in presidential elections. To Norton's dismay, conservative Democrats chairing District sub-committees pigeonholed these measures.

In 1935, Norton claimed unsympathetic members throttled sixty-one bills. She implored "the Ways and Means Committee appoint to the District Committee only those members who were interested in District affairs." In order to expedite committee work on political reform bills by the entire committee, she dissolved the standing subcommittees and selected ad hoc special committees comprising those genuinely interested in District affairs to handle each measure. "It was," Norton admitted, "a rather daring step for the first woman chairman of an important committee to take, I suppose, but I got away with it."[12]

On the House floor, conservative Southern Democrats often thwarted Norton's District legislative measures. Anti–New Dealers, led by Democrat Thomas Blanton of Texas, frequently delayed or blocked floor action by delivering lengthy speeches. Norton complained that Blanton "seemed to make a point of opposing everything I advanced to help the District. It might have been dislike of having a woman chairman of the committee. Or it might have been just his peculiar disposition. Whatever it was, he gave me plenty of trouble, and the people of the District seemed to be his pet aversion." Blanton requested repeated quorums and roll calls when presence of the members on the floor was unnecessary, delaying House action on District legislation. Norton, perturbed by Blanton's strategy, lamented, "It is a device sometimes used to embarrass members, and it is this device Mr. Blanton used when bills important to the District were being debated. I never objected to members disagreeing with me, but I did object to dilatory tactics."[13]

Shortly after assuming the committee chairmanship in 1931, Norton denounced Blanton's ploys on the House floor. She wanted the House to debate twenty-four District measures, but Blanton blocked floor action. Blanton, who nicknamed her "Bloody Mary," used parliamentary strategies to derail her District bills. Norton, chagrined, reminded Blanton that "while he constantly preached economy when such matters as old page pensions and appropriations for badly needed improvements in the District were being considered, he did not seem to think that taxing his own constituents for useless pages of his remarks—at $60 a page—in the *Congressional Record* should be curtailed." Blanton denied her charges and, following adjournment, insisted she remove the remarks from the *Congressional Record*. Norton declined to comply, further irritating Blanton, who replied she "was the first member who had ever refused him such a request." Texans unseated Blanton in the 1936 House elections partly because he had wasted taxpayers' money with *Congressional Record* space.

Blanton tried to stereotype Norton on the House floor. During one heated floor exchange, he repeatedly referred to her as "the lady" and sarcastically said that he would "yield to the lady." "Norton, adept at navigating toward power within the institution, captured that spirit most succinctly" by rebuffing Blanton. She "insisted upon entering the rough and tumble of debate as an equal and scorned any deference because of her sex." Norton interjected, "I'm no lady, I'm a member of Congress, elected by the citizens of the 13th District in New Jersey, and I'll proceed on that basis!" She added, "I expected the same consideration as any other member of Congress." "Her remark encapsulated the belief shared by most of her female contemporaries on the Hill—Democrat and Republican—that the surest way for women to attain power and influence in Congress was to work within the prescribed system to mitigate gender differences." [14] Norton's retort did not dissuade Blanton from calling her "the lady," but the exchange amused both House colleagues and the media.

In 1936 Blanton and other anti–New Dealers delayed House action on the Ellenbogen bill. Democrat Henry Ellenbogen of Pennsylvania introduced legislation to establish a rent control commission in Washington D.C. Blanton's conservative faction denounced the measure and insisted upon numerous quorum calls. Norton obtained a special rule limiting House floor debate on the Ellenbogen bill to 90 minutes. The *Washington Post* observed, "Such unusual consideration for a District bill establishes a valuable precedent," applauding her move as "an emancipation proclamation for the District insofar as it strikes directly at the attempt of one man or any minority to run the city" and wondering why "the District leaders waited until now to ask for a special rule." "If similar consideration is shown other District measures," the *Washington Post* added, "it will no longer be possible for a small group of obstructionists to tie up the entire program of local legislation." The House, however, disappointed Norton, rejecting the Ellenbogen measure, 196 to 85. [15]

The following year, Norton fought with conservatives over the Sisson measure. Democrat Frederick Sisson of New York had introduced legislation to withhold pay from District employees found teaching anything about communism. Norton opposed the Sisson bill because Blanton attached a rider insisting that District teachers also sign an affidavit that they had not taught or advocated communism during the preceding pay period. Although Norton denounced the rider as an infringement of constitutional liberties, Blanton insisted upon its inclusion and blocked House action on the Sisson legislation. Massachusetts Democrat John McCormack negotiated a compromise permitting District teachers to teach about, but not advocate, communism. The House on February 8 accepted McCormack's compromise version.

As the District of Columbia Committee head, Norton affectionately acquired the nickname "Aunt Mary." Marion McDonagh Burke, her niece and committee clerk, initially gave her that moniker. The young Washington newspaper reporters, including James Chinn of the *Washington Star*, James Secrest of the *Washington Post*, Una Franklin of the *Washington Herald*, Louis Whyte and Julie Bonwit of the *Washington Times*, and Ralph Palmer of the *Washington News*, also called her "Aunt Mary" and reported her work as the District's unofficial mayor. "They always played fair with me, as well as with the papers they represented," Norton remembered. "I grew very fond of them."[16]

The *Washington Star* arranged for Norton to deliver progress reports on legislation affecting the District of Columbia twice a month on Saturday afternoons over their radio station. During a May 1, 1937, broadcast, Norton heard telephones ringing constantly in the adjacent studio. After finishing her address, she asked the young receptionist in the next studio what had happened. "I've had such a terrible fifteen minutes," the receptionist replied, "everybody jumping on me for putting you on!" Norton's address had prevented the station from broadcasting the Kentucky Derby. The station manager had forgotten to change the time for Norton's program. "I could imagine how little interest anyone would have in a report from Congress when the Kentucky Derby was on," she admitted. One irate listener wrote her, "Who the H--- did I think I was" to take up radio time when the Kentucky Derby was being run."[17] War Admiral, ridden by Charles Kurtsinger, won the Kentucky Derby and later captured the Preakness Stakes and Belmont Stakes, becoming only the fourth horse to win the Triple Crown.

Norton resigned her District of Columbia Committee post on June 30, 1937, to become chair of the House Labor Committee. During her final year as chair, she had introduced over twenty bills in her committee. The Washington press corps gave her an inscribed gavel and scroll on which was engraved, "May this gavel, fashioned from one of the beams in the old White House roof assist you in wrapping out as much constructive legislation in your new post, chairman of the Labor Committee, as you achieved in your six years as 'Mayor of Washington' at the head of the District Committee. May this little token also be a symbol of the deep affection in which you are held by the boys and girls of the local Press." Norton had the scroll framed and hung in her office and used the gavel when she chaired the Labor Committee. Mrs. Lewis Ottenberg, president of the District's League of Women Voters, wrote her, "We regret exceedingly the loss which is ours in the fact that you have had to give up the Chairmanship which for six years you held with such credit to you and to the District of Columbia." Besides thanking Norton for her "many courtesies and endeavors in behalf of our program," Ottenberg concluded, "We know that tho' we may not continue to be your major interest, you will be a friend in the halls of Congress whom we can count as loyal and understanding."[18]

Norton steadfastly championed home rule for the District residents. In a 1944 article entitled "Democracy's Stepchild," she lamented that District residents still lacked congressional representation in battling "appalling slums," overcrowded schools, inadequate recreational and day care centers, tuberculosis, juvenile delinquency rates, and other critical urban problems. Norton claimed that District inhabitants "might as well still be living under King George the Third" because they were not consulted about taxation, did not have self-government, and could not choose their president, local health, law enforcement, and educational officials.[19]

The New Jersey Democrat also opposed having the legislative branch continue to govern the District. Although admitting that "congressmen assigned to the (District) committee do as good a job in attempting to govern Washington as is possible under the circumstances," Norton asserted, "the circumstances do not make sense." Congress, she argued, handled so many important national and international issues that it too often subordinated municipal issues. "Frequently on District Day the calendars were so long," Norton complained, "that worthwhile legislation which had been the subject of careful consideration in committee, had to be shelved because of any unexpected controversy over some minor bill."

Norton especially lamented that all legislation to grant District residents self-government and the right to vote had been sidetracked. To her chagrin, representatives frequently lacked expertise in resolving District problems. "Many of those men and women," Norton charged, "have had no experience in municipal government, yet they are expected to act intelligently on problems concerning schools, hospitals, police and fire departments, street maintenance, waterworks, and the thousands of other services needed in large cities. Is it any wonder that conditions are hideous?" In addition, she argued that U.S. congressmen were elected primarily to represent their own district and should not be expected to serve another one, too. "The double responsibility," Norton contended, "is unfair to them, to their constituents, and to the people of Washington."[20]

In 1947, Norton trumpeted the Auchincloss home rule bill. Republican James Auchincloss of New Jersey, a House District of Columbia Committee member, proposed a measure granting District of Columbia residents authority to handle strictly local legislation and to draft a home rule Municipal Charter form of government. Congress would have retained the power to review major District policy decisions affecting the nation. Norton defended the Auchincloss bill on the House floor, claiming that Congress lacked time to act as a local legislature. Congress, she bemoaned, "being immersed in national and international problems, always regarded the municipal problems of the District as secondary." Norton, therefore, favored relieving Congress of the responsibility of handling legislation of a "purely local nature." She admitted, "There are few of us, not members of the District Committee, who can say that we have not looked upon District Day as a day when we could well afford to be absent from the floor to attend to other business." Norton warned, "Both local and national issues often suffer from our attempts to serve two masters, the electorate of the nation and the residents of the District of Columbia." The District's rapid population growth from 170,000 in 1873 to nearly one million in 1947 had compounded its legislative needs. Norton hoped the Auchincloss legislation would bring "a measure of democracy to the only corner of our country where democracy in local matters does not exist today" and claimed, "We are being a little hypocritical in preaching democracy abroad without first practicing democracy in the capital of our own nation." The Auchincloss bill, however, suffered the same fate as earlier abortive attempts to grant Washingtonians home rule. Although the Senate passed its version of home rule, the House rejected the Auchincloss measure. Norton's proposals to give the District national representation and a vote for the president likewise failed. Washington, D.C., women, though, rallied behind her efforts and held an annual Mary Norton Day in her honor.

Washingtonians eventually attained greater self-rule. The Twenty-Third Amendment, adopted in 1961, granted Washington residents the right to vote for president and vice president. In 1973, Congress adopted the District of Columbia Home Rule Act, permitting Washington, D.C., residents to elect their own mayor and a 13-member legislative city council. The District also won the right to levy taxes, but Congress retained power to veto council actions and approve the city budget.[21]

Norton, meanwhile, frequently visited the White House on political and legislative matters during the New Deal years, but shunned the Washington social scene. "She can't be dragged to the big formal affairs everyone is supposed to attend," *Current Biography* noted. "To snooty Washington society," writer Duff Gilfond observed, "she is a business school graduate, Tammany and Catholic and hence unacceptable."[22] Niece Marion McDonagh Burke recalled, "Norton did not socialize. She was tired when she got home." Norton occasionally invited political friends to her apartment for relaxing conversation and an informal meal, which she usually cooked. Evenings usually were spent reading newspapers and legislative reports or writing political speeches. Norton enjoyed few hobbies, occasionally reading religious history and detective stories, attending theater plays and operas, and driving through rural Maryland and Virginia.[23]

Norton remained active in national party affairs, supporting Al Smith's quest for the Democratic presidential nomination in 1932. Smith, a Roman Catholic, battled New York Governor Franklin D. Roosevelt and U.S. House Speaker John Nance Garner of Texas for the Democratic Party nomination. Party regulars began bolting to Smith's campaign for Roosevelt in the primaries, disappointing Norton. During an April 1932 wom-

en's gathering at the Statler Hotel in Boston, Massachusetts, Norton protested, "The political charlatans who have deserted Governor Smith are
mad." She warned that, "like weakened traitors, their day of reckoning is
not far away." Massachusetts' voters resoundingly backed Smith in the
April primary. "The Democrats," Norton wrote Smith, "are, at last, awak-
ening to the fact that in you they have or could have a real leader. Let us
hope that they shall avail themselves of their greatest opportunity for
service in the country by selecting you as our Standard Bearer and deliverer of a country that is crying aloud for leadership." Smith replied, "I
heard from all over the country about the radio speech, and it seems to
have taken very well."[24]

Norton served as a delegate-at-large for the third time at the 1932
Democratic Party Convention in Chicago, Illinois. She termed the gathering "one of the most fateful national conventions ever held by my party."
Governor Joseph Ely of Massachusetts placed Smith's name in nomination, with Norton seconding it. Norton already had prepared a ten-min-
ute speech trumpeting Smith's accomplishments, but the convention
chairman limited her talk to five minutes. The Smith team drafted a short
speech denouncing Roosevelt that Norton read. "When I finished reading
that speech to the convention," Norton admitted, "I felt thoroughly
ashamed of it. And it did not make me feel any better when (Jersey City)
Mayor (Frank) Hague told me he had not even seen it!"[25]

Hague and the New Jersey delegation steadfastly backed Smith during the spirited, all-night battle with Roosevelt for the Democratic presidential nomination. Smith had helped Hague win appointment as vice
chair of the Democratic National Committee. "As a staunch Roman Catholic, Hague identified with Smith's opposition to Prohibition, which
some held was directed toward the new European immigrants." Norton
recalled, "We kept our promise and remained loyal to him." The weary
delegates, however, selected Roosevelt on the fourth ballot as their 1932
presidential nominee. Norton was the first woman to be considered,
however symbolically, for a vice-presidential nomination. New Jersey
Democrats wanted to nominate Norton for the vice presidency, but she
gracefully declined because a majority of convention delegates already
supported Garner. "Women deluged me with letters," Norton disclosed,
"criticizing me for what they regarded as a betrayal of the cause of wom-
en." Norton claimed, however, that the nomination would have been
only "a grand gesture" and stressed that "she had no desire to receive
concessions because of her sex."[26]

When Hague abruptly switched his support to Roosevelt, Norton followed suit and dutifully campaigned for Roosevelt in New Jersey and
New England. "Indignant as she was at the defeat of her hero, Governor
Smith, at the Chicago Convention, she was nevertheless convinced that
further opposition to Roosevelt would only aid his opponent." Hague
phoned Norton in late August, "We may land on our heads out in Forty-

Third Street, but you and I are going hand in hand over to the Biltmore and offer to help in this campaign. Roosevelt is our candidate, and we're going to do everything we can to elect him." Norton met Hague and his son, Frank, Jr., for lunch at the Biltmore. Hague organized a huge rally of 120,000 for Roosevelt on August 27 at Sea Girt, New Jersey, the summer mansion of New Jersey governors, and brought in supporters from Hudson and Essex County on 100 chartered trains and 50 buses.

Joseph Maynard, Massachusetts State Democratic party chairman, asked Norton that fall to address a large gathering of Boston women, who were still upset about Smith losing the nomination. Norton tried to persuade them that Roosevelt deserved their backing. "I convinced most of them," Norton recollected, "that it had been a clean fight and that Roosevelt deserved their support." Norton also helped organize numerous Roosevelt meetings across New Jersey. "I enjoyed the campaign," she reflected, "and gave it everything I had to give."[27]

Norton welcomed Roosevelt's landslide victory over Republican incumbent Herbert Hoover in the 1932 presidential election. Roosevelt routed Hoover, 22.8 million to 15.7 million, in the popular vote and 472 to 59 in the Electoral College. "He had a keen mind and more courage than any other person I have ever known," Norton observed. "It was this courage, coupled with exceptional ability, that made it possible for him to lead our country safely through the worst depression it had ever experienced."

New Jersey gained two new congressional districts because of population growth reflected in the reapportionment from the 1930 census. The New Jersey Democrats picked up two seats, as William Sutphin and Edward Kenney joined the House from the Third and Ninth Districts, respectively. Norton appealed to a heavily Democratic Party constituency from the newly drawn Thirteenth District, which elected her to a fifth consecutive House term. She trounced Republican Mortimer Neuman, 73,779 to 27,964, picking up 72 percent of the popular vote, and trailed only Republican Charles Wolverton from the First District and Democrat Oscar Auf der Heide from the Fourteenth District numerically.[28] Roosevelt's landslide victory; the unstinting support of the Hague machine, women, and Irish, Roman Catholic, working-class constituents; the increasing severity of the economic depression; Norton's unwavering support of federal economic relief and recovery measures beneficial to her constituents; and her growing leadership role in Congress contributed to her resounding victory at the polls.

Norton worked diligently in 1933 and 1934 for the passage of President Roosevelt's First New Deal legislation, a sweeping package of economic relief and recovery programs and regulatory policies to help alleviate the economic depression. By March 1933, around 5,500 banks had closed, over 25 percent of Americans were unemployed, the gross national product had plunged almost 33 percent, and farm prices had plummeted. These changes affected virtually every aspect of American life, including banking, stock market regulation, public works, labor practices, agriculture, and transportation.

The House passed the Agricultural Adjustment Act in May 1933 and the National Recovery Act in June 1933, the foundation measures of the First New Deal legislation. The National Recovery Act authorized industrial organizations to formulate codes to govern pricing, production, trade practices, and labor relations in their respective industries, thus securing the fair competitive behavior and enlightened labor practices thought necessary to restore economic prosperity. The Agricultural Adjustment Act encouraged farmers to restrict agricultural production, thereby increasing farm prices, and to receive subsidy payments, financed by a special tax on processors. Representatives also approved the Federal Emergency Banking Relief Act, the Civilian Conservation Corps Reforestation Relief Act, the Federal Emergency Relief Act, the Tennessee Valley Authority Act, the Securities Exchange Act, the Home Owners Loan Corporation Act, the Glass-Steagall Banking Act, and other relief and recovery measures in 1933, plus the Federal Deposit Insurance Act and the Securities Exchange Commission Act in 1934. These various economic relief and recovery programs and regulatory policies received Norton's wholehearted support. "At the time of Roosevelt's election," Norton recollected, "the condition of the country couldn't have been much worse." She welcomed Roosevelt's visionary, pragmatic programs, reflecting, "He has done tremendous things for the American people. His ideas are so revolutionary that they have kept us from something that might have been much more terrifying." Norton reflected, "The period following the inauguration of President Roosevelt in 1933 will always stand, I believe, as one of the most eventful and inspiring in our national history, and I shall always feel a deep sense of gratitude to the people in my district who were responsible for the privilege I had of voting for the humane and constructive legislation that was passed."[29]

Norton returned weekends to Jersey City in May 1934 to spend as much time as possible with her ill husband, Robert, at their apartment. Robert, who served on the Board of Directors of the Lincoln Building and Loan Association of Jersey City, had developed a heart condition, exacerbated by the anxiety of the economic depression. During the week, Norton phoned him daily from her Washington, D.C., office. A housekeeper and nurse cared for Robert at considerable expense, draining their savings. Norton acknowledged, "There were times when the strain became so great that I thought I could not go on." House Speaker Homer Rainey of Illinois gave her a three-week leave of absence from her congressional responsibilities from late May until mid-June to be at Robert's bedside.[30]

Robert died on June 16 at the Norton's Allenhurst, New Jersey, summer home. "I was more or less prepared for the end," Norton explained, "but those things are terribly hard, even when you have faced them for many months. It was a great satisfaction to me to have had those last three weeks with him, completely free from my work." To compound the tragedy, two members of Robert's family were killed in an automobile accident en route to his funeral. "I have often thought that having the responsibility of a campaign that fall was probably the best thing that could have happened to me," Norton reflected. "A very busy person cannot let down and give in completely to grief." Norton's autobiography reveals little about Robert's illness and death. Washington political life so engrossed Norton that she did not dwell much on Robert's situation. Robert had chosen to stay far from the Washington political scene and maintained such a low profile that the media referred to Norton as being a widow long before she became one.

Norton continued living in Washington, D.C., with her sister, Anne Hopkins, after Robert's death and summered at East Quogue, Long Island. Her other sister, Loretta, and brother-in-law, Joseph McDonagh, had bought a large house on the southern shore near the Atlantic Ocean. Norton loved the cool, steady breeze blowing off the water. "After hot, sticky Washington," she sighed, "the place used to seem like Heaven!" The vacation spot provided Norton valuable respite from the rigors of Washington life.[31]

From late September to early November 1934, Norton campaigned throughout New Jersey for Democratic Party congressional candidates backing President Roosevelt's First New Deal programs. State rallies were well attended and "very enthusiastic," but she detected increased anti–New Deal sentiment among large businessmen. "Just recently," Norton warned Roosevelt, "there seems to be a decided underground propaganda to the effect that Industry is not getting a square deal. Of course you know in this Industrial state, that kind of talk is apt to do much damage. We are doing everything possible to combat such propaganda, but the sentiment seems to be growing." She requested Roosevelt to "say something reassuring to business . . . upon which I could base an argument to disprove this widespread propaganda."[32]

Roosevelt quickly alleviated Norton's fears. "Quite frankly," the president responded, "I don't feel that there is any particular reason for worrying over the situation, and even if there is I do not believe that it would be dissipated by any mere statement that I might make." He observed, "Just what should be said that would be reassuring to business no one seems to know," and insisted, "I believe that what is being done and the results that are being obtained is not only the best, but the only means of reassuring those timid souls." Roosevelt detected, "There is, apparently much less of this feeling of fear than there was a few weeks ago when there appeared to be a sort of what you might call mob psychology." The president added, "I believe that what is being done and the results that are being obtained is not only the best, but the only means of reassuring those timid souls." He concluded, "Actions and results are the things that will count and I do not believe that any more statements would have any particular effect on 'reassuring business.'"

New Jersey Democrats experienced mixed results in the November 1934 elections. They easily elected A. Harry Moore to the U.S. Senate, but William Dill lost to Harold Hoffman in his bid to become governor. Norton concluded, "Apparently people were not nearly so much interested in how their tax money was spent or in how their government functioned as they were in Harry Moore's stories." In the Thirteenth District, Norton overwhelmed Republican Anthony Montelli, 73,342 to 26,447, for a sixth congressional term, amassing 73 percent of the popular vote. She again tabulated the third highest number of votes among the New Jersey delegation, trailing only Wolverton from the First District and Democrat Edward Hart from the Fourteenth District. Norton retained overwhelming support from the Hague machine and her constituents, who benefited from various First New Deal relief and recovery measures. Democrats, though, still held only 4 of the 14 New Jersey House seats, with Hart replacing Auf der Heide.[33]

Norton steadfastly supported Roosevelt's Second New Deal domestic measures. The Second New Deal, begun in 1935, shifted the focus to reform and social justice legislation, providing a long-term economic safety net for all Americans, granting labor greater recognition, and promoting old-age pensions, public works, and the arts. Norton backed the landmark Wagner Act of 1935, Social Security Act of 1935, Works Progress Administration, and other social justice and reform measures. The Wagner Act gave official government recognition to labor unions and authorized collective bargaining between labor and management. As a Labor Committee member, Norton helped sponsor the Wagner Act and lauded it as "the greatest boon to organized labor in all its history" and welcomed the National Labor Relations Board to oversee administration of the measure. The Wagner Act, however, encountered formidable congressional resistance. "This bill," Norton conceded, "was fiercely and relentlessly opposed, and it was only through the courage and persistence of Senator Wagner, Representative William P. Connery Jr., of Massachusetts, then Chairman of the House Labor Committee, and the support of progressives in both parties that it finally became law." The Social Security Act of 1935 provided old-age pensions, excluding farm laborers, domestic workers, public employees, and educational and religious personnel, instituted unemployment insurance, and provided assistance to families of dependent children. The Works Progress Administration (WPA), created by Congress in 1935, employed over eight million people on public works construction and community service projects.[34]

Although her workload as House District of Columbia Committee chairman limited the amount of time she could devote to constituent matters, Norton sought New Deal funds to alleviate the unemployment crisis in her district. She used her House seniority to help attain WPA and other federal funds for the expansion and completion of Mayor Hague's Medical Center Complex, providing numerous jobs for unemployed Hudson County residents. The complex, the nation's third largest hospital and New Jersey's biggest hospital, already had become "one of the city's most visible and recognizable landmarks." Free state-of-the-art health care was given to those Jersey City residents who could not afford to pay. Hague had renovated the original double-wing, six-story Jersey City Hospital building, situated at Montgomery and Baldwin Avenues, and built a new twenty-three-story facility, which opened in 1931. By 1934, the Medical Center Complex had 750 employees and treated around 900 patients daily.

Federal funding brought rapid expansion of the Medical Center Complex. In 1934, a nearly $3 million loan from the Reconstruction Finance Corporation enabled the construction of the Pollak Hospital, a new Hudson County tuberculosis hospital noted for the treatment of chest diseases. In March 1936, Hague urged Norton to secure additional funding for the expansion of the Margaret Hague Maternity Hospital. "I want you to take this matter to Harry Hopkins (WPA director) yourself," he wrote Norton, "and stay with it until you put it over." He added, "I know of your interest in this hospital" and penned, "It would be a nice thing if you were to finish the job by obtaining approval of the project." Furthermore, Hague wanted her to get federal monies for the completion of the Pollak Hospital and a home for the Maternity Hospital and Hudson County Tuberculosis Hospital nurses. "Both of these improvements are urgently needed," Hague concluded, "and you know what a deep personal interest they have for me. I wish you would do everything in your power to get them approved so that we can go ahead with the work." Secretary of Interior Harold Ickes's office, meanwhile, told Norton that the State Office had approved but not yet sent those projects to Washington. Norton wrote Hague, "I well know of your personal interest in this hospital and naturally I have a certain pride in my original act as a Freeholder to 'carry on' to completion." She assured Hague, "I will do my utmost with the officials here." The WPA allocated substantial grants and loans for these projects, putting unemployed residents to work and benefiting Jersey City citizens. The maternity hospital added an Eleanor Roosevelt Nursery that provided day care for children of mothers in the hospital and offered extended visiting hours to working fathers. A psychiatric hospital and an outpatient clinic were built. President Roosevelt, who welcomed Hague's political support and Norton's legislative work, dedicated the Medical Center Complex on October 2, 1936, before 200,000 people. Hague later wrote Roosevelt, "The people of this city will be forever grateful to you for the help and assistance that you gave to make the existence of this hospital possible."

Hospital funding for continued construction remained through the late 1930s. The House rejection of an $870 million measure to increase the lending powers of the U.S. Housing Authority in August 1939 endangered but did not stop the $463,000 federal hospital funding. Norton hurriedly wrote Hague on August 5, "I have just heard we shall receive the hospital award anyway." She enthused, "I am simply overjoyed, as I feared it was 'all over' when the Lending Bill was defeated," and added, "I sincerely hope some of our worries will be at an end." Norton conferred extensively with Colonel E. W. Clark, acting commissioner of Public Works for the Federal Works Agency and General Edwin "Pa" Watson of the White House staff to get $463,000 for completion of the maternity hospital. She wrote Watson on November 10, "Nothing will make me happier than to know that we shall secure this very much needed $463,000." Norton contacted Clark the same day, "The completion of this project is very close to my heart. I know what the maternity hospital has done for women" and stressed, "It is the realization of a dream." She concluded, "I have watched the progress though the years and feel that it was a great welfare project."

The Medical Center Complex was nearly completed by November 1940. Jersey City had invested over $25 million in the Medical Center Complex with over 3,500 beds and 23 operating rooms. Hague in November sought Norton's assistance in securing $3.5 million in additional federal funding for completing the Medical Center Complex by building housing with 1,000 beds for maternity hospital nurses and 150 beds for a doctor's staff house for resident physicians. He wrote Norton, "I do not have to tell you of my interest in this important matter." Hague asked Norton and Representative Ed Hart to meet with Roosevelt "to further the program." He added, "I am sure you will again be successful if you put the same energy in this last appeal as you have done on previous occasions." Norton already had planned to confer with the president on labor legislation. "I feel," she replied, "that would be the most advantageous time to discuss the matter." Hague penned President Roosevelt that the Medical Center Complex "when completed will be one of the outstanding hospitals of this country and the most completely equipped and efficient Medical Center in all of the United States." He vowed that the facility "will stand as a monument to the human interest which you have always exhibited in the development of this hospital."

In April 1941, Frank Eggers, Hague nephew and assistant, sent Norton the amendments the Jersey City mayor desired and stressed the amendments would "give the President the necessary authority to help us out in the completion of the Jersey Medical Center, which so far has progressed so favorably." He concluded, "It is absolutely necessary that we secure the balance of funds necessary to complete the job." Norton urged the Public Buildings and Grounds Committee to approve those amendments and notified its chairman Democrat Fritz Lanham of Texas, "The suggestions offered in these amendments will prove of vital importance in connection with our National Defense program." The federally funded WPA provided abundant grants and loans for the completion of the Medical Center Complex. Murdoch Hall was erected in 1941 and served as the residence for graduate and student nurses at the facility.

The costly Medical Center Complex, however, sparked some criticism. WPA funds, historian Thomas Fleming wrote, enabled Hague "to complete his medical center on a scale so large that the hospital's staff frequently outnumbered the patients." Jack Alexander assailed the complex as "a costly experiment in socialized medicine" that was "disproportionately magnificent for the size of Jersey City, and it is a financial white elephant."[35]

Norton, meanwhile, helped obtain federal financing for the construction of Roosevelt Stadium in Jersey City. Hague applied for WPA and Civil Works Administration funds for the construction of a municipal sports stadium at Drayer's Point. The Art Deco, bowl-shaped facility, named after President Roosevelt and built for $1.5 million, was one of Hudson County's largest funded projects under the WPA. The 24,500 seat stadium, constructed of steel and concrete in the mid-1930s, provided 2,400 jobs for the Hudson County unemployed and was designed as a multisport edifice. Frank Bixby of the *New York Times* called Roosevelt Stadium, "the paradigm of elegance in a blue-collar town" and "a center of the socio-economic-political fabric of Jersey City." The stadium became the home baseball field of the Jersey City Giants of the International League from 1937 to 1950. Jersey City lost to the Rochester Red Wings, 4 to 3, in the stadium's first game on April 13, 1937, before an overflow crowd. Jackie Robinson, the first African-American to play modern major league baseball, made his minor league debut there with the Montreal Royals against Jersey City on April 18, 1946, clouting a three-run home run, making three other hits, scoring four times, and driving in three runs. Boxing matches, track and field meets, and high school football also were held there.[36]

Throughout her tenure in the U.S. Congress, Norton also worked diligently to fulfill the needs of her constituents and other New Jersey residents. Lucille Considine, Norton's niece and office secretary, summarized the New Jersey Democrat's extensive constituent work: "She is concerned not only with general legislation but hundreds of letters cross her desk dealing with individual cases, all of which require immediate attention. She is well known in the various Government departments for the personal work that she does in behalf of individual constituents. At times when New Jersey has had no Democratic representation in the Senate Mrs. Norton has handled matters not only for her own constituents but for citizens of New Jersey as a whole who have no Democratic representation in Congress."

In 1936, Mayor Hague encouraged Norton to become the Democratic Party candidate for the U.S. Senate to challenge first-term Republican William Warren Barbour. He warned Norton that she would be surrendering her safe House seat and risking possible defeat. "This looks like a good Democratic year," Hague prophesied, "but of course I can't absolutely guarantee that you'd make it. You certainly do deserve the nomination if you want it, and, if you do, I'll do everything in my power to put you over." After weighing the pros and cons for about a week, Norton declined Hague's overture. "I could not afford to take the chance of defeat," she explained, "particularly as I really liked being in the House. And I knew I would have two strikes against me—being a woman and also a well-known Catholic."

During the Fall 1936 campaign throughout New Jersey, Norton organized Democratic Party meetings for Roosevelt's reelection. House Speaker William Bankhead of Alabama asked Norton on October 9 if she wanted a letter from him "endorsing your splendid record in Congress, your high standing with your colleagues and your record of loyalty to the program of the Administration." He also requested Norton's assessment of the political situation in her district regarding the presidential campaign. Norton replied October 16, "Of course, I would be delighted to receive the letter you suggest as I know it would be most helpful to me in my campaign." But she assured Bankhead, "I do not anticipate any trouble," noting "my district is overwhelmingly Democratic and my constituents seem to be well pleased with the service I have rendered them." Norton then evaluated the New Jersey political situation. "My entire time has been devoted to the Presidential campaign in the state," Norton wrote. "I have arranged meetings in all of the counties and shall continue to do so." She added, "The President has as good a chance, if not better, than in 1932, bearing in mind, of course, that this is an overwhelmingly Republican, industrial state. However, while the industrialists are all opposed to Roosevelt, the average citizen seems to be greatly in favor of the policies of the administration. Since they have numerical strength, we feel that we have a chance to carry the state."[37]

Roosevelt won a second presidential term by a landslide over Republican Alf Landon in November, capturing 62 percent of the popular vote. He nearly swept the Electoral College, 523 to 8, carrying 46 of 48 states. Roosevelt received 59.6 percent of the New Jersey vote, while Landon got only 39.6 percent. Democrats in the New Jersey delegation capitalized on Roosevelt's landslide victory. Democrat William Smathers triumphed over Barbour for the Senate seat. The Democrats gained three congressional seats in New Jersey, equaling the Republicans for the first time in nearly two decades. Elmer Wene, Edward O'Neill, and Frank Towey, Jr. unseated Republicans in the Second, Eleventh, and Twelfth Districts, respectively.

Jersey City and Bayonne voters decisively reelected Norton for a seventh consecutive House term, giving her 77 percent of the popular vote, 4 percent better than in 1934. Norton tallied 93,702 votes to just 27,615 for Republican John Grossi and 2,099 for National Social Justice candidate Charles McCarthy. She tabulated the second highest popular vote among the New Jersey delegation, trailing only Hart.[38] Roosevelt's landslide victory, the enormous popularity of his Second New Deal programs, the steadfast support of the Hague machine and women, Norton's adept legislative skills in securing federal funding for projects benefiting her Roman Catholic, working-class constituents, and her enhanced leadership role in Congress contributed to her resounding triumph at the polls.

Two years later, however, the Republicans gained eighty House seats nationally and four House seats in New Jersey. Norton, Sutphin, and Hart were the only New Jersey Democrats to retain their House seats. The economic recession of 1937 to 1938, along with a backlash against Roosevelt's Supreme Court and executive reorganization plans and party realignment attempts, triggered the Republican resurgence. Despite the Republican gains, however, the Democrats still retained a comfortable majority of 262 to 169 in the House.

Norton maintained her broad base of political support, being decisively reelected for an eighth straight House term. She tallied 89,287 votes to just 22,459 for Republican T. Burton Coyle, amassing 80 percent of the popular vote. Norton's prominent leadership role in steering House passage of the landmark Fair Labor Standards Act of 1938 impressed her Irish, Roman Catholic, working-class constituents. Speaker Bankhead congratulated Norton upon her resounding victory. "We all, of course," he wrote, "regret our losses in the House, but this fact, I am sure will tend to strengthen Democratic solidarity in the next House." Roosevelt's leadership continued to impress Norton. During the 1938 congressional campaign, Norton wired Roosevelt, "Thank you so much for all you have meant to all of us who have been inspired by our fine leadership."[39]

Norton maintained few personal friendships in Washington, D.C. Her small clique of notable Washington women friends included Eleanor Roosevelt, first lady, humanistic reformer, and consummate politician; Lorena Hickok, an Associated Press reporter from 1928 to 1933 and chief investigator for the Federal Emergency Relief Administration from 1933 to 1940; and Molly Dewson, who headed the Women's Division of the National Consumer League. Roosevelt impressed Norton as a very unprejudiced, compassionate person who loved people and promoted welfare programs. Hickok later helped Norton draft an autobiography, while Dewson shared Roosevelt's interest in general welfare.[40] These friends proved invaluable support as she faced the biggest legislative battle of her political career.

NOTES

1. Mary T. Norton, "Madam Congressman: The Memoirs of Mary T. Norton of New Jersey," (Hereafter cited as "Memoirs"), Mary T. Norton MSS, New Jersey Collection, Archibald Stevens Alexander Library, Rutgers, The State University of New Jersey, pp. 98–100; *Washington Post*, August 3, 1959, p. B2; National Women's History Museum, "Women Wielding Power: Pioneer Female State Legislators: New Jersey," http://www.nwhm.org; Featured House Publications, *Women in Congress, 1917–2006*, April 27, 2007, 108th Cong., 1st sess., H. Doc. 108–223, http://www.gpo.gov.; Annabel Paxton, *Women in Congress* (Richmond, VA: The Dietz Press, 1945), p. 33; Marcy Kaptur, *Women of Congress: A Twentieth Century Odyssey* (Washington, D.C.: Congressional Quarterly, 1996), p. 41; Phyllis J. Read and Bernard L. Witlieb, *The Book of Women's Lists* (New York: Random House, 1992), p. 317.

2. Norton, "Memoirs," pp. 101–3; Congressional Research Service, *Women in the United States Congress: 1917–2011*, March 18, 2011, p. 62, http://www.crs.gov; Angeline Bogucki, "Summary of the Legislative Career of Representative Mary T. Norton," Legislative Reference Service, Library of Congress, Washington, D.C., November 3, 1950, p. 9.

3. Hope Chamberlin, *A Minority of Members: Women in the U.S. Congress* (New York: Praeger Publishers, 1973), p. 56; Paxton, *Women in Congress*, p. 33.

4. Helen Meagher, "Notes of Interview with Mary T. Norton," *Women's Voice*, March 26, 1931, Norton MSS, Box 1, General Correspondence, 1931–1936; Chamberlin, *Minority of Members*, p. 55; Featured House Publications, *Women in Congress, 1917–2006*.

5. Norton, "Memoirs," pp. 111–12; *Washington Post*, Aug. 3, 1959, p. B2.

6. *Chicago Herald*, May 10, 1933; "Lady Mayor Makes Good, 1931," Norton MSS, Box 4, Personal, Biographical Material; Bogucki, "Summary," p. 7; *Washington Post*, Aug. 3, 1959, p. B2; Kaptur, *Women of Congress*, p. 46.

7. *Washington Post*, July 25, 1932; "Lady Mayor Makes Good," 1931; Bogucki, "Summary," p. 5.

8. Norton, "Memoirs," pp. 103–4; *Washington Post*, Aug. 3, 1959, p. B2; Bogucki, "Summary," pp. 5–6.

9. Norton, "Memoirs," p. 109; *Washington Post*, Aug. 3, 1959, p. B2; Bogucki, "Summary," p. 6.

10. Norton, "Memoirs," pp. 109–11.

11. Norton, "Memoirs," pp. 112–13.

12. *Washington Evening Star*, November 29, 1936; Norton, "Memoirs," pp. 101–3; Bogucki, "Summary," pp. 8–9.

13. Norton, "Memoirs," pp. 105–6.

14. Norton, "Memoirs," pp. 107–8; Featured House Publications, *Women in Congress, 1917–2006*; *Washington Post*, Aug. 3, 1959, p. B2.

15. *Washington Post*, April 17, 1936; Bogucki, "Summary," pp. 7–8; Norton, "Memoirs," p. 108.

16. Norton, "Memoirs," p. 114; Bogucki, "Summary," p. 8.

17. Norton, "Memoirs," pp. 114–15.

18. Bogucki, "Summary," p. 9; Mrs. Lewis Ottenberg to Mary Norton, June 25, 1937, Norton MSS, Box 1, Gen. Corr., 1937.

19. Mary T. Norton, "Democracy's Stepchild," *Woman's Home Companion* 71 (August 1944), p. 19.

20. *Washington Post*, Aug. 3, 1959, p. B2; Mary T. Norton, "Home Rule and Reorganization of the District of Columbia," Speech, Washington, D.C., undated, Norton MSS, Box 5, Speeches, n.d.; Norton, "Democracy's Stepchild," 1944.

21. Norton, "Home Rule and Reorganization"; *Washington Post*, Aug. 3, 1959, p. B2; Reva Beck Bosone to the Readers of the *American Fork Citizen*, "Life With Congress," April 9, 1949, Norton MSS, Box 1, Gen. Corr., 1949; Bogucki, "Summary," p. 9; Michael K. Fauntroy, *Home Rule or House Rule: Congress and the Erosion of Local*

Governance in the District of Columbia (Lanham, MD: University Press of America, 2003), p. 33.

22. "Mary T. Norton," *Current Biography* 5 (1944), p. 503; Duff Gilfond, "Gentlewoman of the House," *American Mercury* 18 (October 1929), p. 160.

23. "Mary T. Norton," *Current Biography*, p. 503; Margot Gayle, "Battling Mary Retires," *Independent Woman* 29 (July 1950), p. 200; Marion McDonagh Burke, Interview with Author, August 7, 1981.

24. *New York Times*, April 25, 1932; Mary Norton to Shallow, April 25, 1932, Norton MSS, Box 1, Gen. Corr., 1931–1938; Mary T. Norton to Alfred E. Smith, May 23, 1932, Norton MSS, Box 1, Gen. Corr., 1931–1938; Alfred E. Smith to Mary T. Norton, May 27, 1932, Norton MSS, Box 1, Gen. Corr., 1931–1938.

25. Norton, "Memoirs," pp. 119–20.

26. Maureen Rees, "Mary Norton: A 'Grand Girl'," *The Journal of the Rutgers University Libraries* 47 (December 1985), pp. 59–75; Carmela Ascolese Karnoutsos, "Mary Teresa Norton, 1875–1959," in Joan N. Burstyn, ed., *Past and Promise: Lives of New Jersey Women* (Syracuse, NY: Syracuse University Press, 1997), pp. 368–70; Carmela Karnoutsos, "Frank Hague, 1876–1956," *Jersey City Past and Present Home Page*, New Jersey Historical Commission, http://www.njcu.edu.

27. Norton, "Memoirs," pp. 121–22; Maxine Davis, "Five Democratic Women," *Ladies Home Journal* 50 (May 1933), p. 22; Bob Leach, *The Frank Hague Picture Book* (Jersey City, NJ: Jersey City Historical Project, 1998), p. 70.

28. Norton, "Memoirs," pp. 121–22; "Statistics of the Congressional and Presidential Election of November 8, 1932," (Washington, D.C.: U.S. Government Printing Office, 1933), p. 22; Featured House Publications, *Women in Congress, 1917–2006*.

29. Featured House Publications, *Women in Congress, 1917–2006*; Eleanor Andrews to Elenere Kellogg, undated, Norton MSS, Box 4, Personal Biographical Material; Norton "Memoirs," pp. 124–25; David M. Kennedy, *Freedom from Fear: The American People in Depression and War, 1929–1945* (New York: Oxford University Press, 1999).

30. Kaptur, *Women of Congress*, p. 42; Norton, "Memoirs," p. 128.

31. Norton, "Memoirs," pp. 128–29, 168; National Women's History Museum, "Women Wielding Power."

32. Mary T. Norton to Franklin D. Roosevelt, October 19, 1934, Franklin D. Roosevelt MSS, President's Personal File 5418, Norton.

33. Franklin D. Roosevelt to Mary T. Norton, October 22, 1934, FDR MSS, PPF 5418, Norton; Arthur M. Schlesinger, Jr., *The Age of Roosevelt: The Coming of the New Deal* (Boston, MA: Houghton Mifflin Company, 1958), p. 501; Norton, "Memoirs," p. 128; "Statistics of the Congressional Election of November 6, 1934," (Washington, D.C.: U.S. Government Printing Office, 1935), p. 18.

34. Norton, "Memoirs," p. 125; Schlesinger, *The Age of Roosevelt*, pp. 501–2; Michael Parrish, *Anxious Decades: The United States, 1920–1941* (New York: W. W. Norton, 1994), pp. 382–83; Mary T. Norton Labor Record, circa 1949, Norton MSS, Box 4, Personal Biographical Material; Featured House Publications, *Women in Congress, 1917–2006*.

35. Kennedy, *Freedom from Fear*, pp. 271–72; Karnoutsos, "Frank Hague"; Carmela Karnoutsos, "Medical Center Complex," *Jersey City Past and Present Home Page*, New Jersey Historical Commission, http://www.njcu.edu; Carmela Karnoutsos, "Margaret Hague Maternity Hospital," *Jersey City Past and Present Home Page*, New Jersey Historical Commission, http://www.njcu.edu; Antoinette Martin Martin, "A New Lease on Life for Jersey City Complex," *New York Times*, February 27, 2005; Leonard F. Vernon, *Images of America: Jersey City Medical Center* (Portsmouth, NH: Acadia Publishing, 2004); Karnoutsos, "Mary Teresa Norton, 1875–1959"; Frank Hague to Mary T. Norton, March 23, 1936, Norton MSS, Box 1, Gen. Corr., 1931–1936; Mary T. Norton to Frank Hague, March 24, 1936, Norton MSS, Box 1, Gen. Corr., 1931–1936; Mary T. Norton to Frank Hague, August 5, 1939, Norton MSS, Box 1, Gen. Corr., 1939; Mary T. Norton to Edwin M. Watson, November 10, 1939, Norton MSS, Box 1, Gen. Corr., 1939; Mary T. Norton to Colonel E. W. Clark, November 10, 1939, Norton MSS, Box 1, Gen. Corr.,

1939; Frank Hague to Mary T. Norton, November 25, 1940, Norton MSS, Box 1, Gen. Corr., 1940; Mary T. Norton to Frank Hague, November 29, 1940, Norton MSS, Box 1, Gen. Corr., 1940; Frank Eggers to Mary T. Norton, April 19, 1941, Norton MSS, Box 1, Gen. Corr., 1941; Mary T. Norton to Fritz Lanham, April 28, 1941, Norton MSS, Box 1, Gen. Corr., 1941; Thomas Fleming, "I Am The Law," *American Heritage* XX (June 1969), p. 42; Jack Alexander, "King Hanky-Panky of Jersey City," *The Saturday Evening Post* 26 (October 1940), pp. 121–22.

36. Carmela Karnoutsos, "Roosevelt Stadium," *Jersey City Past and Present Home Page* New Jersey State Historical Commission, http://www.ncju.edu; Frank Borsky, "Park of an Era Will Fall with Roosevelt Stadium," *New York Times*, July 1, 1984; "Jersey City to Get WPA Stadium Fund," *New York Times*, September 26, 1935; "Jackie Robinson Made History Here First," *Jersey Journal*, April 13, 2007; Jules Tygiel, *Baseball's Great Experiment: Jackie Robinson and His Legacy* (New York: Oxford University Press, 2000).

37. Lucille Considine Memorandum for Mr. Casey, February 21, 1944, Norton MSS, Box 4, Personal Biographical Material; W. B. Bankhead to Mary T. Norton, October 9, 1936, Norton MSS, Box 1, Gen. Corr., 1931–1936; Mary T. Norton to W. B. Bankhead, October 16, 1936, Norton MSS, Box 1, Gen. Corr., 1931–1936.

38. Norton, "Memoirs," pp. 133–34; "Statistics of the Congressional Election of November 3, 1936," (Washington, D.C.: U.S. Government Printing Office, 1937), p. 21.

39. "Statistics of the Congressional Election of November 8, 1938," (Washington, D.C.: U.S. Government Printing Office, 1939), p. 15; James T. Patterson, *Congressional Conservatism and the New Deal* (Lexington, KY: University of Kentucky Press, 1967), pp. 288–291; W. B. Bankhead to Mary T. Norton, November 13, 1938, Norton MSS, Box 1, Gen. Corr., 1938; Mary T. Norton to Franklin D. Roosevelt, November 5, 1938, FDR MSS, PPF 5418, Norton. Chapters 4 and 5 discuss Norton's role in the passage of the landmark Fair Labor Standards Act of 1938.

40. Burke, Interview with Author, Aug. 7, 1981.

FOUR

The Labor Committee Years

During the late 1930s, Norton shifted her attention to the House Labor Committee and landmark legislation setting national labor standards. She had served on the Labor Committee since joining the U.S. Congress in 1925 but had played a minimal role in her first six years when Republicans controlled it. The media did not consider the Labor Committee important in the business-dominated 1920s. "During my first years in Congress under a Republican administration," Norton lamented, "I cannot recall a single law passed in the interest of the working men and women of this country."

Norton became the second ranking Democrat on the Labor Committee in 1928 and ranking majority member in 1931 when the Democrats gained control of the House. She served a highly industrialized area and understood worker's problems. "The 13th District, which I represented, takes in eight wards of Jersey City and all of Bayonne and is heavily industrialized," she explained. "My constituents were mostly working people." Marion McDonagh Burke, Norton's niece, recalled "Battling Mary" was "a reformer who fought for the labor and the working-class interests of her urban New Jersey district" for over two decades. "Blue-collar concerns" defined her career.[1]

Due to chairing the House District of Columbia Committee from 1931 through 1937, Norton devoted relatively little time to Labor Committee issues even after Democrat William Connery of Massachusetts became its committee chairman in 1931. Norton, who recollected the "difficult task" of chairing the District Committee "occupied my entire time" said, "I suggested to Bill Connery, the chairman, that I resign so he could have another member, who would have more time to give to it." Connery countered, "I'd rather have you than anyone else because I know I can count on you to back me up if I need you, even though you can't come to all the meetings." Although attending few meetings, Norton remained on the Labor Committee. "She was a savvy and determined politician, a staunch member of the Democratic Party, and liked to think of herself as a champion for working class men and women."

During the 1930s, the Labor Committee played a crucial role in restructuring relations between labor, business, and government, handling landmark legislation designed to help the American worker and unions. The stock market crash of October 1929, the deepening economic depression in the 1930s, the alarming increase in national unemployment to over 25 percent by 1932, and the election of Franklin Roosevelt as president in 1932 put the Labor Committee on center stage with the New Deal programs. The First New Deal in 1933 and 1934 concentrated on economic recovery, relief, and regulatory measures, including the National Recovery Act and the Agricultural Adjustment Act. The Second New Deal shifted the focus in 1935 to reform and social justice legislation with the Works Progress Administration, the Social Security Act, and the Wagner National Labor Relations Act.[2]

By early 1937, national attention shifted to President Roosevelt's dramatic proposal to enlarge the U.S. Supreme Court and lower federal courts. The U.S. Supreme Court had declared unconstitutional the National Recovery Act, the Agricultural Adjustment Act, and other First New Deal relief and recovery measures, contending that executive agencies created by them were assuming quasi-legislative powers. "The Court's interpretation of the commerce clause and the taxing power indicated that it was prepared to invalidate much of the rest of the New Deal when statutes such as the Social Security Act and the National Labor Relations Act (the Wagner Act) reached it in 1937." President Roosevelt in February 1937 asked Congress for authority to increase the U.S. Supreme Court by up to six members for every justice who declined to retire within six months after reaching the age of 70. "FDR's proposal sent shock waves through the nation, not only because of the boldness of the scheme, but because it came with almost no warning." Critics accused him of trying to reorganize the judiciary "to insure approval of New Deal laws" and began denouncing it as "the Court-packing plan." Congress rejected Roosevelt's judicial reorganization plan, but the U.S. Supreme Court began declaring Roosevelt's Second New Deal legislation constitutional when some conservative justices died or retired.

Congress, meanwhile, began considering wage and hour legislation in 1937. The Democrats in 1936 pledged to enact a Wage and Hour Bill as part of Roosevelt's Second New Deal. In a special message to Congress in late May 1937, Roosevelt urged Congress to pass a measure guaranteeing workers minimum wages and maximum hours and restricting child labor. He encouraged Congress to increase wages and shorten hours for American workers so as to prevent the downward spiral of wages. Roosevelt, noting the plight of some 20 million unorganized American laborers, protested that workers were toiling long hours for poor wages under substandard conditions. Roosevelt said, "We have promised it (legislation). We cannot stand still."[3]

Roosevelt administration assistants Benjamin Cohen and Thomas Corcoran, along with Secretary of Labor Frances Perkins, already had drafted a labor standards bill. Their measure proposed establishing a Labor Standards Board with unlimited authority to set the minimum wage at what it deemed appropriate and to set different work week standards. In mid-May, Roosevelt met first with William Green, American Federation of Labor (AFL) president, and then with John L. Lewis, United Mine Workers head, and Congress of Industrial Organizations (CIO) president, and Sidney Hillman, Amalgamated Clothing Workers of America head, to discuss the draft legislation.

Senator Hugo Black of Alabama and Representative Connery of Massachusetts on May 22 introduced a bill incorporating the Roosevelt administration's ideas. Black and Connery chaired the Senate and House Labor Committees, respectively. The Black-Connery measure empowered Congress to set compulsory minimum wage and maximum hours standards for all industries involved in interstate commerce. The legislation primarily was designed to cover nearly all workers engaged in interstate commerce and increase the wages and regulate the hours of the working poor.

The Black-Connery bill proposed creation of an independent, five-member Labor Standards Board, appointed by the president with Senate consent and spread geographically across the United States, with each receiving a $10,000 annual salary. The board was directed to set a minimum wage of 40 cents an hour for all workers in interstate commerce industries, thus guaranteeing any laborer toiling 40 hours for 50 weeks at least $800 annually. The minimum wage was created on the basis of occupation rather than gender. The board also was instructed to establish a maximum work week as close to 40 hours as economically feasible without curtailing either earning power or reducing production. It was authorized to raise work standards after conducting hearings, if collective bargaining already had failed. Exemptions were made for seamen, common carriers, railroad workers, and other workers already covered under previous legislation. The measure also prohibited the employment of children under age 16 in interstate commerce industries unless they received special permission from the chief of the Children's Bureau or the hiring of youths under age 18 in hazardous occupations. It also banned wage differentials, thus preventing southern industries from paying lower wage scales than other geographical regions.[4]

The Senate and House Labor Committees conducted three weeks of joint hearings on the Black-Connery bill. Black and Connery presided over the joint hearings. Assistant Attorney General Robert Jackson, the lead Roosevelt Administration witness, argued that the legislation was anchored in the federal government's authority to regulate interstate commerce rather than the police power of the state to regulate health. Secretary of Labor Perkins strongly supported the measure, but disliked exempting small employers. Women's organizations backed giving the Labor Standards Board authority to set wages, while civil rights organizations likewise endorsed the Black-Connery legislation. Norton, with the assistance of Gerard Reilly of the National Labor Relations Board, gathered statistics showing wage discrimination against African-American workers affiliated with the Brotherhood of Railroad Car Porters.

The Black-Connery bill, meanwhile, sharply divided organized labor. Hillman favored the bill, but AFL president Green disliked letting the Wage Standards Board intervene in the wage-bargaining process and set regional wage differentials. Green feared that such government power would diminish collective bargaining and strikes, warned that the composition of the board would shift from one administration to another, and questioned placing statutory limits on wages. He believed that wages and hours should apply to all workers without differentials and was afraid the board would let Southern industries continue to pay lower wages. Green wanted amendments guaranteeing organized labor's newly won collective bargaining capacity and also insisted that the Department of Justice enforce the bill. CIO president Lewis opposed the federal board fixing wage standards because they were below those already achieved by his United Mine Workers and preferred an alternative bill penalizing companies violating the Wagner Act. The metal and building trades and AFL craft unions also opposed the measure. Southern farmers feared the legislation would raise the wages of black workers. "That attitude showed prejudice by Southerners toward black people,"[5] Burke, Norton's niece, reflected.

House Labor Committee Chairman Connery died suddenly of a massive heart attack on June 15, 1937, thrusting Norton into the limelight. The Labor Committee had just completed hearings on the Wage and Hour Bill. According to Burke, "Mary was visiting a veteran's hospital at the time." Connery's death shocked Norton, who wondered whether to resign her District of Columbia chairmanship to take the Labor Committee helm. Norton held seniority on the Labor Committee, having served 12 years. The Washington media, the Associated Press, and the United Press telephoned her in Jersey City inquiring about her preference. "The telephone in my apartment kept ringing late into the night," she remembered. Norton, initially extremely reluctant to accept the Labor Committee chairmanship, confessed being "really scared" and "not well prepared." "Frankly, I did not want to become Chairman of the Labor Committee," she admitted, "for several reasons, the most important being that the Wage and Hour Bill was before the Committee. There had been extended hearings, which, because of my work as chairman of the District

Committee, I had been unable to attend. I really knew very little about the bill. I'd have to take over unprepared." Burke echoed Norton's sentiments. "Connery chaired the proceedings on the bill from the outset to the hearings stage. Mary did not know a thing about the Wage and Hour bill at the time she took over the committee chairmanship and had no interest in the bill at first."[6]

Conservative Southern Democrats portrayed Norton as an uncompromising advocate of social reform and sought to dissuade her from accepting the Labor Committee helm. House Speaker William Bankhead of Alabama telephoned Norton that he wanted to see her. Norton rode the midnight train from Jersey City to Washington, D.C., and saw Bankhead the next morning. Bankhead urged her to decline the Labor Committee post and retain her District of Columbia chairmanship because she had performed excellent work there. According to Norton, "He thought I'd be happier if I stayed there, that the Labor Committee chairmanship would be a terrific tax on my health. He pointed out that I was unfamiliar with the Wage and Hour Bill, and that if I took over now, it would mean eighteen hours a day for weeks, getting caught up." Switching committee chairmanships, however, seemed the right move for Norton to make at that time. Norton told Bankhead that her primary allegiance belonged to her Jersey City and Bayonne constituents. She represented an industrial labor district and affirmed, "The people who elected me to Congress should be my first consideration." Norton explained, "I feel the people of that district have more claims on me than do the people of the District of Columbia. They have returned me to Congress seven times. I would be ungrateful if I did not take advantage of the opportunity better to serve them." Norton claimed, "Their interests would best be served if I were to accept the chairmanship of the Labor Committee." Bankhead warned Norton that she was letting herself in for something very serious, but she retorted, "Nobody knew this better than I did, but I could not afford in conscience to refuse the challenge."[7]

Norton realized that she faced an awesome responsibility at a critical juncture in Labor Committee history. "I am undertaking a very serious and, at this time, responsible job," she affirmed, "but I hope with help of the Lord and all my good friends, that I shall be able to go through with some degree of success." Norton's dynamic personality and important listening skills made her an effective committee head. Burke recalled, "Mary always was very alert and listened intently to what was going on."[8]

Norton resigned the District of Columbia Committee post on June 30 to accept the Labor Committee chairmanship. She assumed the challenging position at age 62, "when most women contemplate devoting their remaining days to a leisurely household routine and the enjoyment of the grandchildren." Upon accepting the Labor Committee assignment, "she plunged into the fight over the wage and hours bill." *Time* wrote Norton "inherited the thankless chore of trying to push a stiff Wages & Hours bill past an unsympathetic Rules Committee and then through a recalcitrant House." Connery had considered the labor legislation his "pet" bill, inspiring Norton to try to save the hotly contested measure. Supporters of the Black-Connery legislation, though, questioned whether Norton possessed "the parliamentary skills, the capacity for rough and tumble debate to shepherd the bill." Burke even admitted, "Mary didn't know a thing about the bill at the time she took it over."[9]

At a very tense cabinet meeting, President Roosevelt defended Norton's ascendancy to the Labor Committee helm. Roosevelt adviser Corcoran, who largely had helped draft the Wage and Hour Bill, vehemently opposed Norton's selection as Labor Committee chairman. According to Norton, "The (cabinet) discussion centered around the fact that I had not attended enough of the hearings on the Bill. But of course the real reason was that the South was so bitterly opposed to it." Roosevelt, who strongly favored the Black-Connery measure, listened very carefully to the cabinet debate and then inquired, "Has she done a good job as chairman of the District Committee?" The cabinet members responded affirmatively. Roosevelt queried, "Then why should she be penalized?"[10]

Government officials, labor leaders, and journalists applauded Norton's selection. Secretary of Labor Perkins, the first female cabinet member in the nation's history, wrote, "It means that the wage earners of the nation will have in this important post a friend who is thoroughly familiar with their problems and sympathetic with their aims and aspirations." Democratic Mayor Edward Kelly of Chicago wired, "I want to extend to you my warm congratulations on this fine recognition of your abilities." M. J. McDonough, Secretary of the Building and Construction Trades Department of the American Federation of Labor, telegrammed Norton, "I . . . desire to offer you my sincerest congratulations and assure you my cooperation." *Newsweek* commented, "Proud that she holds the best post any Congresswoman ever had, proud that she and Secretary of Labor Perkins share two of the Federal Government's key positions in labor relations, she is going to hold the fort of woman hood."[11]

Norton faced an enormous challenge at the Labor Committee helm. She recalled embarking upon "the most strenuous and turbulent period of my career. For ten years I was destined to occupy a position in the center of a prolonged and relentless struggle between two gigantic forces in the economic life of this nation." Norton observed, "Millions of American working men and women battled to gain new rights and privileges and to preserve those they had won during the first Roosevelt administration." She also noted, "Diehards in industry, who resented and feared this new giant, fought back with every resource of power and money they could command, yielding ground inch by inch." Burke recalled, "Labor faced a scary situation."[12]

The Black-Connery Wage and Hour Bill marked Norton's baptism as Labor Committee chairperson. Norton vowed to "place a floor under wages and a ceiling over hours for some twenty million unorganized, exploited, and heretofore defenseless American workers." She understood the controversial nature of the Black-Connery measure. "The idea that the federal government could step in and help these unorganized workers by exercising its authority over inter-state commerce was new and alarming to employers already resentful of the gains organized labor had made, and there was bound to be a fight over it," she observed. "I never sought a fight, but never ran away from one either. My whole heart was in this one."[13]

Republicans and Southern Democrats on the Labor Committee perceived Norton as too protective of organized labor's concerns. Southern Democrats had wanted Democrat Robert Ramspeck of Georgia, who favored less comprehensive legislation, to assume the committee helm. "If he became chairman," Norton feared, "undoubtedly his bill would be the one reported out." She added, "I also knew that many Southern members of the House were violently opposed to the Connery bill." Richard Welch of California, ranking Minority Committee member, and Fred Hartley, Jr. of New Jersey, led the Republican resistance to the measure.[14]

Norton, who had missed most of the joint hearings with the Senate Labor Committee, termed her initial meeting as House Labor Committee head "a terrific strain." Norton disclosed, "I felt a definite under-current of resentment when I called the meeting to order that first day, so decided to appeal to the members for fair play." She explained that her district "was heavily industrialized" and expected her "to accept the chairmanship," adding "I felt I should do so." Norton readily admitted, "I was not very familiar with the Wage and Hour Bill and promised that, if they would give me their confidence, I would not disappoint them."[15]

The Senate Labor Committee, headed by Black, approved a version of the wage and hour measure that lacked the AFL's desired amendments, restricted child labor, and authorized each industry to establish wage and hours standards. Its bill empowered the Labor Standards Board to oversee the increase of wages to 40 cents an hour and reduction of work hours to 40 hours a week, but it could not raises wages above 40 cents an hour or reduce work hours below 40 hours a week. The measure also exempted rural workers, including those on farms or in agricultural-related industries like processing, canning, and warehousing.

The Wage and Hour Bill provoked considerable resistance on the Senate floor but survived. Southern Democrats disliked granting broad authority to the Labor Standards Board. AFL President Green warned Black that the Senate version did "not meet the expectations of labor" and insisted that the measure be amended, while several other AFL leaders wanted the legislation returned to the Labor Committee. After acrimonious debate, the Senate in July rejected a recommittal motion by Democrat

Pat Harrison of Mississippi, 48 to 36, and approved the committee version, 56 to 28.[16]

The House Labor Committee ceased drafting its own bill in August and promptly substituted the Senate measure. The Senate version, Norton affirmed, "greatly raised our hopes of its immediate passage by the House." Southern committee members from low wage states, however, rejected the Senate legislation. Ramspeck introduced an alternate bill granting wage differentials and other concessions to Southern industries. Norton protested that Ramspeck's measure was "so heavily weighted with concessions to the South that I knew it would be unacceptable to employers in the North." Southern industries paid lower wages than northern plants and opposed raising pay scales for workers. Norton told colleagues, "Textile plants and shoe factories in New England were closing down, as Northern capital, lured by the promise of cheap labor, moved down South." The Labor Committee rejected Ramspeck's legislation by six votes after contentious debate. "I had some anxious moments when he offered his bill," Norton admitted, "for I knew that if he won on that vote, I might as well resign as chairman. To my relief I won, with six votes to spare."[17]

Norton spent evenings with Burke and Leo Fee, a Georgetown University Law School student, examining and analyzing all aspects of the Senate measure. According to Burke, "Fee researched the bill and described it to Mary." "There were long hot evenings that summer in Washington," Norton recalled. "Night after night we'd suddenly discover that it was 1, 1:30, 2 a.m. But it really did pay off in the end," she stressed. "I had to know all the answers, because it would be my job to defend it on the floor." Norton read the complete Senate testimony very carefully and practically memorized substantial portions of it. "There must always be an answering argument, which I must know," she insisted. Norton probed wage differentials between the Northern and Southern industries, trying to determine a fair Northern minimum wage and the extent to which, if any, that Southern wages should be lower.[18]

Norton's Labor Committee, which needed to complete action on the Senate legislation and report it to the House floor for debate, met several times each week during July and early August. Burke recalled, "The House Labor Committee hearings on the Wages and Hours Bill were fascinating." Norton admitted, "We were working on the bill in the committee even as I was familiarizing myself with the whole subject!"

On August 6, the Labor Committee decisively approved, 19 to 2, a measure that differed substantially from the Senate legislation. "The bill," Norton recollected, "was amended again and again with concessions to the South, to agriculture, to labor, before we reported it out." The controversial wage differentials section was removed, permitting Southern industries to pay lower wages than other geographical regions. To further placate the Southern industries, the child labor restrictions were deleted.

The section creating a Labor Standards Board was removed because AFL President Green had objected to that group as an enforcement agency. Norton instead empowered a U.S. Department of Labor administrator to create a Wage and Hour Board to establish fair standards within each industry.[19]

The National Consumers League disliked Norton's concessions to Southern industries and charged that the New Jersey representative was impeding its national campaign to enact wages and hours legislation. In July 1937, Clara Beyer, assistant director of the Bureau of Labor Standards, complained that Norton "is proving even worse than anticipated. She is definitely opposed to the wage and hour bill and has done all that she could to obstruct it in the committee." Norton, Beyer protested, had cast the crucial vote to delete the child labor provisions from the bill. Beyer, though, did not realize Norton's dilemma. "Norton, under pressure from Southern members of her own committee, was in fact walking an uncomfortable tightrope, juggling the interests of every imaginable constituency as she tried to satisfy an administration that desperately wanted the bill."[20]

A Paterson, New Jersey, factory owner was irate that the Labor Committee allowed the Southern industries to pay lower wages than those from other geographical regions. He insisted that Norton restore the section mandating uniform wage standards across the United States. According to Burke, "The factory owner wanted things put back in the bill that she was not going to put in. He even offered her a bribe, but she turned him down."[21]

Norton's views on the wage and hour legislation clashed with those of Mayor Hague. The Jersey City mayor held a "lukewarm" attitude toward labor unions as "he hoped to lure additional industrial plants to his working class community." Norton and the CIO supported the House Wage and Hour Bill, while Hague and the AFL opposed it. Burke recollected, "CIO lobbyists had worked very well with Mary on the legislation." Hague, who "constantly feuded with the CIO on the Wages and Hours bill," had sought to prevent the CIO from organizing in Jersey City in 1937. The CIO had formed in 1935 and attempted to expand industrial unionism across the United States. It questioned the constitutionality of Hague's local anti-littering ordinance banning the distribution of circulars without a police permit. The CIO had wanted to distribute pamphlets explaining the rights of citizens to collective bargaining under the Wagner Act. Hague, who allegedly once boasted, "I am the law" to assert "his unchallenged authority," fought the CIO's attempt to interfere with the governance of Jersey City.[22]

Hague, termed "Labor's No. 1 bete noire" by *Time,* tried to change Norton's stance on the wage and hour measure. Before House floor debate began, he telephoned Norton from Jersey City reprimanding her. "I understand," he snapped, "you are in charge of a labor bill that is obnoxious to the American Federation of Labor." When Norton inquired which legislation he meant, Hague replied that he did not know the specific measure, but indicated her committee had approved it and sent it to the House floor for debate. Norton identified the legislation as the Wage and Hour Bill and assured him that he would like it. Hague, however, countered that the AFL disliked the measure and that AFL President Green had told him that Norton should not oppose them. "What are you trying to do to the A. F. of L.?" he queried. "You know it's against this bill you are working for." He declared, "You have control of the bill. It must not be adopted."

Norton was surprised that Green opposed the measure and assured Hague, "I had cooperated with President Green and even succeeded in getting five amendments suggested by him into the bill." Burke remembered, "Green usually had worked very well with Mary." Norton stressed the significance of the labor legislation to unorganized, poorly paid workers and "appealed to him in the name of humanity to understand what was at stake." Hague retorted, "You are wrong. They are opposed to your bill, and in fact I have been told that you betrayed labor." He reminded her, "The A. F. of L. has always been our friends and my friends" and added, "It is the first time I ever asked you to do anything for me." When Norton still refused to comply with the mayor's request, Hague declared, "He was ashamed of me—that I had double crossed the A. F. of L."

Norton, unaccustomed to taking orders from Hague, confessed, "I was speechless. I realized that someone had reached my chief to try to get him to influence me—in other words, I was being double-crossed. I hung up the phone, too angry to speak. It was the first and only time in my twenty-six years in Congress that Frank Hague ever tried to influence my actions." She knew that somebody was attempting to undermine her. "Someone," Norton figured, "was evidently trying to discredit me in a very devious way, attempting to make trouble between me and the man everyone knew I considered my friend. I was completely aroused and angry." Norton immediately summoned Green to her congressional office. Green arrived around one hour later. Norton told Green what had transpired and asked the AFL president "to contact him (Hague) immediately and tell him the truth." She insisted Green tell Hague that she "had done everything possible to work with him in the consideration of the bill." Green, plainly embarrassed, replied, "Frank probably doesn't understand. I'll explain when I see him." The impatient Norton, however, did not want to wait and telephoned Hague. Green told Hague that there was a misunderstanding and indicated that Norton "had cooperated with him and had never betrayed his organization." Hague agreed that there must be a misunderstanding and added, "He did not believe I would betray anyone or anything." The mayor never told Norton who had tried to discredit her. Norton, who termed the disagreement "the only real dispute I ever had with him," revealed the incident "left me with a big scar." Thereafter, "Norton seemed to walk a tightrope between the Roosevelt administration, which badly wanted a bill to regulate wages and hours, and the AFL, which would accept only a bill that stringently protected the battered remnants of its voluntarist philosophy."[23]

Green's resistance to the Wage and Hour Bill, Norton later learned, was triggered by William Hutcheson, Carpenter and Joiners of America head. Hutcheson's union, the most powerful within the AFL, opposed increasing the wages of unorganized labor. Norton was not prepared to "take advice even from Hague" and held a personal stake in not conceding to Hague on this issue. "That if it was the last thing I ever did in Congress," she vowed, "I would do everything possible to put this bill through which meant, and has meant so much to the unorganized people who had neither money nor an organization to support them." Norton, of course, realized the potential risks of differing with Hague and following the dictates of her conscience. "It was a very serious decision for me to make politically and personally," she acknowledged. "My husband had died and I was obliged to support myself."[24]

Although organized labor remained unenthusiastic about the wage and hour measure, AFL President Green mildly endorsed it on August 9. He called the legislation "reasonably acceptable and fairly satisfactory to labor" but hoped that the House members would significantly alter it.

That evening, Norton passionately defended the Wage and Hour Bill on the NBC National Radio Forum. She pictured the legislation as a "modest" beginning toward providing relief for those desperate Americans trying to recover from the most severe economic depression in American history. Norton described receiving "pathetic" letters from numerous downtrodden Americans, laboring 70 to 80 hours a week for under 10 cents an hour and for just $5 a week. Some businessmen, whom she denounced as "chiseling employers," had begun arousing American public sentiment against the wage and hour measure. "Do not let propaganda against this bill, led by a few selfish people, scare you," Norton warned. "This bill is not communistic, fascistic, bureaucratic or autocratic." She insisted that the legislation would protect constitutional rights and increase the economic power of unorganized American workers. She concluded, "It is surely and clearly the duty of the legislative body to carry out the principles of true friendship for our neighbor by legislation such as this."[25]

The House Rules Committee posed the next major hurdle for the wage and hour measure. Before the House could consider the bill, it needed to give its consent. The Rules Committee determined what legislation would be debated on the House floor. Anti–New Deal conservatives, led by Chairman John O'Connor of New York, dominated the fourteen-member Rules Committee and sternly resisted the wage and hour measure. "Mary despised O'Connor," recalled Burke. "She waged a desperate struggle to unleash the Labor Committee's version from a southern-dominated Rules Committee." Norton asked to testify before the Rules Committee to obtain a special rule under which the legislation could be debated. The Rules Committee, though, not only refused to grant a special rule for the House to consider the bill, but even denied Norton's request to testify. *Time* wrote, "Wages & Hours lay as dead as a roast chicken" and added, "By its refusal to give Wages & Hours a rule last week the Committee had effectively bottled up the bill until 1938." "Months went by," Norton lamented, "and I wasn't able to get a hearing." O'Connor told her, "It would be impossible to get a favorable rule because a majority of the members were opposed to it."[26]

Five Southern Democrats aligned with four Republicans to give conservatives control of the Rules Committee. *Time* noted, "Four are Republicans naturally opposed, five are Democrats from the South, whose industrial ambitions hinge on attractively cheap labor which the Black-Connery Bill aims to end." Democrats Howard Smith of Virginia, Edward Cox of Georgia, and Martin Dies of Texas led the Rules Committee resistance to the wage and hour measure. Besides fearing that labor unions would destroy Southern industries, they lacked sympathy for government regimentation, urban life, labor officials, and immigrant workers. Cox, "whose most notable efforts during 12 years in Congress were confined to peanut growers' legislation until Labor got under his skin last week," warned "(United Mine Workers head) John L. Lewis and his Communistic cohorts that no second 'carpetbag expedition' in the Southland, under the red banner of Soviet Russia . . . will be tolerated." Democrats William Driver of Arkansas and J. Bayard Clark of North Carolina charged that the bill would hurt Southern industries. House Majority Leader Sam Rayburn, a Democrat of Texas, quietly arranged to drop any further consideration of the wage and hour measure.[27]

New Deal Democrats explored two alternatives for reviving the wage and hour legislation. They contemplated seeking House consideration of the bill under suspension of the rules, a procedure which limited floor debate to forty minutes and required a two-thirds affirmative vote. Rayburn, however, already had promised the Rules Committee that he would not utilize that strategy. Many representatives had left Washington and President Roosevelt wanted certain changes made in the wage and hour measure. Norton instead circulated a petition for a Democratic caucus to bind the party to support the wage and hour legislation. Only 157 Democrats attended the August 19 caucus, eight short of the majority required to transact party business. Around twenty-five to thirty Democrats, mostly Southern conservatives, roamed in the cloakrooms or loitered in the corridors during the caucus.[28]

Norton, therefore, resorted to a little-used parliamentary procedure, the discharge petition, to compel House consideration of the wage and hour legislation. "Only by resort to the extraordinary proceeding of a discharge petition," Norton explained, "was the House enabled to consider the bill." Still determined to secure floor debate and action on the measure, she placed a discharge petition on Speaker Bankhead's desk. "If Rules refuses a rule, proponents of the bill can bring it to the floor by discharging the Committee through petition of half the membership, but only after an interval of 30 days." Norton needed to obtain the signatures of 218 members, a majority of the 435 House members, on the petition to discharge the measure from the Rules Committee. The House adjourned, however, before 218 members signed the petition. Norton lamented, "We went home on August 26th with heavy hearts at our failure to enact this much-needed legislation." [29]

Norton delivered two passionate radio addresses urging House adoption of the Wage and Hour Bill. She, in September, declared that the legislation's passage was "very near and dear" to President Roosevelt, who deplored "the presence of misery and degradation engendered by too low wages and too long hours." Numerous unorganized workers, Norton stressed, toiled long hours under unsanitary conditions for "miserable" wages and were forced to send their "emaciated" youngsters into the work force. "Do you not every day," she asked, "meet the man who is old beyond his years from struggling desperately to make enough so that his family may eat, so that his wife and children may not too be sacrificed to the greed for money of some unscrupulous employer?" According to Norton, the measure would "surely go a long way toward bettering the lot of the workers now employed at low wages and long hours and the elimination of cut-throat competition in industries engaged in interstate commerce." [30]

On October 5, Norton again fervently appealed via radio for House approval of the Wage and Hour Bill. The legislation, she insisted, would create more uniform labor standards in interstate commerce and help workers attain at least a minimum standard of living. "We can never be a progressive nation and rightfully the leader of the world," Norton warned, "while some of our people are exploited, starved, robbed of health, happiness and beaten into submission." Federal government intervention, she argued, was essential because so many workers either were exploited or unemployed. The measure, Norton predicted, would "give relief, justice, and courage" to over one-fourth of the nation's population. [31]

President Roosevelt, meanwhile, on November 15 summoned Congress into special session to enact the Wage and Hour Bill and other measures. The congressional rejection of Roosevelt's Supreme Court reorganization plan, the economic recession, the continued stock market struggles, and the rising unemployment had weakened the president's bargaining position. Roosevelt urged Congress to adopt fair labor standards legislation. "This did not mean," he stressed, "that legislation must require immediate uniform hour or wage standards; that is an ultimate goal." The president wanted Congress to be flexible, enabling industries to adjust to standards, and to grant a coordinating agency sufficient inspection and investigation authority to ensure effective enforcement.

Secretary of Labor Perkins asked Labor Department Solicitor Reilly to draft a substitute Wage and Hour Bill based on the British Board of Trade Act. Reilly helped Norton gather statistics to justify the legislation. The AFL and most CIO unions gave only tepid support to the measure. The AFL insisted on amendments exempting unionized industries. Perkins advised Norton that it was better to include those AFL amendments rather than incite active labor opposition on the House floor.

The Rules Committee, however, still refused to grant a special rule for the House to debate the Wage and Hour Bill. The committee resistance extended this time beyond the South to include Democrat Lawrence Lewis of Colorado. Norton, therefore, on November 16 placed another discharge petition on Speaker Bankhead's desk. "This time we met with success in securing the necessary signatures," she recollected, "although it took some time to do it." After securing 153 of the required 218 signatures the first week, she maneuvered to round up the remaining names. The list grew to 193 names the next week, but Cox of Georgia claimed that at least ten signers had promised him to withdraw their names from the list, if necessary.[32]

Norton intensified her campaign for House action on the wage and hour measure. In an attempt to placate AFL President Green, she introduced an amendment replacing the five-man board with a one-man administrator in the U.S. Labor Department. Norton and other urban representatives also threatened to block impending agricultural legislation unless more rural congressmen signed the discharge petition. Martin Dies of Texas and other conservatives, though, objected to this behind-the-scenes maneuvering. "They have swapped everything today but the Capitol," Dies asserted. "They have traded and promised everything to get them on that petition."[33]

Several Southern Democrats endorsed the discharge petition this time, forcing the Wage and Hour Bill out of the Rules Committee. Although still against the legislation, they believed that the House should vote on it. Democrat Joseph Mansfield of Texas, confined to a wheelchair, rolled to the well of the House on December 2 and affixed the final signature to force House floor action. The 218 signers included 196 Democrats, 9 Republicans, 8 Progressives, and 5 Farmer-Laborites. "It took seventeen days," Norton tabulated, "to get the required signatures on that bill." It had taken her three months to secure floor debate on the wage and hour measure.[34]

AFL President Green, to Norton's chagrin, defected to the opposition camp. After Green mildly endorsed the wage and hour legislation in August, the AFL withheld its approval of the bill at its national convention. Norton claimed that the AFL members still backed the measure but conceded that some AFL officials directed the resistance. She asserted, "Strong Republican opposition reached the delegates through some of those officers, many of whom were Republicans." Green feared that a one-man administrator within the U.S. Labor Department might arbitrarily set unsatisfactory wage standards and instead preferred enforcement by the U.S. Department of Justice. The legislation, he added, should establish a flat 40-hour maximum work week and 40 cent an hour minimum wage. Green adamantly rejected regional wage differentials, thus intensifying Southern and rural resistance.[35]

The fate of the Wage and Hour Bill rested in the House. Although many liberal urban Democrats helped the House approve farm legislation, conservative rural Democrats still fought the wage and hour measure. "The passage of this measure," Cox of Georgia warned, "is the worst thing that could take place at this time. It could throw a million out of work." Dies of Texas invoked racial overtones, contending, "You cannot prescribe the same wages for the black man as for the white man."[36]

Norton led the House floor battle for the wage and hour legislation. On December 12, she presented a motion, backed by the 218 petition signers, to bring the measure out of the Rules Committee for floor consideration. "Very seldom—I think only once since I came to the House—had the Rules Committee been as arbitrary in the consideration of a bill as it has been in this case," Norton claimed. The House resoundingly backed her motion, 285 to 123, allowing floor debate.[37]

The House floor debate on December 12 and 13 stirred considerable passion. The representatives split into five factions on the wage and hour issue. Norton, who never missed one minute of floor debate, led those members backing the entire House Labor Committee version. "Mary never minded speaking on the floor of the House," Burke recalled. "She would speak animatedly. The press loved it." Democrats Arthur Healey and Joseph Casey of Massachusetts, Michael Bradley and James McGranery of Pennsylvania, and Raymond McKeough of Illinois gave her invaluable support. Democrats Jennings Randolph of West Virginia, Matthew Dunn of Pennsylvania, William Fitzgerald of Connecticut, Edward Curley of New York, Jerry Voorhis of California, Reuben Wood of Missouri, and Kent Keller of Illinois also lent assistance.

The other four factions held widely diverse views on the wage and hour legislation. The first group favored making only moderate changes in the House Labor Committee version. The second faction supported labor in principle but wanted the House Labor Committee Bill completely rewritten. The third group opposed the House Labor Committee version as detrimental for the nation but argued their case in a dispassionate, methodical, logical manner. The final faction vehemently fought against any wage and hour measure. Democrats Cox of Georgia, Dies of Texas, Smith of Virginia, Sam McReynolds of Tennessee, Graham Barden of North Carolina, and Sam Hobbs of Alabama, along with Republicans

John Taber and Hamilton Fish of New York, and Hartley of New Jersey, led the die-hard opponents. These dissenting factions represented the AFL, agriculture, and the South. "These three powerful forces and others less forceful but just as determined fought us for five days on the Floor of the House," Norton recollected.

Contentious issues highlighted the two-day floor debate. Conservative Southern Democrats insisted upon retaining wage differentials because employers in their region paid lower wages than their Northern counterparts. Norton tried to accommodate them by continuing to allow different wage standards between the North and the South. "But even this great concession, so unappetizing to Northern employers," she lamented, "did not appease the South" altogether. Conservative Southern Democrats also protested granting so much authority to one U.S. Labor Department administrator and the Wage and Hours Board. The farm bloc disliked the exemption of agricultural processors. Dies, who represented Southwestern farmers, denounced the wage and hour legislation as "an ill-prepared and half-baked measure designed to humbug labor." The testy floor debate drained Norton's physical strength. "So heated was this debate," Norton recalled, "that I never dared leave the floor and went without lunch those days. It was a long, hard grind, but I was so absorbed in the proceedings that I never realized how tired I was until it was all over."[38]

Green's AFL persuaded Democrat John Dockweiler of California to introduce alternative wage and hour legislation protecting craft unions. The Dockweiler measure left enforcement to the U.S. Department of Justice rather than one U.S. Department of Labor administrator, established a 40-hour workweek standard, set a uniform minimum wage at 40 cents an hour for workers in non-unionized plants, and rejected regional wage differentials. CIO leaders Lewis and Hillman opposed the Dockweiler measure, however, preferring instead flexible standards set by a board. "One of the things that hurt most was the opposition of the American Federation of Labor" to the wage and hour measure, Norton conceded. She also lost a valuable ally when Republican Richard Welch of California, ranking minority Labor Committee member, rallied behind Dockweiler's bill. The House, though, on December 15 rejected the Dockweiler AFL measure by a 162 to 131 margin. Norton's faction aligned with conservative Southern Democrats and the agricultural bloc to defeat the Dockweiler bill.

The House weakened the original Labor Committee measure, however, with numerous other amendments exempting certain industries. "By this time," Norton complained, "the bill carried so many amendments that it had lost most of its character." But she remained undaunted, remarking, "Those of us who believed in a Wage and Hour bill still fought on, in the hope that we could get it through."[39]

Floor debate shifted to the original House Labor Committee version, favored by the CIO. AFL President Green, still distrustful of the Labor Committee version, telegrammed House members urging recommittal of the entire bill to allot for amendments. He denounced the creation of a Wage and Hour Board, claiming, "Labor, industry and the public are fed up with boards." At the 1938 AFL Convention, he assailed the CIO for supporting the original Labor Committee version. "No matter how objectionable a proposed wage and hour bill might be," he moaned, "the CIO favored it." Green's organization, "having failed to get the changes it sought, torpedoed the effort by inviting congressmen to vote to recommit it." Secretary of Labor Perkins wrote that Green "threw the whole weight of his organization against the bill."

Norton's faction resisted further attempts to recommit the wage and hour measure. Democratic Majority Leader Rayburn warned that recommittal would signify "the death of Wage and Hour legislation in Congress," while Democrat O'Connor of New York reminded colleagues that American workers wanted his party to fulfill its campaign pledge to establish a minimum wage and set a ceiling on working hours. He praised the Labor Committee version as a "progressive step toward . . . taking care of the people who are underpaid and who are compelled to work unconscionable hours." O'Connor cautioned colleagues, "When you vote to recommit this bill, you give the bill a stab in the back. You sound its death knell."[40]

To the dismay of Norton's faction, however, the House on December 17 voted 216 to 198 to return the wage and hour legislation to the Labor Committee. According to *Time*, "Aunt Mary's colleagues upset the applecart by voting it down." "A deathly hush," Norton recalled, "pervaded the chamber—not even in the galleries which were packed with onlookers was there a sound, as the Clerk (South Trimble) read the names. As he progressed through the roster of Members of the House we could see we were doomed to defeat."[41]

The Roosevelt administration had suffered a devastating setback on the recommittal tally. Sharp sectional and geographical divisions split the Democrats, causing Roosevelt's once formidable coalition to disintegrate. Speaker Bankhead and 27 other petition signers, including 15 rural and Western Democrats, 6 Southern Democrats, and 3 Republicans, voted to kill the measure. The 216 members favoring recommittal included 133 Democrats, around 40 percent of Norton's party. Backing recommittal were 81 of the 99 Southern Democrats and 20 of the 53 Western Democrats. Only 31 of the remaining 177 Democrats opted to recommit the bill. Rural Democrats supported recommittal, while urban Democrats opposed that move. Only 6 Republicans aligned with Norton's faction.[42]

Several other factors doomed the Wage and Hour Bill. Critics warned that the measure would not solve the recession and might even worsen economic problems. Increasing the wages of workers when prices were falling, they cautioned, might drive many marginal industries out of business. "If this bill is recommitted," one conservative congressman had predicted before the vote, "You will see a change for the better in two days." The AFL also contributed to the recommittal. AFL President Green feared that the influence of craft workers would be undermined if salary increases and protections were given unorganized workers. President Roosevelt, whose prestige declined on the judicial reorganization question, wielded less political clout than on earlier New Deal measures.[43]

The House setback chagrined but did not discourage Norton. "A turnover of nine votes," she observed, "would have meant victory. It was the greatest disappointment of my Congressional career." Norton, who had wanted to outlaw sweatshops, starvation wages, and child labor, declared, "The unhappy experience served to make me more insistent than ever on getting another bill through Congress." Norton remembered, "The bill was not rejected by the House but was recommitted to the Labor Committee, obviously for further consideration in light of those debates." According to Norton, "The Committee went back to work on it that very night." President Roosevelt telephoned Norton the next morning, "Sorry about the bill," and inquired what she planned to do next. To Roosevelt's delight, Norton immediately replied, "Give you another bill, Mr. President, one that I hope we'll get through." Roosevelt promised to help Norton if she needed it and stressed, "That bill is a must."[44] Cohen, a Brain Trust member and able Roosevelt administration lawyer, could provide Norton legal assistance in helping frame a new wages and hours measure.

NOTES

1. Mary T. Norton, "Madam Congressman: The Memoirs of Mary T. Norton of New Jersey," (Hereafter cited as "Memoirs"), Mary T. Norton MSS, New Jersey Collection, Archibald Stevens Alexander Library, Rutgers, The State University of New Jersey, p. 125; Marion McDonagh Burke, Interview with Author, August 7, 1981; Angeline Bogucki, "Summary of the Legislative Career of Representative Mary T. Norton," Legislative Reference Service, Library of Congress, Washington, D.C., November 3, 1950, p. 5; National Women's History Museum, "Women Wielding Power: Pioneer Female State Legislators: New Jersey," http://www.nwhm.org; Featured House Publications, *Women in Congress, 1917–2006*, April 27, 2007, 108th Cong., 1st Sess., H. Doc.108–223, http://www.gpo.gov. For labor legislation in the 1930s, see David R. Roediger and Philip S. Foner, *Our Own Time: A History of American Labor and the Working Day* (Westport, CT: Greenwood Press, 1989), pp. 243–57.

2. National Women's History Museum, "Women Wielding Power"; Featured House Publications, *Women in Congress, 1917–2006*; Norton, "Memoirs," p. 135; Mary T. Norton, "Speech on Wage and Hour Bill," Washington, D.C., October 19, 1938, Norton MSS, Box 5, Speeches, 1927–1940; Lisa Kutlin, "Congresswoman Mary T. Norton: Matriarch of the Living Wage," Georgetown Law Library, Gender and Legal History MSS, 2004, http://www.ll.georgetown.edu.

3. Norton, "Memoirs," p. 139; James T. Patterson, *Congressional Conservatism and the New Deal* (Lexington, KY: University of Kentucky Press, 1967), p. 149; James Mac-

Gregor Burns, *Roosevelt: The Lion and the Fox* (New York: Harcourt, Brace & World, 1956), p. 311.

4. "Troubled passage; the labor movement and the Fair Labor Standards Act," http://www.thefreelibrary.com; Katie Loucheim, ed., *The Making of the New Deal: The Insiders Speak* (Cambridge, MA: Harvard University Press, 1983), p. 172; Norton, "Wage and Hour Bill," Speech, October 19, 1938. For a history of the act, see Patterson, *Congressional Conservatism*, pp. 149–54, 179–83, 193–98, 242–46; James MacGregor Burns, *Congress on Trial* (New York: Harper, 1949), pp. 68–82; Paul Douglas and Joseph Hackman, "The Fair Labor Standards Act of 1938 I," *Political Science Quarterly* 53 (December 1938), pp. 491–515; Paul Douglas and Joseph Hackman, "The Fair Labor Standards Act of 1938 II," *Political Science Quarterly* 54 (March 1939), pp. 29–55; and J. S. Forsythe, "Legislative History of the Fair Labor Standards Act," *Law and Contemporary Problems* 6 (1939), pp. 464–90.

5. "Troubled passage"; Burke, Interview with Author, Aug. 7, 1981. For the joint committee hearings, see Douglas and Hackman, "The Fair Labor Standards Act I," pp. 491–515; and Forsythe, "Legislative History," pp. 464–90.

6. William E. Leuchtenburg, "Court-Packing Plan," in Otis L. Graham, Jr. and Meghan Robinson Wander, eds., *Franklin D. Roosevelt: His Life and Times* (Boston, MA: G.K. Hall & Company, 1985), pp. 85–87; Kutlin, "Congresswoman Mary T. Norton"; Burke, Interview with Author, Aug. 7, 1981; RBC, Associated Press Release, Washington, D.C., January 1951, Norton MSS, Box 2, General Correspondence, January-June 1951; Mary T. Norton to Edward J. Kelly, June 28, 1937, Norton MSS, Box 1, Gen. Corr., 1937.

7. Norton, "Memoirs," pp. 136–137; Bogucki, "Summary"; *Washington Post,* August 3, 1959, p. B2; Chamberlin, *A Minority of Members: Women in the U.S. Congress* (New York: Praeger Publishers, 1973), p. 57.

8. "Mary T. Norton," *Current Biography* 5 (1944), p. 501; Burke, Interview with Author, Aug. 7, 1981.

9. Joan Lovero, "Life of Mary Norton," Jersey City Public Library, Jersey City, NJ, p. 12; *Washington Post,* August 3, 1959, p. B2; Chamberlin, *Minority of Members,* p. 56; Burke, Interview with Author, Aug. 7, 1981.

10. Joseph Lash, *Dealers and Dreamers: A New Look at the New Deal* (New York: Doubleday & Company, 1988), p. 330; Norton, "Memoirs," p. 138.

11. Frances Perkins to Mary T. Norton, June 22, 1937, Norton MSS, Box 1, Gen. Corr., 1937; M. J. McDonough telegram to Mary T. Norton, June 24, 1937, Norton MSS, Box 1, Gen. Corr., 1937; Edward J. Kelly to Mary T. Norton, June 24, 1937, Norton MSS, Box 1, Gen. Corr., 1937; Chamberlin, *Minority of Members,* p. 58.

12. Norton, "Memoirs," p. 139; Marcy Kaptur, *Women of Congress: A Twentieth Century Odyssey* (Washington, D.C.: Congressional Quarterly, 1996), p. 43; Burke, Interview with Author, Aug. 7, 1981.

13. Norton, "Memoirs," p. 140.

14. Norton, "Memoirs," p. 137; Burke, Interview with Author, Aug. 7, 1981.

15. Alice Kessler-Harris, *In Pursuit of Equity* (New York: Oxford University Press, 2001), pp. 102–3; Norton, "Memoirs," pp. 140–43; Frank Freidel, *F.D.R. and the South* (Baton Rouge, LA: Louisiana State University Press, 1994), p. 75; Burke, Interview with Author, Aug. 7, 1981.

16. Patterson, *Congressional Conservatism,* pp. 149–54; "Troubled passage"; Norton, "Wage and Hour Bill," Speech, Oct. 19, 1938.

17. Loucheim, ed., *Making of the New Deal,* p. 172; RBC Press Release, January 1951, Norton MSS, Box 2, Gen. Corr., Jan.-June 1951; Norton, "Wage and Hour Bill," Speech, Oct. 19, 1938; Norton, "Memoirs," p. 141.

18. Burke, Interview with Author, Aug. 7, 1981; Norton, "Memoirs," p. 143.

19. Burke, Interview with Author, Aug. 7, 1981; Norton, "Memoirs," p. 144.

20. Clara Beyer to Mary W. Dewson, July 27, 1937, Mary W. Dewson MSS, Carton 1, Wages and Hours File; Kessler-Harris, *Pursuit of Equity,* pp. 104–105.

21. Burke, Interview with Author, Aug. 7, 1981.

22. *New York Times,* April 25, 1952, p. 14; Burke, Interview with Author, Aug 7, 1981; Carmela Karnoutsos, "Frank Hague, 1876–1956," *Jersey City Past and Present Home Page,* New Jersey State Historical Commission, http://www.njcu.edu; Alfred Steinberg, *The Bosses* (New York: Macmillan Publishing Company, 1972), p. 56; Jack Alexander, "King Hanky-Panky of Jersey City," *The Saturday Evening Post* 26 (October 1940), p. 122.

23. Norton, "Memoirs," pp. 144–46; Mary T. Norton, "Handwritten Notes for Autobiography," Norton MSS, Box 6, Autobiography; "Aunt Mary's Applecart," *Time* 31 (May 16, 1938), p. 15; Burke, Interview with Author, Aug. 7, 1981; Kessler-Harris, *Pursuit of Equity,* p. 104.

24. Norton, "Handwritten Notes," Norton MSS, Box 6, Autobiography.

25. Mary T. Norton, "The Wage and Hour Bill," Speech, NBC, Washington, D.C., August 9, 1937, Norton MSS, Box 5, Speeches, Labor, 1937–1949.

26. Featured House Publications, *Women in Congress, 1917–2006;* Burke, Interview with Author, Aug. 7, 1981; "National Affairs: Roast Chicken," *Time* 30 (August 23, 1937), http://www.time.com; Norton, "Memoirs," p. 147; Kessler-Harris, *Pursuit of Equity,* p. 105.

27. Patterson, *Congressional Conservatism,* pp. 181–82; "National Affairs," *Time,* Aug. 23, 1937; Mary T. Norton Notes, March 23, 1943, Norton MSS, Box 4, Personal Biographical Material.

28. Patterson, *Congressional Conservatism,* p. 183; Mary T. Norton to Franklin D. Roosevelt, April 29, 1938, Norton MSS, Box 1, Gen. Corr., 1938.

29. Norton, "Memoirs," p. 147; "National Affairs," *Time,* Aug. 23, 1937.

30. Mary T. Norton, Radio Speech, undated, Norton MSS, Box 5, Speeches, Labor, 1937–1949.

31. Mary T. Norton, Radio Speech, Herald Tribune Forum, New York City, October 5, 1937, Norton MSS, Box 5, Speeches, Labor, 1937–1949; "Troubled passage"; Franklin D. Roosevelt, *The Public Papers and Addresses of Franklin D. Roosevelt.* ed. by Samuel I. Rosenman, Vol. 1, 1937 (New York: Macmillan, 1938), p. 497.

32. Loucheim, ed., *Making of the New Deal,* p. 172; Norton, "Wage and Hour Bill," Speech, Oct. 19, 1938; Norton to Roosevelt, Apr. 29, 1938; *New York Times,* December 1, 1937, p. 19.

33. *New York Times,* December 2, 1937, p. 13.

34. *New York Times,* December 3, 1937, p. 1; Norton, "Memoirs," p. 147; Kessler-Harris, *Pursuit of Equity,* p. 105; Office of the Clerk, U.S. House of Representatives, "The Fair Labor Standards Act," http://www.artandhistory.house.gov; "Aunt Mary's Applecart," *Time,* May 16, 1938, p. 14.

35. Norton, "Memoirs," p. 150; Patterson, *Congressional Conservatism,* pp. 194–95.

36. Patterson, *Congressional Conservatism,* p. 195; Norton Notes, Mar. 23, 1943.

37. Norton, "Memoirs," pp. 147–48; Norton Notes, Mar. 23, 1943.

38. Burke, Interview with Author, Aug. 7, 1981; Norton, "Wage and Hours Bill," Speech, Oct. 19, 1938; Norton to Roosevelt, Apr. 29, 1938; Kaptur, *Women of Congress,* p. 44; Norton, "Memoirs," pp. 148–51; Norton Notes, Mar. 23, 1943.

39. Norton, "Memoirs," p. 151; "Troubled passage."

40. "Troubled passage;" Frances Perkins, *The Roosevelt I Knew* (New York: Viking, 1946), p. 260; Norton, "Memoirs," pp. 152–53; Norton, Notes, Mar. 23, 1943; Kessler-Harris, *Pursuit of Equity,* p. 105.

41. Norton, "Wages and Hours Bill," Speech, Oct. 19, 1938; "Aunt Mary's Applecart," *Time,* May 16, 1938, p. 14.

42. Patterson, *Congressional Conservatism,* p. 196; "Troubled passage."

43. Patterson, *Congressional Conservatism,* p. 197.

44. Norton, "Memoirs," p. 153; Norton to Roosevelt, Apr. 29, 1938; Kaptur, *Women of Congress,* p. 44; Norton Notes, Mar. 23, 1943; Mary T. Norton Labor Record, circa 1949, Norton MSS, Box 4, Personal Biographical Material; Eleanor Roosevelt and Lorena Hickok, *Ladies of Courage* (New York: E. P. Putnam, 1954), p. 165.

FIVE

The Greatest Victory

Norton renewed her battle on wage and hour legislation when the Seventy-fifth Congress reconvened in January 1938. She still claimed, "A majority desired a Wage and Hour Bill, although there was a wide difference of opinion as to the form the bill should take." President Franklin Roosevelt and Secretary of Labor Frances Perkins "leaned heavily on Norton to bring the bill up again." Norton worked with Perkins "to truly reshape the American economy."[1]

In 1938, the prospects improved for adoption of a wage and hour measure. The Roosevelt administration again urged Congress to pass minimum age and maximum hour legislation. During his State of the Union address in January, Roosevelt, aware of the discontent of the American Federation of Labor (AFL) leaders, explained, "We are seeking, of course, only legislation to end starvation wages and intolerable hours." He added, "More desirable wages are and continue to be the product of collective bargaining." After attending a White House conference later that month, seven Southeastern state governors backed a Wage and Hour Bill in principle. In January, New Deal Democrat Lister Hill also triumphed against strident conservative J. Thomas Heflin in an Alabama Senate primary.

Norton's House Labor Committee started drafting completely new legislation because the recommitted wage and hour measure had been amended too much. "As we studied the recommitted bill, which had been so loaded down with amendments that little was left of it," Norton recalled, "we realized that we must write an entirely new bill." She soon realized, "It would be impossible for 22 men to come to an agreement" and selected a seven-member subcommittee to draft legislation. Norton recollected, "We met every day for many weeks and during that time had before us every type of bill." Several labor organizations played significant roles in helping the Labor Committee frame the measure. The AFL maneuvered "to shape a bill that it could support" and persuaded the Labor Committee to accept a modified version of the 1937 legislation. "CIO (Congress of Industrial Organizations) lobbyists worked very hard with Mary, too," Marion McDonagh Burke, Norton's niece and House Labor Committee clerk, recalled. "The Shirtwaist factory union also had a great role to play."[2]

Norton's subcommittee weighed the merits of a fixed, universal wage and hour standard, preferred by the AFL, against the establishment of a National Labor Standards Board with limited power to establish standards on an industry basis, an approach favored by the CIO. The subcommittee framed legislation containing a wage board, but the AFL and National Association of Manufacturers objected. "For the first time in years," Secretary Perkins observed, "Congress was treated to the spectacle of the AFL and the NAM fighting cordially on the same side." By April, the conscientious subcommittee reported back a new measure to the full committee.

Norton, meanwhile, suffered a temporary setback when the House on April 8 rejected President Roosevelt's plan to reorganize the executive branch, endangering the prospects for a Wage and Hour Bill. Roosevelt had recommended that most autonomous agencies and branches be consolidated into cabinet rank departments, urged the selection of six administrative assistants, proposed the replacing of the Civil Service system with one personnel officer, and favored transferring the Budget Bureau from the Treasury Department to the White House. The Senate approved the reorganization measure, 49 to 42, but the House rejected it, 204 to 196. "Congressional disenchantment with bureaucracy and the growth of presidential power, coupled with the growing conservative mood nationally, had prevented Roosevelt from restructuring the executive branch," marking "the low point in his Presidential career." Norton feared that the House action might stymie the wage and hour measure. "Up until last night," she wrote, "I had every reason to think that the committee was very anxious to report a wage-hour bill . . . but now it is difficult to tell."

The Labor Committee, though, approved wage and hour legislation more acceptable to the AFL. It dropped regional wage differentials between the North and the South, equalizing wages nationally, and eliminated sex-based pay differentials, benefiting women. The measure authorized the Secretary of Labor to impose definite minimum wage and maximum work hours standards for the entire nation on an industry basis, exempting specific businesses where such tight standards could not be applied. Agricultural workers, transportation employees, local retail store personnel, and public employees were exempted. Minimum worker salaries would start at 25 cents an hour and increase 5 cents annually until reaching 40 cents, while maximum work hours would begin at 44 hours weekly and decrease 2 hours a year until reaching 40 hours, both done on an industry basis. Workers engaged in interstate commerce would be paid at least 25 cents an hour for a maximum 44-hour work week the first year, 30 cents an hour for a 42-hour work week the second year, 35 cents an hour for a 40-hour work week the third year, and 40 cents an hour for a 40-hour work week thereafter. Employees would be paid time and a half for overtime hours. Persons toiling an entire year would earn at least $572 the first year, $655 the second year, $728 the third year, and $832 per year thereafter.

The Labor Committee measure also regulated the employment of children and contained enforcement mechanisms. Children under 16 could not be employed, except by a parent or guardian. Fifteen-year-old children could work if given a special certificate from the Children's Bureau. Youth between ages 16 and 18 could not be hired in occupations deemed hazardous by the Children's Bureau. Goods produced under substandard conditions could not be transported in interstate commerce. The Secretary of Labor would be empowered to investigate any violations and conduct hearings to determine whether the law was applicable to any given industry. Any industry dissatisfied with the Secretary of Labor's decisions could appeal them in the courts. President Roosevelt welcomed Norton's persistence in drafting the wage and hour legislation, stating, "It is always a source of encouragement to know that I can rely upon your loyal support." [3]

House Labor Committee conservatives opposed granting Secretary of Labor Perkins broad discretionary enforcement powers. Norton attributed their resistance to Perkins being a woman. "I know," she charged, "that most men—and even some women—still cling to their illogical belief that no woman is capable of holding a so-called big job." Norton insisted, "They are going to have to get over it in a very short time" and lauded Perkins as "an extraordinarily capable and intelligent person." [4]

The wage and hour measure, however, commanded little support from Southern Democrats. Southern moderates, including Speaker William Bankhead of Alabama and Robert Ramspeck of Georgia, refused to endorse the bill because it did not allot for wage differentials. Ramspeck, who represented Atlanta, introduced substitute legislation restoring regional wage differentials and establishing an independent five-man commission. Organized labor, though, fought wage differentials and disagreed over an independent commission. AFL President William Green still opposed restoring regional wage differentials on principle and feared that an independent commission would undermine union power and favor the rival CIO. CIO and United Mine Workers President John L. Lewis rejected regional wage differentials, but backed an independent commission. The Labor Committee, convinced that no legislation would pass without AFL support, rejected Ramspeck's alternative measure, 10 to 8, on April 14 and decisively approved Norton's version, 14 to 4, on April 21. [5]

The House Rules Committee granted the wage and hour measure a hearing this time but protested the elimination of regional wage differentials. By a narrow 8 to 6 margin on April 29, the Rules Committee, "influenced by Ramspeck's opposition," again prevented the Labor Committee bill from reaching the House floor. Eight Rules Committee members denied the House an opportunity to consider the legislation. Five Southern Democrats, including Edward Cox of Georgia, Martin Dies of Texas, and Howard W. Smith of Virginia, aligned with three Republicans to stymie the wage and hour legislation. The Southern members complained the bill "lacked the regional differential which had been its predecessor's concession to Southern industry's cherished conviction that climatic and racial conditions below the Mason & Dixon line entitle its workers to a lower wage scale." Republican Joseph Martin Jr. of Massachusetts, cognizant that New England mill owners disliked regional wage differentials, broke with his three Minority Committee colleagues on this issue. Norton conceded, "The conservative opposition in the committee was too strong."[6]

Norton on April 29 began to circulate another discharge petition. The Rules Committee, she wrote Roosevelt, again had denied the 435 House members the right to "express themselves on this important legislation." Norton assured the president, "The Labor Committee has done its utmost to reconsider the bill." She stressed, "Many members of the House, besides myself, consider this arbitrary action of the Rules Committee a failure of the democratic process" and vowed, "The requisite 218 signatures to this petition will be obtained."

Roosevelt the next day supported Norton's move to post another discharge petition, deeming "the continuing fairness of the legislative process" as "the foundation of enduring democracy." The president regarded the measure "of undoubted national importance" because it related to major government policies and affected "the lives of millions of people." He, therefore, insisted that the entire House should debate it. Roosevelt pointed out that the Democratic Party supported wage and hour legislation in its national platform and stressed that "a large majority of the membership of the House believes that the House as a whole should pass its judgment on such legislation." The president concluded, "I still hope that the House as a whole can vote on a Wage and Hour Bill—either by reconsideration of this action by the Rules Committee itself or by the petition route." Roosevelt's letter, publicized widely by the press on May 2, boosted the legislation's prospects. Democrat Claude Pepper, who strongly favored the wage and hour measure, upset two-term conservative Representative James Wilcox in the May 3 Florida Senate Primary, indicating that the legislation even appealed to voters in the Deep South.[7]

A rejuvenated Norton walked again to the well of the House at noon on May 6 and placed another discharge petition on Speaker's Bankhead's desk. She still needed 218 House members to sign the discharge petition to bring the bill out of the Rules Committee to the House floor for debate. Norton exuded more confidence this time, buoyed by Roosevelt's letter and convinced that Pepper's upset victory had changed the House sentiment. Some conservative Southern Democrats feared that voters might punish them if they continued resisting the wage and hour measure. Norton stressed, "Many members realized that the salvation of the working man lay in a bill to lower his hours of work and raise his wages. I felt sure that a petition would meet with success and so would the bill."[8]

House colleagues quickly rallied behind Norton's discharge petition this time. "A swarm of Representatives was already beginning to crowd the well of the House" to sign the petition, "jostling each other in an unusually boisterous atmosphere on the House floor." When Norton handed her fountain pen to nearby representatives, the scene became chaotic. The sergeant at arms forced those waiting to sign the petition to form "a queue," which gradually wound half way around the chamber. "So many members were in so much of a hurry to put their names on the petition" that Bankhead, after repeatedly calling for order, suspended regular business. The House did not transact any further business that afternoon until 218 members had signed the petition. "Whenever a Southerner or a Republican joined the line, supporters of the bill cheered." Within 40 minutes, 140 representatives endorsed the petition. In the first 90 minutes, 200 representatives signed the petition. When Democrat Sam Rayburn of Texas, who had vowed not to sign the petition, became the 203rd signer, Norton cried, "It's all over now!" After a lull, the entire eight-member Louisiana delegation walked down the aisle.[9]

Within a record two hours and twenty-two minutes, 218 members had endorsed Norton's discharge petition. The signers included 183 Democrats, 22 Republicans, 8 Progressives, and 5 Farmer-Laborites. Eighteen of the Republicans came from more urban northeastern states, while the other four represented California. Twenty-two southern Democrats, including Rayburn, Maury Maverick, and Lyndon Johnson of Texas, also inked the discharge petition. Democrat Robert Mouton of Louisiana, the final signer needed, gallantly kissed Norton. Colleagues congratulated her on breaking the previous record of 100 signatures in one day. Norton observed, "The aisle was still filled with members who wanted to be counted. I was pleased and excited, for I knew that now the bill would go through." Norton, cognizant that it had taken 17 days in 1937 to secure 218 signatures, had wired Democrat Virginia Jenckes of Indiana "to make a special trip from home to sign her name. Mrs. Jenckes flew East but she arrived at the Capitol in time only to witness the celebration of an astounding victory." Jenckes, "disappointed that it was too late for her signature to be added to the list," flew back to Indiana later that day.

Several factors triggered the dramatic House turnaround on the discharge petition this time. *Time* attributed "the sensational transformation of Aunt Mary's capsized bandwagon" partly to her "efforts and those of her steering committee, headed by Democrat Arthur Healey of Massachusetts." But *Time* added "the real reasons" were Roosevelt's letter to Norton "in effect urging members to heed her petition" and the Florida primary "which had the result of urging members to heed Franklin Roosevelt." The sudden turn of events enabled the House to reconsider the wage and hour legislation and gave Norton "great hopes that the bill would be passed equally quickly." [10]

Before the House floor debate, Norton on May 15 appealed over the Mutual Broadcasting System for radio listeners to urge their representatives to support the wage and hour legislation. The measure, she stressed, would establish a minimum wage for two million American workers, including 100,000 New Jersey laborers, who were "exploited by chiseling employers in the sweated industries" under substandard conditions. The severe economic recession had forced employers to slice wages, causing "a vicious spiral of deflation" that threatened government institutions. Numerous American laborers had written her describing "terrible," almost "unbelievable" working conditions. Norton warned the radio audience, "Our country is in danger when we permit a large part of our population to exist in conditions which would be a disgrace to even an uncivilized country." President Roosevelt, labor organizations, American workers, and many employers strongly supported the Wage and Hour Bill. Norton pleaded with the radio audience to "join with us in Congress who are waging the battle for the rights and protection of the underprivileged." [11]

During Norton's radio message, Democratic Senator James Pope of Idaho asked her why House sentiment had shifted on the wage and hour measure. She replied, "The bill had been rewritten to remove some of the objections." Constituents had written numerous opponents of the original bill, urging them to support the wage and hour legislation because "the people of the United States wanted sweatshops, starvation wages, and child labor abolished by the federal government." During an election year, she argued, "Few people had any sympathy with members who did not support a living or near living wage for working men and women." [12]

By a decisive 322 to 73 margin, the House on May 23 approved Norton's motion to bring the wage and hour measure to the floor for debate. Norton planned the floor strategy for proponents of the legislation. "We knew," she explained, "the opponents were going to use every trick in the book to destroy our bill with amendments if they couldn't defeat it any other way, and we had to be ready for them." Norton told colleagues a tragic story about a female New Jersey toy factory worker, who earned only $3.45 one week for six days work. She was paid by each piece produced and received no pay for days when material shortages held up work, although required to stay there.[13]

The wage and hour measure still pitted Northern industrial progressives against Southern rural conservatives, but the two-day floor debate lacked the rancor of the 1937 encounters and survived numerous attempts to weaken it. The House defeated 23 of 26 amendments, decisively rejecting, 139 to 70, a substitute bill by Ramspeck of Georgia granting concessions to the South. Representatives attached three amendments exempting agricultural workers, fishing industry employees, weekly newspaper personnel, and child actors and actresses. "The three (amendments) that did get by," Norton claimed, "did not injure the bill materially." A persuasive, lucid, and witty debater, she knew "when to yield a point and when to fight back."[14]

At 10:45 p.m. on May 24, the House overwhelmingly approved the wage and hour legislation, 314 to 97. As Labor Committee chairperson, Norton oversaw House passage of the nation's first minimum wage law. The measure, which Norton "personally shepherded through committee and onto the House floor for a vote," marked her "crowning achievement." Democrats resoundingly favored the measure, while Republicans split sharply. The proponents included 256 Democrats, 46 Republicans, many of whom represented labor districts, and 12 third party members. Of the 97 opponents, 41 were Republicans. Only 56 Democrats objected, 77 fewer than in December. Fifty-two, led by Cox, Dies, and Smith, came from southern states. Norton boasted, "Many members who had been against the first bill because they thought it was badly written, or because they did not like some particular provision, although they agreed with the idea behind the legislation, were now definitely in our corner."[15]

Norton was House manager on a conference committee that resolved significant differences between the 1938 House and 1937 Senate versions. New Dealers Benjamin Cohen, who had "talked with Mary for hours about the Wages and Hours bill," and Gerard Reilly served as principal legal advisers. The Senate legislation had provided for an independent five-man board and regional differentials, whereas the House measure contained neither. Southern senators threatened to filibuster if the conferees approved the House version and insisted "that any measure contain some opportunity for regional differentials in wages." House conferees, who wanted to finish the congressional session and return home, were willing to compromise on the Senate-House differences if the labor unions consented, while most Senate conferees wanted to resolve the Senate-House differences before the November elections.[16]

The conferees on June 14 accepted a compromise between the House and Senate legislation, ending a year of intense congressional maneuvering. The compromise version, thereafter called the Fair Labor Standards Act, established a maximum 44-hour work week and a minimum 25 cents an hour wage for the first year. Industrial committees could recommend higher standards. A wage-hour administrator in the U.S. Department of Labor could approve or reject, but not alter, those suggestions. Employers were given three years to reduce the maximum work week to 40 hours, with overtime pay set at time and a half. The minimum hourly wage was put at 30 cents an hour for the second year. Certain firms could pay their workers 30 cents an hour for up to five years, when the minimum hourly wage would climb to 40 cents in every industry. The hours and salaries of service or domestic workers were not affected. The bill established the minimum working age at 16, but numerous exceptions were made. Intrastate retail and service industry workers, most transportation workers, agricultural workers, government employees, domestic servants, weekly or semiweekly newspapers with small circulations, food processors, seamen, non-profit organization employees, and numerous small business workers were exempted. Senate conferees agreed to let one person in the U.S. Department of Labor administer the act, while House conferees relented on regional wage differentials. In most interstate occupations, advisory wage boards were permitted to determine competitive conditions as affected by transportation, living, and production costs. The compromise also provided strong enforcement, authorized the administrator to rule on differentials, eliminated classifications by sex for wage purposes, and prohibited child labor in interstate commerce.

Although seeing many of its demands met, the organized labor lobby reacted to the conference committee compromise in a mixed fashion. The CIO, whom Secretary Perkins said "claimed full credit for its passage," welcomed the conference committee version more enthusiastically than did the AFL. At its 1938 convention, the CIO passed a resolution lauding passage of the bill "after an intensive struggle by organized labor in the face of the most reactionary opposition." The CIO, however, warned that maximum hours needed to be lowered further to alleviate the unemployment problem. Sidney Hillman, whose low-paid clothing workers were among the most likely to benefit from the legislation, especially backed the measure. Although not opposing the conference committee version, AFL President Green complained that its terms "did not comply fully with the wishes of the AFL" and pledged to seek corrective amendments. He urged AFL affiliates to set wage rates "as high as all available facts can justify" and to secure "labor standards higher than the minimum standards." Southerners grudgingly concurred with the committee compromise, too.

Both houses accepted the conference report on June 15, the House by a 290 to 89 tally and the Senate on a voice vote. Norton termed the conference committee version "a composite of the best features of the House and Senate bills" and "as near perfect as we could make it." She proclaimed, "The long arm of Uncle Sam reached out to protect the unorganized working men and women of this country." Norton concluded,

"The time had come when this country could no longer support the conditions prevailing in many parts of the nation with regard to sub-standard wages." [17]

President Roosevelt on June 25 signed the Fair Labor Standards Act, sighing, "That's that." The New Dealers had prevailed over a relentless, bipartisan conservative coalition. Norton likewise admitted, "It was a long hard battle, which at times seemed to be a losing fight," but proclaimed, "Those of us who had persevered for the cause of the workers of the country, were victorious against that minority which led the fight to keep the workers of the country in peonage." [18]

The Fair Labor Standards Act, known as labor's "Bible," differed markedly from Roosevelt's original request, exempting numerous industries. The measure "only dimly reflected the hopes of its originators." Its provisions covered only 20 percent of the 55 million American workers. Southern and rural members secured exemptions for many agricultural and domestic workers and let many businesses postpone paying what progressives deemed a living wage. The legislation included only 14 percent of working women, 25 percent fewer than working men. African-Americans, who comprised a disproportionate percentage of domestic servants and agricultural workers, received few protections. Burke recalled, "President Roosevelt was very active behind the scenes" rallying support from Southern congressmen, intimating "he may have made promises or concessions to them." [19]

Nevertheless, the Fair Labor Standards Act marked a significant milestone for the fledgling organized labor movement as the last major Second New Deal measure. Isadore Lubin, Commissioner of Labor Statistics in the U.S. Department of Labor, lauded it as "the most vital social legislation in the nation's history both in its 'philosophic basis' and 'in the numbers affected,' every worker in interstate commerce in the United States." By placing a ceiling on hours and a floor on wages, the legislation provided a foundation for future legislation benefiting workers. In 1937 over 11 million industrial employees, including all Southern textile workers, earned less than 25 cents an hour. According to Norton, "Hundreds of thousands of unorganized workers were paid as little as $4 and $5 in many parts of the United States—not only in the South, where Northern capital exploited cheap Southern labor in the textile mills." For the first time in the nation's history, she maintained, "Those workers of the country who had been paid starvation wages and were worked fantastically long hours by the chiseling employers, were, by law, given a small part of what they justly deserved in the form of minimum wage and maximum hours to work." The act placed men and women workers on a more equitable playing field, mandating maximum hours and minimum wages. The measure brought, Norton argued, "salvation to hundreds of thousands of workers in this Country who have no one to protect them." [20]

Although criticized by labor for making too many concessions, Norton played the most crucial role in securing House passage of the Fair Labor Standards Act. "Mrs. Norton's name will ever be associated with labor's first gains on a national basis." The measure, "the only significant New Deal reform to pass in President Franklin Roosevelt's second term," signified the crowning achievement of her legislative career, consuming most of her time and energy for nearly one year. Norton had worked diligently to frame the legislation in the House Labor Committee, posted two discharge petitions to overcome resistance by the Rules Committee, and directed the spirited floor battles for the measure. "It was surely a hard struggle," she recollected, "but the fact that we won the fight more than makes up for some of the disappointments and for all the hard work." Norton not only portrayed the Fair Labor Standards Act as her "legislative memorial," but as "one of the most important labor bills ever enacted." "I'm prouder of getting that bill through the House," she boasted, "than of anything else I've ever done in my life."[21]

House colleagues, along with labor officials, admired Norton's persistent, determined efforts in guiding the Fair Labor Standards Act through the Labor Committee. "I," Speaker Bankhead wrote Norton, "congratulate you upon the very fine service which you have rendered to the country in the enacting and arduous duties which have fallen upon you as chairman of the Committee on Labor, as well as for your excellent services on all legislation coming before the House. It has been a deep and genuine satisfaction for me to serve with a woman of your high character and great ability."[22] Democrat John McCormack of Massachusetts echoed similar sentiments. "In that fight Congresswoman Norton played a heroic part." Besides calling Norton "a great legislator" and "a fighter," he reflected, "She certainly did a great job when the Fair Labor Standards bill was up for consideration and debate in the House." According to McCormack, Norton deserved "gratitude from labor, both organized and unorganized, and to the people of the United States."[23] Edward Keating, managing editor of *Labor*, wired the New Jersey legislator, "You did a great job," while New Jersey Commissioner of Labor John J. Toohey Jr., commented, "Time, I know, will in the sphere of social and political economics, place your name in a well deserved niche for your masterly direction of the Wage and Hour Bill to its ultimate enactment into the Law of the Land."[24]

McCormack and Democrat Arthur Healy of Massachusetts also played pivotal roles in securing House passage of the Fair Labor Standards Act. McCormack, an Irish Roman Catholic presided over the House floor debate, while Healey headed the steering committee preparing the agenda. McCormack confessed, "It was a very hard legislative fight. It was one of the hardest legislative battles I have ever been engaged in and I have engaged in a great many." Norton recollected, "Representative Healy was a very great help to me in the Floor passage of the

Fair Labor Standards Act." According to McCormack, Healy "played a heroic part" in securing House adoption of the measure. "Healy, in my opinion, is entitled to second credit," he wrote.

Norton, meanwhile, cited President Roosevelt's role in securing adoption of the landmark Fair Labor Standards Act. Roosevelt had recommended on at least five separate occasions that Congress enact legislation putting a floor under wages and a ceiling on hours for interstate commerce workers. The president, she observed, had engaged in a "long and courageous fight to assure the working men and women of our country a standard of minimum wages and hours." Norton claimed that the legislation marked "one of the brightest pages in our history" and insisted "full credit can be given to only one man"—namely Roosevelt. "In all sincerity," she penned the president, "you gave me the inspiration to carry the fight to victory. The people of our country have only you to thank for your clearness of vision and foresight to establish this splendid law for our people." Roosevelt appreciated Norton's "splendid message" and replied, "It gave me a great deal of pleasure."

The Fair Labor Standards Act soon brought significant improvements in both wage and hour standards, alleviating the concerns of organized labor. By 1941, the Wage and Hours Division of the U.S. Department of Labor reported that wage orders had brought 700,000 workers above the 25-cent minimum. The Labor Department claimed that all workers would be covered by the 40-cent minimum two years before the deadline mandated by the law. The 69 industry committees completed their work on implementing standards by 1943.[25]

Norton, meanwhile, lost her valuable, longtime clerk and speechwriter, Marion McDonagh. The New Jersey congresswoman always wrote her own speeches except from 1932 to 1937, when McDonagh drafted them. "Marion is the only person," Norton said, "who has ever been able to say for me what I wanted to say better than I can say it myself." McDonagh, Norton's niece, married 35-year-old Edmund Burke Jr., a lawyer for the Public Works Administration, at Quogue, Long Island, New York, on July 18, 1939. Burke, a Princeton University graduate, had worked six years for a New York City law firm and later became the youngest member of the Securities and Exchange Commission. Lucille McDonagh, Marion's younger sister, became Norton's House Labor Committee clerk. "Lucille," Norton remembered, "was bright and quick" and "keenly interested in labor problems." Lucille, according to Norton, "filled the job with great ability," and was her "constant and faithful ally through many a battle."[26]

In January 1939, Norton and the New Deal Democrats suffered a major setback on a related labor issue, namely unemployment relief. President Roosevelt on January 5 warned that funds for the Works Progress Administration (WPA) would evaporate within one month and requested Congress allocate $875 million to keep the WPA in operation for the rest of the fiscal year. The WPA, established in April 1935, had employed over three million persons on various public works projects. The House Appropriations Committee reduced the WPA allocation to $725 million. Norton backed an amendment by Democrat Clarence Cannon of Missouri to restore the original $875 million amount on the House floor, but the conservative coalition decisively rejected that proposal, 226 to 137. Nearly one-third (107) of 226 Democrats opposed the White House this time, joining 119 of the 123 Republicans to doom the Cannon amendment. The House and the Senate ultimately approved the $725 million amount. Roosevelt later requested restoration of the $150 million, but Congress agreed on just $100 million. The WPA votes meant that the New Dealers might have difficulty keeping intact the Fair Labor Standards Act.

Norton, meanwhile, hoped to strengthen the Wagner National Labor Relations Act of 1935 and the Fair Labor Standards Act of 1938. She championed shorter work hours, higher pay, and better working conditions for employees and resisted all attempts to weaken the Wagner Act. "We knew," Norton explained, "we could improve both the NLRA (National Labor Relations Act) and the Wage and Hour Law by amending them. We prepared amendments in the Labor Committee, constructive amendments designed to correct the inequities and misinterpretations in the laws."

The Roosevelt administration proposed several ways to strengthen the Fair Labor Standards Act. In January 1939, Elmer Andrews, administrator of the Wage and Hour Division, drafted amendments eliminating inequities and hardships and removing certain problems in administering the law. By a 16 to 2 margin, Norton's House Labor Committee resoundingly approved those amendments. "The Labor Committee," Norton conceded, "did go somewhat beyond the recommendations of Mr. Andrews—but not very—and it was very difficult to hold the committee down to just what was suggested." It reported the bill "with a certain amount of trepidation," however, fearing conservatives would attempt to derail the 1938 measure.[27]

The House leadership abandoned plans to broaden the scope of or otherwise strengthen the Fair Labor Standards Act because of the Republican resurgence and obstructionist tactics by Rules Committee members. The Republicans had nearly doubled their numerical strength from 89 to 169 members in the November 1938 elections. "The difficulty in the House," Norton wrote Roosevelt, "is considerably greater this year because in addition to the group of a certain section of the country who are strongly opposed to the law there is now added a group of Republicans and they have considerably strengthened the opposition."

Norton resisted attempts by Southern conservatives to weaken the Fair Labor Standards Act. Anti–New Dealers, she charged, made "a determined effort to substitute amendments of their own which would have destroyed the laws we had fought so hard to get on the books." Southern conservatives sought to exempt telegraph messengers, industrial home workers, and other employees from the legislation. Democrat Graham Barden of North Carolina introduced an amendment exempting over one million industrial workers preparing and processing agricultural products from the wage and hours benefits. Norton protested, "Groups of diehards, reactionaries and many real enemies of the law" had sought "to emasculate the Act ever since its enactment and seized upon the Committee's attempt to strengthen it to attempt their deliberate sabotage of it." She affirmed, "I, for one, did not and will not stand idly by while the opponents of the Wage and Hour legislation attempt to destroy it, by this or any other means."[28]

The Roosevelt administration again defended Norton. Wages and Hours Administrator Andrews warned President Roosevelt that conservative Southern representatives were trying to alter drastically the Fair Labor Standards Act and stressed that his Wages and Hours Division unalterably opposed granting exemptions weakening the Fair Labor Standards Act. Andrews drafted a letter, endorsed by Roosevelt, declaring that the White House strongly reject any amendments exempting specific industries. In May 1939, Roosevelt forwarded Andrews' letter to Norton.[29]

Norton welcomed the White House assistance and staunchly resisted any changes not recommended by Andrews. "There has been tremendous pressure brought to bear on Members of Congress," she warned the president, "all of which is coming from the same selfish sources which opposed the enactment into law of this wage and hour legislation." Cox's obstructionist strategy especially irked Norton. Cox, Norton wrote the president, was "doing everything in his power to get a resolution through the Rules Committee to bring out an open rule which would emasculate the law." "If there is any thing further you think I can do in the matter," she asked Roosevelt, "please advise me."[30] Norton also showed Roosevelt's letter to Majority Leader Rayburn. She worked hard to protect the act and "guarded zealously the gains made by labor" for the remainder of the 1939 session, preventing the conservative coalition from weakening the Fair Labor Standards Act. In October 1939, Norton claimed that the legislation already had "accomplished more for the benefit of the exploited wage earners and the underprivileged men and women of America than has any other law passed by Congress." She and Abe Sabath of Illinois, who had replaced Democrat John O'Connor of New York as Rules Committee Chairman in January 1939, deftly used parliamentary maneuvers to prevent undermining of the landmark New Deal legislation.

The conservative coalition introduced numerous measures between 1939 and 1947 to limit the Fair Labor Standards Act, but none emerged from Norton's Labor Committee. When these representatives proposed legislation weakening the 1938 measure, "they were drafted by their authors as to by-pass the Labor Committee and referred to other committees of the House, where labor did not have so staunch a friend." Norton insisted that her committee had "honorably fought for legislation we considered to be for the best interests of our country" and urged House colleagues not to bypass her committee on labor legislation.

In July 1939, meanwhile, Smith sought to weaken or even repeal the Wagner Act of 1935. Norton had cosponsored the 1935 legislation, which had granted workers the right to organize unions and bargain collectively through their own representatives and created the National Labor Relations Board to administer the law. Businesses, industry lobbyists, and trade associations claimed that the Wagner Act revolutionized national labor policy, sparked the surge of labor militancy, and spurred the rapid growth of the CIO. Smith introduced a resolution to establish a special committee to investigate the National Labor Relations Board.[31]

Smith's resolution aroused spirited House debate on July 20. Southern Democrats and conservative Republicans rallied behind Smith's proposal. Republican Earl Michener of Michigan charged that the National Labor Relations Board sought "arbitrarily to organize labor throughout the country and set about the objective of organizing labor rather than presenting a forum whereby labor could organize itself." Liberal Democrats assailed the Smith measure. Sabath warned that Smith's resolution would establish a dangerous precedent. Thomas Ford of California claimed that the Smith proposal would emasculate the National Labor Relations Act, while John Cochran of Missouri denounced the Smith resolution as "a slap at a standing committee of this body." Norton assured colleagues, "If it is necessary to amend the law, your Committee on Labor will certainly do just that."[32]

Despite these objections, the House overwhelmingly approved the Smith resolution, 254 to 134. Speaker Bankhead selected a five-member committee to investigate the National Labor Relations Board and designated Smith as chairman. Republicans Charles Halleck of Indiana and Harry Routzohn of Ohio aligned with Smith, giving conservatives control of the investigatory committee. Democrats Healey of Massachusetts and Abe Murdock of Utah, the remaining committee members, opposed probing the National Labor Relations Board. "The committee," Norton complained, "definitely was stacked in favor of its chairman."[33]

Norton welcomed the end of the 1939 regular session in August. "I am very tired and must have complete rest," she wrote Mayor Hague, "as I am sure from reading the newspapers you know, I have been in fights. However, I am glad to say I came out victorious on the Wage and Hour Bill, and it has not been amended. I am going home very happy over the result, so far as I am concerned, of this Session."

Toward the end of the 1939 regular session, though, the New Dealers suffered three major legislative setbacks. In early August, the House rejected Roosevelt's proposals to allocate $3.86 billion for self-liquidating public works projects and $800 million to increase the lending powers of the United States Housing Authority. Republicans and conservative Democrats had struck various items from the self-liquidating projects bill until only $1.6 billion remained before deciding, 193 to 167, to scrap the measure altogether. All 146 Republicans opposed the self-liquidating projects legislation. Norton was "terribly disappointed that the Lending Bill and Housing Bill failed." She also was dismayed that the House on July 20 wholeheartedly approved, 241 to 134, the Hatch Act prohibiting federal employees, including workers on government relief projects, from participating in presidential and congressional campaigns. Norton charged that the measure was designed to retaliate against the growing power of the executive branch and warned President Roosevelt that it was "gotten up to destroy you." Nearly 40 percent of Norton's Democratic colleagues, though, aligned with the Republicans to adopt the Hatch measure.[34]

During 1940, Norton thwarted more attempts by the conservative coalition to overhaul the Fair Labor Standards Act. Anti–New Dealers introduced numerous amendments to exempt specific industries from the wage requirements. Conservative Democrats, along with Republicans, exploited the growing split between legislators representing rural farm districts and those serving urban industrial districts. They argued that organized labor was gaining economically at the expense of businessmen and farmers because higher wages increased the costs of manufactured goods, which farmers purchased. Many rural districts lacked heavy industry, but housed sawmills, pulpwood processing, tobacco processing, pecan shelling, sugar, packing, canning, and other light industries. Employers from those industries resisted minimum wage and maximum work hour requirements. Many Southerners complained that the 1938 legislation deprived their geographical region of wage differentials, its chief advantage in attracting Northern industry.[35]

Barden sponsored several amendments exempting agriculture from the Fair Labor Standards Act and decisions by the Wages and Hours Administration. Norton tried to block congressional consideration of those amendments, but the House Rules Committee submitted a special rule that circumvented the Labor Committee and brought the Barden amendments directly to the House floor. By a slim 189 to 185 margin, the House agreed to debate the Barden amendments. The bipartisan conservative coalition, augmented by some farm state representatives, appeared to have the numerical strength to weaken or overhaul the Fair Labor Standards Act.[36]

The Barden amendments aroused spirited House floor debate on April 23. Barden claimed his proposals would "provide more protection for the agricultural situation and for the producers of agricultural products." Sabath countered that farmers were already included in the Fair

Labor Standards Act, charging, "The Barden Bill is seeking these exemptions in the name of the farmer but the farmer is not involved. It is the packing, canning, sugar and cotton lobbies who are seeking this legislation." Norton and Majority Leader McCormack fended off conservative's attempts to dilute the measure. Norton "scolded her colleagues for trying to reduce the benefits to working class Americans" earning just "a $12.60 weekly minimum wage." She reminded members that the minimum wage was "a pittance for any family to live on." Norton told colleagues, "That is really our fight—whether Congress wanted to go on record as believing that less than $12.60 is sufficient for the ordinary American workers." She added, "When members get their monthly check for $833, they cannot look at the check and face their conscience if they refuse to vote for American workers who are getting only $12.60 a week."[37]

Although the anti–New Dealers wielded the numerical advantage, Norton's effective counter-strategy prevented the undermining of the Fair Labor Standards Act. Norton's badly outnumbered pro-labor forces lost nearly every roll call, but the special rule permitting floor debate on the Barden amendments also allowed floor counter amendments. Colleagues riddled the Barden amendments with so many exemptions and provisions that it became a monstrosity. Norton and McCormack kept amending each anti–New Deal amendment until the final revision was unacceptable to the House. McCormack, whom Norton termed "one of the best strategists ever to serve in the House," "beat off an attack by offering amendments to each destructive amendment proposed by the opposition, until the final revision was such a hodgepodge that the House voted to retain the original act!" Barden even asked the House to kill his measure because of the numerous amendments.[38]

During the spring of 1940, Norton's committee conducted hearings on proposed amendments to the Wagner National Labor Relations Act. Norton conceded, "Some mistakes were made" in the original legislation and realized, "They should have been corrected." The Labor Committee approved several minor amendments, but rejected any major changes. Norton admitted, "I felt very uneasy about bringing out any amendments to the act" and insisted, "The basic right guaranteed (to organize without interference from employers and to bargain collectively) should and would be unimpaired."[39]

The Smith Committee, though, held extensive hearings that diminished public support for the Wagner Act. Conservatives Smith, Halleck, and Routzohn sought to emasculate the National Labor Relations Board, overriding the protests of New Dealers Healey and Murdock. The Smith Committee realized that outright repeal of the National Labor Relations Act was impossible, but Smith proposed amendments to terminate the economic division of the National Labor Relations Board and permit employers to refuse collective bargaining with labor. It also sought to restrict to one year the period for which the board could order back pay and file charges of violations. The National Association of Manufacturers and the U.S. Chamber of Commerce, two business-oriented lobbying groups, zealously supported the Smith amendments. Norton's Labor Committee sought unsuccessfully to block the Smith amendments from reaching the House floor. "The Smith Amendments lived up to my worst fears," Norton lamented. Smith, Halleck, and Routzohn, she recalled, "picked at the Act" and "reshaped its substance and its purpose. The guarantee of labor's right to organize was rendered largely meaningless, and enforcement of the guarantee was almost impossible."[40]

The National Labor Relations Board sparked contentious floor debate from June 4 through June 6. Smith asserted that the board encouraged radicalism, punished business, and was staffed by bureaucrats who did not fully espouse capitalism. He concluded, "We are confronted by the greatest emergency of our national life" and warned, "No agency of this Government must be permitted to stir up strife or to strafe, or hamstring, or persecute the industries of the country upon which our safety now depends." Hoffman of Michigan charged that the board was hindering national defense. "One of the greatest obstructions to . . . preparedness," he contended, "is the unfairness of the National Labor Relations Act and the arbitrary and unjust acts of the N.L.R.B."[41]

New Deal Democrats adamantly defended the Wagner Act and especially the National Labor Relations Board. Norton feared that the Smith amendments would "practically repeal the law" and would destroy collective bargaining between business management and labor unions. Murdock claimed that the World War II experience verified the need for the labor board to mediate industrial disputes and maintain uninterrupted defense production. Frank Hook of Michigan declared that the Wagner Act symbolized the democratic values that made American society worth protecting against the Nazi peril. He warned, "If we fail to defend the rights of free men and women in a democracy, if we take away the social legislation previously enacted, if we take away the labor legislation that has been placed on the statute books, if we take away the rights of collective bargaining, we are not defending democracy as it should be defended."[42]

AFL President Green aroused Norton's ire by endorsing the Smith Committee amendments. Green accused the National Labor Relations Board of favoring the rival CIO over his AFL. Norton claimed Green's move was "apparently because of a last minute deal with Mr. Smith to make certain changes in his bill." She explained, "It was a definite breach of faith to a committee that had always tried loyally to support the AF of L."[43]

Norton, furious over Green's defection, made an impassioned plea to her House colleagues as debate closed. Several hundred AFL rank and file members had written her urging preservation of the Wagner Act and rejection of the Smith amendments. "It is your funeral, not mine," Norton cautioned House members. "I have made as good fight as I know how to make, with the cards all stacked against the Labor Committee." She assured American workers, "The Labor Committee has kept faith with them. We shall continue to do so."

Despite Norton's fervent pleas, the House, nevertheless, on June 7 resoundingly approved the Smith amendments, 258 to 129. A bipartisan coalition of 116 Democrats, including 75 of the 100 Southern Democrats, and 142 Republicans, backed the Smith amendments. "The combination of the president of the American Federation of Labor, the National Association of Manufacturers and the U.S. Chamber of Commerce," Norton lamented, "had proved to be too much for the majority of the members of the House to withstand." The Senate Labor Committee, however, pigeon holed the Smith amendments, preserving the Wagner Act.[44]

The Smith Committee continued to assail the Wagner Act and especially the National Labor Relations Board for the remainder of the 1940 session. Smith, Halleck, and Routzohn in late December issued a scathing report attacking New Deal labor policy. They charged that the "coddling" of labor had caused violent, illegal strikes and the spread of working-class militancy and urged curbing the Wagner Act "lest industrial peace, and with it the entire program of national defense, be jeopardized."[45]

Roosevelt, meanwhile, sought an unprecedented third term as president in 1940. World War II had erupted when Germany attacked Poland in September 1939, influencing the president's decision to remain in office. The Republicans in June 1940 selected utilities magnate Wendell Willkie of Indiana as their presidential candidate at their national convention in Philadelphia, Pennsylvania, while the Democrats in July renominated Roosevelt at their national convention in Chicago, Illinois. "From the start," Norton acknowledged, "we knew we were going to nominate Roosevelt. It would have been political suicide to do anything else." She added, "And there were a great many of us who sincerely believed that it would be dangerous to send a new and inexperienced man to the White House, no matter how able or well-meaning he might be."[46]

Some conservative delegates revolted when Roosevelt named liberal Secretary of Agriculture Henry Wallace as his vice-presidential candidate. "The din had grown to a point," Norton recalled, "where it began to look as though the convention was getting out of control." Eleanor Roosevelt quieted the rebellious crowd with a short speech stressing that the president needed dependable, cooperative subordinates. "It was a simple speech, very brief, apparently entirely extemporaneous," Norton observed, "but it was one of the most effective speeches I ever heard at any convention. By the time she (Eleanor) finished, you could have heard a pin drop anywhere in that huge place."[47] The delegates quickly rallied behind Wallace as vice president candidate.

During the fall campaign, Republicans railed against granting Roosevelt an unprecedented third term as president. In November 1940, though, Americans easily reelected Roosevelt. Roosevelt prevailed by a near-landslide margin this time, capturing 54.7 percent of the popular vote and trouncing Willkie in the Electoral College, 449 to 82. "He was trusted," Norton explained, "not only by the American people, but by the British, fighting for their existence. Millions whose countries had been over-run by Hitler's armies looked to him as their deliverer." Mayor Hague lauded Roosevelt on his "wonderful victory" and wrote, "I feel sure that it was the fact that you came out and presented yourself to the people in the closing days of the campaign, and the great Americanism that you displayed which was the spark that inspired us all to drive through to victory."

Thirteenth District constituents reelected Norton to a ninth consecutive congressional term, as she trounced Republican Raymond Cuddy, 92,356 to 39,274. Norton tallied 70 percent of the popular vote. Republican Charles Wolverton from the First District alone outpolled her among the New Jersey delegation. Norton's staunch defense of the legislative interests of her Irish, Roman Catholic, working-class constituents, continuing congressional leadership, and the unstinting support of the Hague machine and women, combined with Roosevelt's near landslide victory, brought her another decisive victory. Democrats regained one seat in the New Jersey delegation when Elmer Wene defeated Walter Jeffries in the Second District, but Republicans still wielded a 10 to 4 numerical advantage. Democrats William Sutphin and Edward Hart retained their seats in the Third and Fourteenth Districts, respectively. Nationally, Democrats remained in control of both the Senate and the House, picking up five seats to give them a 267 to 162 numerical advantage in the latter. Majority Leader Rayburn wrote Norton, "It is a pleasure to serve with you and I trust that your people will return you here as many times and as often as you will allow them."[48]

Following the 1940 election, Norton sent another inspirational message to President Roosevelt. She wired Roosevelt, "It was a great battle nobly fought and nobly won." Roosevelt likewise admired Norton. "Not the least of the Norton fans," one writer commented, "was F.D.R. himself." Roosevelt, who commended Norton's personal qualities, human compassion, and committee and political leadership skills, responded, "Your kind words and your good wishes are appreciated more than I can say."[49] Norton and Roosevelt both sorely needed inspiration and courage as they faced the critical World War II problems both abroad and at home.

NOTES

1. Mary T. Norton to Franklin D. Roosevelt, April 29, 1938, Mary T. Norton MSS, New Jersey Collection, Archibald Stevens Alexander Library, Rutgers, The State University of New Jersey, Box 1, General Correspondence, 1938; National Women's History Museum, "Women Wielding Power: Pioneer Female State Legislators: New Jersey," http://www.nwhm.org.

2. Franklin D. Roosevelt, *Public Papers and Addresses of President Franklin D. Roosevelt*, ed. by Samuel I. Rosenman, Vol. 2, 1938 (New York, Macmillan, 1939), p. 6; "Troubled passage: the labor movement and the Fair Labor Standards Act," http://www.thefreelibrary.com; Mary T. Norton, "Madam Congressman: The Memoirs of Mary T Norton of New Jersey," (Hereafter cited as Memoirs), Norton MSS, p. 154; Alice Kessler-Harris, *In Pursuit of Equity* (New York: Oxford University Press, 2001), p. 105; Marion McDonagh Burke, Interview with Author, August 7, 1981.

3. "Troubled passage"; Frances Perkins, *The Roosevelt I Knew* (New York: Viking, 1946), p. 262; Norton, "Memoirs," p. 154; Kessler, *Pursuit of Equity*, p. 105; Franklin D. Roosevelt to Mary T. Norton, April 16, 1938, Norton MSS, Box 2, Gen. Corr., Franklin D. Roosevelt, 1928–1945; Mary T. Norton, "Wage and Hour Legislation: The 'Object of the Law,'" Radio Speech, WOR Forum, New York City, May 15, 1938, Norton MSS, Box 5, Speeches, 1927–1940 in *Vital Speeches of the Day* 4 (June 1, 1938), p. 435; Mary T. Norton, "Speech on Wage and Hour Bill," Washington, D.C., Oct. 19, 1938, Norton MSS, Box 5, Speeches, 1927–1940; Angeline Bogucki, "Summary of the Legislative Career of Representative Mary T. Norton," Legislative Reference Service, Library of Congress, Washington, D.C., November 3, 1950; *New York World-Telegram*, April 9, 1938, p. 5. For executive reorganization, see David L. Porter, *Congress and the Waning of the New Deal* (Port Washington, NY: Kennikat Press, 1980), pp. 90–91 and Richard Polenberg, *Reorganizing Roosevelt's Government 1936–1939* (Cambridge, MA: Harvard University Press, 1966), p. 180.

4. Norton, "Memoirs," p. 155; "Troubled passage"; "Aunt Mary's Applecart," *Time* 31 (May 16, 1938), p. 14.

5. James T. Patterson, *Congressional Conservatism and the New Deal* (Lexington, KY: University of Kentucky Press, 1967), p. 242; *New York Times*, April 15, 1938, p. 42; Burke, Interview With Author, Aug. 7, 1981.

6. *New York Times*, April 30, 1938, p. 1; "Troubled passage"; Patterson, *Congressional Conservatism*, p. 243; "Aunt Mary's Applecart," *Time*, May 16, 1938, p. 14; Norton, "Memoirs," p. 155.

7. Norton to Roosevelt, Apr. 29, 1938; Franklin D. Roosevelt to Mary T. Norton, April 30, 1938, Norton MSS, Box 1, Gen. Corr., 1938; Patterson, *Congressional Conservatism*, p. 243.

8. Norton, "Memoirs," p. 156.

9. Office of the Clerk, U.S. House of Representatives, "The Fair Labor Standards Act," http://www.artandhistory.house.gov; "Troubled passage"; Patterson, *Congressional Conservatism*, p. 244; *Time* 31 (May 9, 1938), p. 11; *New York Times*, May 7, 1938, p. 1; *Washington Star*, May 4, 1938, p. A–11; Bogucki, "Summary."

10. Norton, "Memoirs," p. 156; "Aunt Mary's Applecart," *Time* May 16, 1938, pp. 14–15; Norton, "The Wage and Hour Bill," Speech, Oct. 19, 1938; Mary T. Norton, Notes, March 23, 1943, Norton MSS, Box 4, Personal Biographical Material.

11. Norton, "Wage and Hour Legislation," Speech, May 15, 1938.

12. Norton, "Memoirs," pp. 156–57.

13. Norton, "Memoirs," p. 158.

14. Norton, "Memoirs," pp. 157–58; "Mary T. Norton," *Current Biography* 5 (1944), p. 503.

15. Norton, "Memoirs," p. 157; Featured House Publications, *Women in Congress, 1917–2006*, April 27, 2007, 108th Cong., 1st Sess., H. Doc. 108–223, http://www.gpo.gov; "Troubled passage"; Patterson, *Congressional Conservatism*, p. 245; Lisa Kutlin, "Congresswoman Mary T. Norton: Matriarch of the Living Wage," George-

town Law Library: Gender and Legal History MSS, 2004, http://www.ll.georgetown.edu; Norton Notes, Mar. 23, 1943.

16. Patterson, *Congressional Conservatism*, p. 245; Kessler-Harris, *Pursuit of Equity*, p. 105.

17. Patterson, *Congressional Conservatism*, pp. 245–46; Norton, "The Wage and Hour Bill," Speech, Oct. 19, 1938; "Troubled passage"; Norton, "Memoirs," p. 158; Kessler-Harris, *Pursuit of Equity*, p. 105; Mary T. Norton to John W. McCormack, June 14, 1950, Norton MSS, Box 1, Gen. Corr., Feb. 1950.

18. Kessler-Harris, *Pursuit of Equity*, p. 105; William Leuchtenburg, *Franklin D. Roosevelt and the New Deal 1932–1940* (New York: Harper & Row, 1963), p. 262; Mary T. Norton to Edward Keating, June 21, 1938, Norton MSS, Box 1, Gen. Corr., 1938.

19. Clerk, House, "The Fair Labor Standards Act"; Kessler-Harris, *Pursuit of Equality*, pp. 107–8; Burke, Interview with Author, Aug. 7, 1981.

20. Marcy Kaptur, *Women of Congress: A Twentieth Century Odyssey* (Washington, D.C.: Congressional Quarterly, 1996), p. 43; Norton, Memoirs, p. 158; Mary T. Norton Labor Record, circa 1949, Norton MSS, Box 4, Personal Biographical Material; Mary T. Norton, "The Defense of the Federal Wage and Hour Law from Attack," Speech, National Consumers League, New York City, December 8, 1939, Norton MSS, Box 5, Speeches, Labor, 1937–1949. For analysis of the Fair Labor Standards Act, see James MacGregor Burns, *Congress on Trial* (New York: Harper, 1949), p. 77, and O. R. Altman, "Second and Third Sessions of the Seventy-fifth Congress, 1937–38," *American Political Science Review* 32 (December 1938), p. 1105.

21. Featured House Publications, *Women in Congress, 1917-2006*; Norton to Keating, June 21, 1938; Kaptur, *Women of Congress*, p. 43; Norton, "Memoirs," p. 159; *New York Herald Tribune*, August 3, 1959, p. 2B; Kutlin, "Congresswoman Mary T. Norton"; Clerk, House, "Fair Labor Standards Act."

22. Clerk, House, "Fair Labor Standards Act"; W. B. Bankhead to Mary T. Norton, June 23, 1938, Norton MSS, Box 1, Gen. Corr., 1938.

23. Burke, Interview with Author, Aug. 7, 1981; John W. McCormack to Howard D. Samuel, June 20, 1950, Norton MSS, Box 1, Gen. Corr., February 1950.

24. Edward Keating to Mary T. Norton, June 17, 1938, Norton MSS, Box 1, Gen. Corr., 1938; John J. Toohey, Jr. to Mary T. Norton, November 10, 1938, Norton MSS, Box 1, Gen. Corr., 1938.

25. Norton to McCormack, June 14, 1950; McCormack to Samuel, June 20, 1950; Mary T. Norton to Franklin D. Roosevelt, October 24, 1938, Franklin D. Roosevelt MSS, President's Personal File 5418, Norton; Franklin D. Roosevelt to Mary T. Norton, October 28, 1938, Norton MSS, Box 2, Gen. Corr., Franklin D. Roosevelt, 1928–1945; "Troubled passage."

26. Norton, "Memoirs," p. 160; Margot Gayle, "Battling Mary Retires," *Independent Woman* 29 (July 1950), p. 200; *Washington Post*, August 3, 1959, p. B2; *New York Times*, May 17, 1993. For the House role on the WPA issue, see Porter, *Waning of the New Deal*, pp. 61–71.

27. Norton, "Memoirs," p. 160; Burke, Interview with Author, Aug. 7, 1981; Norton, "Defense of the Federal Wages and Hours Law," Speech, Dec. 8, 1939.

28. Norton, "Memoirs," pp. 160–61; Mary T. Norton to Franklin D. Roosevelt, May 16, 1939, Franklin D. Roosevelt MSS, President's Secretary's File, Container 140, Congress; Norton, "Defense of the Federal Wage," December 8, 1939.

29. Elmer F. Andrews to Franklin D. Roosevelt, April 17, 1939, FDR MSS, PPF 5418, Norton; Franklin D. Roosevelt to Mary T. Norton, May 15, 1939, FDR MSS, PPF 5418, Norton.

30. Norton to Roosevelt, May 16, 1939; Edwin M. Watson to Franklin D. Roosevelt, FDR MSS, PSF, Container 113; Richard N. Chapman, *Contours of Public Policy, 1939–1945* (New York: Garland Publishing, 1981), pp. 85–86.

31. Eric F. Goldman, *Rendezvous with Destiny* (New York: Alfred A. Knopf, 1952), p. 365; Norton, "Defense of the Federal Wages and Hours Law," Speech, Dec 8, 1939; Norton Labor Record, circa 1939; Kenneth G. Crawford, "Assault on the NLRB," *Na-*

tion 149 (December 30, 1939), pp. 726–27; Chapman, *Contours of Public Policy*, pp. 88–89.

32. *Congressional Record*, 76th Cong, 3rd Sess., p. 4538; Norton, "Memoirs," pp. 161–62.

33. Chapman, *Contours of Public Policy*, p. 89; Norton, "Memoirs," p. 162.

34. Mary T. Norton to Frank Hague, August 5, 1939, Norton MSS, Box 1, Gen. Corr., 1939; Patterson, *Congressional Conservatism*, pp. 318–22; "A Congress to Win the War," *New Republic* 106 (May 18, 1942), pp. 700, 703; Porter, *Waning of the New Deal*, pp. 111–21.

35. Christiana M. Campbell, *The Farm Bureau and the New Deal* (Urbana, IL: University of Illinois Press, 1962), pp. 105, 116–17, 186; J. B. Shannon, "Presidential Politics in the South" in Taylor Cole and John H. Hallowell, *The Southern Political Scene, 1938–1948* (Gainesville, FL: University of Florida Press, 1948), pp. 466–67; Irving Richter, "Four Years of the Fair Labor Standards Act of 1938," *Journal of Political Economy* 51 (1943), pp. 98–99; Chapman, *Contours of Public Policy*, pp. 86–87.

36. *New York Times*, April 26, 1940, p. 1; *Congressional Record*, 76th Cong., 3rd Sess., pp. 5045–46, 5051–52; Chapman, *Contours of Public Policy*, p. 87.

37. *Congressional Record*, 76th Cong., 3rd Sess., pp. 4924, 5036; Chapman, *Contours of Public Policy*, pp. 87–88; Featured House Publications, *Women in Congress, 1917–2006*; "Mary T. Norton," *Current Biography*, p. 501.

38. *New York Times*, April 28, 1940, p. 9; *New York Times*, April 29, 1940, p. 6; *Time* 35 (May 13, 1940), p. 20; Chapman, *Contours of Public Policy*, p. 88; Norton, "Memoirs," p. 166; Emily A. Geer, "A Study of the Activities of Women in Congress With Special Reference to the Congressional Careers of Margaret Chase Smith, Mary T. Norton, and Edith Nourse Rogers," (Masters thesis: Bowling Green State University, 1952), p. 134; "Mary T. Norton," *Current Biography*, p. 501.

39. Chapman, *Contours of Public Policy*, p. 89; Norton, "Memoirs," pp. 162–63.

40. U.S. Congress, House of Representatives, Special Committee to Investigate the National Labor Relations Board, 76th Cong., 3rd Sess., *Intermediate Report*, House Report 1902, 1940; Arthur D. Healey and Abe Murdock, statement on the Smith Committee, March 11, 1940, Robert Wagner MSS, Georgetown University Library, Box 709-LA-720; Harry A. Millis and Emily Clark Brown, *From the Wagner Act to Taft-Hartley* (Chicago, IL: University of Chicago Press, 1950), pp. 351–52; Norton, "Memoirs," pp. 163–64.

41. *Congressional Record*, 76th Cong., 3rd Sess., pp. 7715, 7720, 7723; Chapman, *Contours of Public Policy*, pp. 89–90.

42. *New York Times*, March 9, 1940, p. 1; *Congressional Record*, 76th Cong., 3rd Sess., p. 7799; Norton, "Memoirs," pp. 164–65.

43. Norton, "Memoirs," pp. 164–65; Chapman, *Contours of Public Policy*, p. 89; *Newsweek* 15 (June 17, 1940), pp. 67–68; *Time* 35 (March 25, 1940), pp. 21–22.

44. *Congressional Record*, 76th Cong., 3rd Sess., p. 7805; Chapman, *Contours of Public Policy, p. 91*; Norton, "Memoirs," *pp. 165–66.

45. U.S. Congress, House Special Committee to Investigate the National Labor Relations Board, 76th Cong., 3rd Sess., *Report*, H. Report 3109, part 1, p. 1; Millis and Brown, *From the Wagner Act to Taft-Hartley*, p. 353.

46. Norton, "Memoirs," pp. 170–71.

47. Norton, "Memoirs," p. 173; Frank Hague to Franklin D. Roosevelt, November 25, 1940, Norton MSS, Box 1, Gen. Corr., 1940.

48. Norton, "Memoirs," p. 175; "Statistics of the Congressional Election of November 5, 1940," (Washington, D.C.: U.S. Government Printing Office, 1941), p. 19; Sam Rayburn to Mary T. Norton, March 7, 1941, Norton MSS, Box 1, Gen. Corr., 1941.

49. Mary T. Norton to Franklin D. Roosevelt, November 6, 1940, FDR MSS, PPF 5418; Doris Faber, *The Life of Lorena Hickok: E. R.'s Friend* (New York: William Morrow & Company, 1980), p. 286; Franklin D. Roosevelt to Mary T. Norton, November 9, 1940, Norton MSS, Box 2, Gen. Corr., 1940.

"Rep. elect Mary T. Norton of N.J., 12/4/24." Mary Norton, pictured here inside the U.S. Capitol building on December 4, 1924, was elected the previous month to the U.S. House of Representatives from the Twelfth District in New Jersey and served urban, Roman Catholic, working-class constituents from Bayonne and part of Jersey City for 13 consecutive terms from 1925 to 1951. She was the first woman elected to the U.S. Congress from the Democratic Party, the northeastern states, and an urban district east of the Mississippi River. *Source: Library of Congress, Prints & Photographs Division, photograph by Harris & Ewing, reproduction number: LCDIG-npcc-26447.*

"Norton, Mary, Mrs." Mary Norton, shown here in academic regalia in the 1930s, attended Jersey City parochial school only through eighth grade, but later received honorary doctoral degrees from the College of St. Elizabeth in 1930 and Rider College in 1937. *Source: Library of Congress, Prints & Photographs Division, photograph by Harris & Ewing, reproduction number: LC-DIG=hec-21089.*

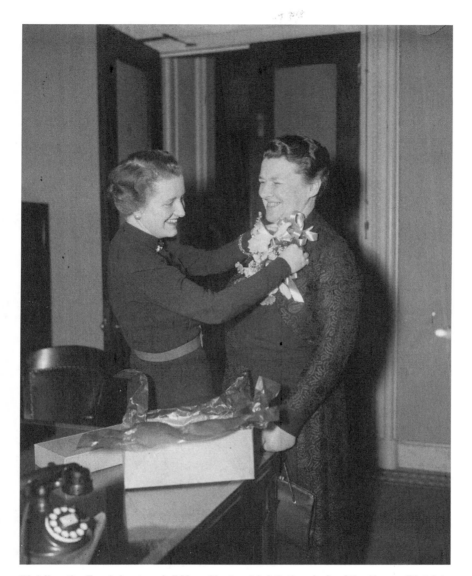

"Adding the Feminine touch." Mary Norton (right), the chair of the House District of Columbia Committee from 1931 to 1937, receives a corsage from her niece, Marion McDonagh Burke (left), in the U.S. Capitol building before the opening session of the Seventy-fifth Congress on January 5, 1937. Burke served as Norton's clerk on the House District of Columbia Committee from 1931 to 1937 and the House Labor Committee from June 1937 to July 1939. *Source: Library of Congress, Prints & Photographs Division, photograph by Harris & Ewing, reproduction number: LC-DIG-hec-21945.*

"New chairman of House Labor Committee." Mary Norton, pictured here walking inside the U.S. Capitol building on June 21, 1937, became Chairman of the House Labor Committee when Democrat William Connery, Jr. of Massachusetts died suddenly six days earlier. *Source: Library of Congress, Prints & Photographs Division, photograph by Harris & Ewing, reproduction number: LC-DIG-hec-22907.*

"Last signature necessary to bring wages-hours bill to floor of house." Democrat Joseph Mansfield of Texas (second right), confined to a wheelchair, on December 2, 1937 became the last of the 218 signers of Norton's petition needed to discharge the wage and hour bill from the House Rules Committee, which had pigeon-holed the measure since August. The discharge petition sent the measure to the floor of the House of Representatives for debate. The historic photo, taken in the well of the House in the U.S. Capitol building, also pictures Mary Norton (left), House Speaker Democrat William Bankhead of Alabama (back middle), and House Majority Whip Democrat Patrick Boland of Pennsylvania (right). *Source: Library of Congress, Prints & Photographs Division, photograph by Harris & Ewing, reproduction number: LC-DIG-hec-23723.*

"Wage-Hour conferees discuss compromise bill." Conference Committee members Mary Norton (left), Democratic Representative Robert Ramspeck of Georgia (second left), Democratic Senator Allan Ellender of Louisiana (second right), and Democratic Senator Claude Pepper of Florida (right), confer inside the U. S. Capitol building on the wage and hour bill on June 6, 1938. The House and Senate conferees agreed on a compromise version of the wage and hour bill on June 14. The House and Senate approved the historic Fair Labor Standards Act the following day. *Source: Library of Congress, Prints & Photographs Division, photograph by Harris & Ewing, reproduction number: LC-DIG-hec-23723.*

"Principals in wage-hour amendments controversy." Mary Norton (second right) is shown here with Wage and Hour Division Administrator Elmer Andrews (left), Democratic Representative Graham Barden of North Carolina (second left),and Democratic Representative and House Rules Committee Chairman Abe Sabath of Illinois inside the U.S. Capitol building on July 25, 1939. Barden testified the next day before the House Rules Committee on several of his controversial amendments to the Fair Standards Act of 1938. *Source: Library of Congress, Prints & Photographs Division, Photograph by Harris & Ewing, reproduction number: LC-DIG-hec-27043 Image 9 - Number 15 Congresswoman from New Jersey.*

"Congresswoman from New Jersey." Mary Norton, pictured here inside the U.S. Capitol building on July 26, 1939, continued to chair the House Labor Committee during World War II. She supported President Roosevelt's executive order establishing the Fair Employment Practices Committee for the duration of the war, but fought unsuccessfully to make the Fair Employment Practices Committee permanent. *Source: Library of Congress, Prints & Photographs Division, Photograph by Harris & Ewing, reproduction number: LC-DIG-hec-27045.*

"Six members of fair sex now members of National House of Representatives."
Mary Norton (left) is shown here on March 6, 1940 with five other women in the
U.S. House of Representatives, including Democrat Clara McMillan of South Carolina (second left), Republican Frances Payne Bolton of Ohio (third left), Republican Edith Nourse Rogers of Massachusetts (third right), Republican Jessie Sumner of Illinois (second right), and Democrat Caroline O'Day of New York (right).
Norton strongly encouraged other women to enter politics, sought to equalize
employment opportunities for women, and supported federally-funded day care
centers for the children of working-class mothers. *Source: Library of Congress,
Print & Photographs Division, Photograph by Harris & Ewing, reproduction number: LC-DIG-hec-28283.*

SIX

The World War II Years

National attention abruptly shifted from New Deal issues to foreign affairs and defense legislation in 1939. German dictator Adolf Hitler already had rearmed Germany, overtaken Austria and the Sudetenland in 1938, and seized Czechoslovakia in March 1939. Germany attacked Poland in September 1939, triggering World War II. Japan had expanded in the Pacific theater, conquering Manchuria by 1933 and much of China by 1939. Italy had overtaken Ethiopia in 1936. President Roosevelt urged Congress to strengthen American military defense and to provide economic and military assistance to Great Britain, France, and other Allies. Norton wholeheartedly backed Roosevelt's plea, warning, "We could not stand by and watch the Luftwaffe destroy Europe, within shooting distance of our own country."

During the 1930s, isolationists had determined American foreign policy. They charged that President Woodrow Wilson's pro-Allied stance, along with American banks and munitions makers, had drawn the United States into a very costly World War I and wanted America to avoid participation in another war. Between 1935 and 1937, Congress enacted several neutrality measures that banned arms trade with warring nations, the extension of credit to belligerent countries, travel on belligerent ships, and the arming of American merchant ships. The Neutrality Act of 1937 permitted warring countries to purchase nonmilitary goods on a cash and carry basis, requiring that goods be paid for when they purchased and transported on the belligerent country's own vessels.

In the late 1930s, isolationists resisted President Roosevelt's pleas to provide American economic and military assistance to Great Britain and France short of war. Roosevelt favored removing the arms embargo, but the House on June 30, 1939, approved, 214 to 173, an amendment by isolationist Republican John Vorys of Ohio, banning the export of arms and ammunition to belligerent nations. Norton aligned with 165 of the 226 Democrats urging repeal of the arms embargo, but 150 of the 158 Republicans insisted on continuing the arms ban. The amendment prevented the United States from shipping essential supplies to Great Britain and its allies after the outbreak of World War II in September 1939.

Norton sided with the internationalists backing President Roosevelt's foreign policy and defense programs. Following the German attack on Poland, Roosevelt called Congress into special session to revise the neutrality laws. Norton backed amending the Neutrality Act, allowing the United States to sell arms and ammunition on a cash and carry basis to European nations fighting Nazi German aggression. Numerous constituents deluged her office with mail opposing arms embargo repeal as a step toward American involvement in war, but she followed the dictates of her conscience. The House on November 3 decisively rejected, 243 to 181, an amendment by Republican James Shanley of Connecticut to continue the arms embargo and approved munitions sales to warring nations on a cash and carry basis. Only 20 of 160 Republicans, however, favored repealing the arms embargo. Germany spread the war to northern and western Europe in 1940, forcing France to surrender in June and assaulting Great Britain by air that summer. In September 1940, Norton supported the destroyer-base deal, an executive agreement sending fifty overage destroyers to Great Britain in exchange for British naval bases in the Western Hemisphere. The same month, Norton backed the Selective Service Act establishing the nation's first peacetime draft and authorizing the drafting of adult males between the ages of twenty-one and thirty-five for one year of military duty.[1]

In 1941, Norton continued rallying behind President Roosevelt's efforts to aid the Allies short of war. Germany remained on the military offensive, battling British ships in the Atlantic Ocean and attacking the Soviet Union. "For Franklin Roosevelt," Norton contended, "the first ten months of his third term must have been as trying as any he ever experienced." She stressed, "We were in mortal danger all that time."[2]

Norton still sent President Roosevelt inspirational messages backing his internationalist policies and actions. She welcomed Roosevelt's December 1940 radio address urging the United States to lend and lease military and economic supplies to Great Britain and other Allies. "I have heard so many fine comments, even from those rather difficult to please," Norton telegrammed the president, "that it gives me much pleasure to pass them on to you." She added, "I shall feel it a privilege to follow your leadership." When the Seventy-seventh Congress convened in January 1941, Norton gave top priority to securing House adoption of the lend-lease measure. "It is of the greatest importance to let nothing interfere with H. R. 1776 at this time," she wrote Eleanor Roosevelt. "Much opposition is developing to certain parts of the bill and the opposition will try to amend it." Norton also ensured President Roosevelt that Mayor Hague wholeheartedly supported lend-lease. "Orders came from him to myself as leader of the House delegation to do everything possible to insure the passage of H. R. 1776," she confided with the president.

On February 6, Norton aligned with the internationalist representatives to pass the lend-lease measure decisively, 265 to 160. The landmark legislation allowed the sale, lending, or leasing of articles to Great Britain, France, China, and other nations whose defense the president deemed vital to American security. Only 24 of the 159 Republicans supported the legislation. Lend-lease, Roosevelt boasted, made the United States "the arsenal of democracy," providing $48 million in munitions, aircraft, and other military supplies to the Allied nations. Norton lauded Roosevelt's message to the American people following congressional approval of the Lend Lease Act in March 1941 as a "soul searching speech" and the "best I've listened to." The *New Republic* termed the Lend-Lease Act "the most important vote in recent years" amounting "to a declaration that our resources would back the United Nations when their own were exhausted."

The worsening European situation alarmed Norton. Norton reflected, "In our hectic lives here it is difficult to get our minds away from the gigantic problems facing us." She sent Roosevelt another uplifting note before he addressed the nation on May 27. Germany had intensified submarine warfare and sunk an American freighter *Robin Moor* in the South Atlantic Ocean. "Your address tonight is a challenge to the soul of America," Norton wrote Roosevelt. "I know it will inspire great courage and loyalty." The president that night extended American security far beyond its borders and declared "an unlimited national emergency." The following day, Norton penned the president again, "You have answered the prayers of millions. Continue strong and unafraid."[3]

Roosevelt, troubled by the deepening world crisis, welcomed Norton's stirring messages. The president responded that Norton's letters "touched me very deeply," were "a real inspiration," and were "heartening and reassuring." He replied to one note, "I was delighted to hear personally from you the other day and in fact been meaning to let you know of my admiration for the staunch manner in which you have been holding the fort."[4]

Norton also battled for the extension of the Selective Service Act, which was set to expire in December 1941. Roosevelt considered the continuation of the draft for the duration of the emergency vital to national security and in July warned Congress against allowing the "disintegration" of America's comparatively small army. During floor debate on August 12, Norton urged House colleagues to renew the military service period for draftees for eighteen months. Draftees had begun military training in November 1940. Although still hoping the United States would not be plunged directly into World War II, Norton insisted that American aid be given Great Britain and its Allies and that the nation's defenses be strengthened. She proclaimed, "The only way to keep our country free is to first give all possible aid to England, which is our first line of defense, and then to build the defense forces of our country so strong that not even Hitler would dare to challenge us." Although realizing that selective service required tremendous sacrifice, Norton claimed, "No sacrifice on our part would be too great" and argued, "This is not (the) time to gamble with the destinies of a great country." Extending the military service period, she hoped, might "strengthen our defenses," "prevent the necessity of fighting in a ruthless war," and "serve notice on the 'king of gangsters' that America means business."[5]

The House on August 12 barely extended the draft for eighteen months by a 203 to 202 margin, with 182 of the 247 Democrats in favor and 133 of the 154 Republicans against. Representatives nearly disbanded the army less than four months before Japan attacked Pearl Harbor. Speaker Sam Rayburn of Texas "wielded an iron fist to drive the bill through the House by one vote." Norton recounted the day she cast a crucial vote for the defense preparedness advocates and internationalists as "one of the most depressing and alarming days I recall in all the years I was there." "Had we lost," Norton reflected, "the whole story of World War II might be different." Constituents, who deluged her congressional office with correspondence, were sharply divided over the controversial legislation. One mother with four sons in military service wrote staunchly defending the draft, while one critic labeled Norton a "murderess." Roosevelt welcomed Norton's wholehearted support on the draft measure. "You really did a great job," the president wrote her, "and I want you to know that, as always, I appreciate your fine cooperation." Selective service provided the nucleus for the American defense effort in World War II. By December 1941, the War Department trained nearly 1.7 million troops from 36 divisions for combat duty.[6]

Norton also intensified pleas for national preparedness. She in September 1941 urged citizens to sacrifice "to guard our freedoms and maintain our American traditions" and wanted the United States to build "an impregnable defense" so that "not even a Hitler will care to challenge us." Norton also implored the United States to expedite the training of its army. Besides cautioning, "We must be realists, not dreamers," she vowed that Americans must "remain free human beings, not vassals of murdering gangsters." German and Allied sea and air forces engaged in continuous battle on the Atlantic Ocean to control the supply routes to Great Britain. German U-boats sought to prevent American merchant shipping from delivering supplies to the Allies, compelling Congress to further amend the Neutrality Act by removing the ban on arming ships. Norton on October 17 supported legislation allowing American merchant ships to convoy arms, equipment, and other lend-lease material to Great Britain and other attacked nations. The House approved removing the ban, 259 to 136, with 220 of 241 Democrats in favor and 113 of 152 Republicans against.[7] At least 2,200 convoys of 75,000 American merchant ships crossed the Atlantic, protected by U.S. naval forces.

On the domestic front, meanwhile, Norton fought attempts by conservative Southern Democrats to enact antistrike legislation in industries vital to American national defense. In April 1941, Naval Affairs Committee Chairman Carl Vinson, a Democrat of Georgia, introduced legislation outlawing jurisdictional and sympathy strikes and boycotts, prohibiting violence during strikes, mandating registration and accounting of funds of all labor unions, and requiring a twenty-five-day cooling off period before defense workers could strike. His measure also sought to freeze closed and open shop arrangements. Closed shops required union membership as a condition of employment, whereas open shops did not compel union affiliation. Vinson's legislation also prohibited employment in defense industries of those advocating the forceful or violent overthrow of the U.S. Government.

Norton planned to testify before the House Rules Committee against the Vinson bill on April 24, but Dr. George Calver refused to let her appear because of high blood pressure. She instead drafted a written statement denouncing all provisions except the twenty-five-day cooling off period and asked a House Labor Committee colleague to read it. "This bill," Norton asserted, "is clearly an attempt to do by indirection what it would not dare to do by direct procedure." She deemed the open or closed shop as the main issue and claimed, "The strike situation will not be improved by the many unfair provisions of this bill." Besides charging that the Vinson measure was designed to "crush labor" rather than expedite national defense, Norton feared that "hysteria" was replacing "common sense."[8]

Norton's written statement infuriated committee conservatives Edward Cox of Georgia and Howard Smith of Virginia, who "touched the ceiling." The *Washington Evening Star*, the *New York Times*, and other newspapers widely publicized Norton's written Rules Committee statement. "I guess that just 'burned them up,'" Norton noted. "Well it was good for me." She wrote several days later, "I'm feeling better," and vowed, "by the time they report the bill to the House I hope to have my fighting clothes on." Democrat Abe Sabath of Illinois, Rules Committee chairman and bitter foe of the Vinson measure, alerted Norton on April 29 that the conservative majority planned to report the Vinson proposal to the House floor the next day for debate. Norton relayed Sabath's message to White House assistant Edwin "Pa" Watson, denouncing the Vinson bill as "terrible" and urging Roosevelt to intervene immediately.[9]

Norton, meanwhile, encouraged organized labor unions to make peace with management for the duration of World War II. Jurisdictional strikes, she cautioned, might disrupt rearmament programs and antagonize congressional conservatives further. Norton charged that labor unions had acted too hostile toward management leaders, thus hindering defense production and provoking adverse public reaction. "I am burned up over the stupidity of the unions," she wrote to close friend Lorena Hickok. "They are ruining the elaborate cause and alienating the public."[10] Norton advised labor unions to concentrate on preserving earlier gains. Unless an amicable truce was reached, she expected conservatives to restrict or even emasculate other significant labor legislation. "Unless labor unions get together and declare a truce for the duration of the war in jurisdictional disputes, and employers and employees compromise their differences," Norton warned, "it will be impossible for the true friends of labor . . . to prevent this (Vinson anti-strike) legislation or even to preserve the legislation we have worked so hard to enact." Hickok wrote Norton that she shared the latter's words with Eleanor Roosevelt. In late April, Norton replied, "Your letter did give me a bit a shock but I know you were activated by the sincerest friendship so it is all right with me. The only thing that bothers me is that I wouldn't want Mrs. R. or the President to think I was 'a quitter'—that would really hurt. I'm not. I can get a bit low particularly when I'm not feeling fit, but I'll never give up under pressure."[11]

Norton countered Vinson's measure with legislation to create a National Defense Mediation Board, including representatives of labor, business, and the public, to settle disputes in defense industries. If the board was deadlocked, the board member representing the public would settle the industrial dispute. A foe of compulsory arbitration, Norton believed that organized labor was capable of resolving its most serious grievances voluntarily. Her legislation required a sixty-day cooling off period before defense industry employees could strike and permitted the seizure of defense plants not using the Mediation Board to settle disputes. If management or labor refused a cease and desist order, the Attorney General could issue an injunction. Congress did not enact Norton's legislation, but she persistently championed cooperation between management and labor and urged defense workers to concentrate on production rather than grievances. Although recognizing that labor unions often had legitimate complaints, she appealed "for a united front during his great emergency."[12]

In September 1941, Helen Gahagan Douglas, National Democratic Party Committee member from California, invited Norton to address a conference of party labor union leaders from eleven western states at Los Angeles, California. Western defense industries had encountered considerable labor unrest. "Never in my life," Norton confessed, "did I work harder on a speech than I did on that one." She wrote four drafts, but did not know how the party labor leaders would respond. "I really let them have it!" Norton declared. She assailed strike leaders as "no friends of labor" and stressed that labor stoppages had delayed emergency defense work. Norton also warned that the American public frowned upon labor union strikes and cautioned that labor leaders must not "allow anything to interfere with the laws we have established to preserve the progressive dignity of labor, even though sacrifice may be necessary at this time." She admonished labor leaders to "live up to the traditions established by those leaders who fought your battle through the past half century and those of this day who have your real interest close to their hearts."[13]

Labor leaders cheered Norton's message. Douglas whispered to Norton, "They think you're terrific" and ushered her into a smaller private room to talk with them. "Never did I get a warmer welcome," Norton observed, "than the labor leaders gave me that day. Without one dissenting voice, they agreed that I was right." The labor leaders asked Norton how they could help her. One union leader distributed copies of Norton's speech throughout the western region. Norton's speech did not end labor strife on the West Coast, but she "made them think and at least kept the situation from growing worse." Douglas wrote Norton, "You were simply superb and we are ever so grateful for the splendid contribution you made to the conference. Your speech at the luncheon was the perfect note to climax the two day session and we all were deeply moved and inspired by what you had to say."[14]

Growing antilabor sentiment on Capitol Hill, however, alarmed Norton. "I am very unhappy over the turn things have taken," Norton confided. "Between John Lewis, Hillman, etc. we seem in a pretty bad situation," she lamented. "The only bright spot is that we are not in session this week. If it were I believe that Vinson bill would be adopted with a bang. Let's hope that something may change the tide before we meet again to consider legislation."

Norton's House Labor Committee chairmanship seemed more physically demanding and less enjoyable. "What with a meeting of my committee every day and trying to ward off hysterical legislation in my committee it hasn't been any fun," Norton conceded in late November. "We meet on Monday to consider Labor legislation and shall continue every day until we report a bill." "I do not intend to be the 'goat' any longer," she vowed. "I addressed the House on Monday last and spoke my mind. The sniping has been rather bad." Nevertheless, she believed, "It will probably work out o.k. I'm determined not to worry about it."

Norton's fears about the Vinson bill were warranted. Smith of Virginia proposed an amendment curbing organizational or jurisdictional strikes or strikes involving closed shops. Employees could not strike until after a thirty-day cooling-off period. Employees wishing to strike had to give thirty days notice to the Secretary of Labor. Strikes called unlawfully by employees would result in the loss of their National Labor Relations Act rights. The House on December 3 approved the Smith amendment, 229 to 158, with the Republicans solidly in favor and the Democrats split evenly, 113 to 113. Representatives resoundingly adopted the Vinson bill, 252 to 136, suspending the Wagner National Labor Relations Act. The Vinson bill cut across party lines, with 129 Democrats and 123 Republicans in favor. Norton joined the 108 Democrats, 24 Republicans, and 4 third party members opposing the Vinson measure.[15]

The sudden Japanese attack on Pearl Harbor, however, derailed further congressional action on the Vinson antistrike measure. On December 7, 1941, Japanese naval and air forces attacked the American military base at Pearl Harbor, Hawaii. In the devastating attack, 2,403 Americans were killed, 1,178 were wounded, and 19 ships were sunk or damaged. Norton was bedridden with the grippe and a 103-degree fever that fateful Sunday afternoon when newscasters interrupted the philharmonic radio concert with news about the surprise Japanese assault. "I was stunned, like everyone else," she recalled. Norton had believed that the Japanese diplomats, who had met with American Secretary of State Cordell Hull around fifty times in 1941, still wanted to negotiate a peaceful settlement with the United States.

Roosevelt summoned a special joint session of Congress for the next day. Norton wondered if and how she would get to the Capitol. Her sister, Anne, warned that traveling to the Capitol would be too risky for the sixty-six-year-old legislator. "But Dr. Calver," Norton said, "knew me well enough to realize that, if I did not go, it would have a bad effect on me." After Anne picked up medicine at the drug store the next morning, niece Marion McDonagh Burke, who lived in Washington, D.C., drove Norton to the Capitol. "When my sister returned from the drugstore," Norton recalled, "I was on my way." Dr. Calver met Norton at the entrance.[16]

Norton entered the Capitol for the joint session around 12:30 p.m. on December 8. "Every seat in the House Chamber, where joint sessions of Congress are held, was taken—members and ex-members, who are always admitted to the floor, standing in the aisles," she observed. "The galleries were packed, people even sitting on the steps." According to Norton, "The clerk walked in, preceding the President, the Vice-President, and the Speaker of the House, who took their places at the Speaker's desk, high above the tiers of seats. The Chamber was hushed."[17] The members stood, applauded, and cheered when President Roosevelt entered the room.

The senators and representatives listened intently to Roosevelt's solemn address. "The President looked grim," Norton observed, "not the smiling, confident man we had welcomed so many times to the Capitol since 1933." Roosevelt, fulfilling his constitutional authority as Commander-in-Chief of the American military forces, told Congress "how the Japanese had pulled their sneak attack on Pearl Harbor, even while their envoys were here deceiving us with talk of peace" and denounced Japan's "dastardly attack" on "a date which will live in infamy." The president warned, "Our people, our territory, and our interests are in grave danger. With confidence in our armed forces, with the unbounded determination of our people, we will attain the inevitable triumph—so help us

God." Roosevelt urged the Senate and House to declare a state of war against the Japanese Empire. "There were not many dry eyes in the House Chamber," Norton recollected, "and I know my own were moist. I was weak from my illness and fearful that emotion would conquer my determination not to show any emotion." [18]

Congress resoundingly approved Roosevelt's war declaration request. Internationalists and isolationists united behind the war declaration. The Senate unanimously adopted the war declaration resolution in just twenty minutes. The House approved the same resolution in thirty minutes. Republican Representative Jeannette Rankin of Montana, a pacifist Quaker, cast the lone dissenting vote. Norton declared, "Our people finally recognized our danger and became united." Three days later, Roosevelt asked Congress to declare war against Germany and Italy. The Senate and House unanimously adopted those resolutions in just fifty-seven minutes. [19]

Congress, which had sharply divided on foreign policy in the 1937 to 1941 period, united behind Roosevelt's defense requests. Norton solidly backed numerous preparedness measures enacted in the tumultuous days following the Pearl Harbor attack. "At long last," she sighed, "bills to strengthen our weak defenses were rushed through Congress, with Democrats and Republicans united in support our Commander-in-Chief." Norton was convinced that the United States, Great Britain, and the other democratic nations would prevail over the Axis totalitarian powers. She, however, experienced lack of physical stamina. "There are so many things I'd like to do," she declared. "How I wish I were about twenty years younger—but never mind—where there's a will there's a way and I'll find it." Norton, like Roosevelt, hoped that World War II would result in world peace and cooperation. In late December 1941, she predicted, "This may be the beginning of a new world era. At least we can hope and pray that it is." [20]

Lucille McDonagh, Norton's niece and Labor Committee clerk, married William Considine, a Washington lawyer, on January 8, 1942, at the Church of St. John the Martyr in New York City. Considine served as a lieutenant in the U.S. Navy throughout World War II, while Lucille remained as Norton's clerk.

Norton found serving in Congress during World War II both frustrating and heartbreaking. "For a member of Congress with thousands of young men from your district fighting in faraway lands, wounded, killed, or missing in action, and thousands of worried wives and parents desperately appealing to you for news of them, for help in the most difficult and heart-breaking situations, it is unadulterated misery," she lamented. Norton poignantly described the wartime trials and tribulations of serving in the House. "It is to you they turn in their trouble, and there is so little—so very little—you can do. You call the War Department, the Navy, the Air Force, with the boy's name, his serial number, and whatever other information you have. They try to help you, but your case is only one of thousands they get every day. You try to write comforting, reassuring letters. Your own heart is heavy with the knowledge that they can be of little help! Sometimes the recipients get angry, accuse you of not trying. It is always hard for them to understand why you, in our position, can do nothing."[21]

One New Jersey mother lost her eighteen-year-old son in his first military engagement. "The news almost killed his mother," Norton learned. His distraught mother erroneously believed that her only surviving son, who had fought overseas for two years, also had died. "We felt that if she could see him even for a few days," Norton thought, "it might save her life." Norton wanted to visit Secretary of War Henry Stimson at the Pentagon to see if the only surviving son could be brought home on leave, but several officers told her it would be impossible to see the cabinet official. The officers proposed to deliver her message to Stimson instead, but she insisted on seeing him and vowed to wait there all day, if necessary. Norton stayed two hours to see Stimson. After listening to Norton's heart-rending story, Stimson told her, "You are suffering for his good mother. I suffer for all the mothers of the men who are dying in this frightful war. I wish I could help you, but it is impossible." Norton replied, "Now I was going to ask God to send that boy home on a furlough—a furlough that was long overdue." "Keep on praying, Mrs. Norton," Stimson responded. "Who knows?" A week later, Stimson telephoned Norton, "Your prayers may be answered, but I'm not sure." Within a few days, he called again, "John is on his way home, by plane, but you had better not tell his mother—nor anyone else—until he lands in this country." When John arrived in the United States, Norton contacted his parents. "The visit," she rejoiced, "had the effect we had hoped it would. I think it saved her life."[22]

Throughout World War II, congressional members toiled hard under enormous pressure. "We all worked long hours," Norton recollected, "and were constantly worried by the appeals and demands of our constituents, many of whom seemed to think we had open sesame to every suggestion or request." Jersey City and Bayonne residents criticized her earlier votes for fortifying the naval base at Guam, repealing the arms embargo, and extending selective service, but usually agreed with her on other defense preparedness measures. "I was very proud of my constituents, most of whom were fine, loyal Americans,"[23] she recalled.

Norton's position as Labor Committee head increased in importance during World War II because American military success depended upon the volume of its defense production by workers. The "key to victory was attracting enough competent workers to build more planes, ships, and weapons than the enemy did. Norton's position was key to producing that result." Through collaboration with President Roosevelt and Secretary of Labor Perkins, Norton "played a strong role in creating a labor force that brought women and minorities to vital jobs in defense plants."

Congress usually approved defense appropriations and other war-related measures, but Republicans and Southern Democrats still balked at New Deal labor measures. The conservative coalition, Norton lamented, "now scrutinized not only every act of the unions, but the conduct of individuals as well, always looking for something on which it could be charged they were holding up the war effort."[24]

In 1942, conservative Southern Democrats revived their campaign to dilute the working hours section of the Fair Labor Standards Act. Smith of Virginia and Vinson of Georgia cosponsored an amendment to suspend the forty-hour work week restriction in defense plants. They circulated false rumors that the Fair Labor Standards Act prevented defense workers from toiling over forty hours a week, thus slowing American military production. Defense workers typically labored over forty hours a week, earning time-and-one-half for every hour they worked beyond the maximum. Smith and Vinson, Norton contended, really objected to workers receiving overtime wages.

In late March, Norton urged Roosevelt to devote a Fireside Chat to defending the forty-hour week. The president already had championed the forty-hour week at an earlier press conference, but many Americans either missed that event or misunderstood his position. Norton alerted Roosevelt that "feeling is running high in the House on the Republican side and the Southern Democratic side" and assured him, "You only have the complete confidence of the majority of the people." She pleaded with Roosevelt to "combat this surge of misinformation. I have a very great responsibility to the working people of America,"[25] she concluded.

Roosevelt, however, countered that antilabor sentiment already had begun to subside and, thus, declined to devote a special Fireside Chat to the forty-hour week issue. He realized, "There are going to be periods of hysteria, misinformation, volcanic eruptions, etc." and warned, "If I start the practice of going on the air to answer each one, the value of my going on the air will soon disappear." Roosevelt believed, "This particular anti-labor outburst is already beginning to diminish—and will continue to do so unless some new circumstance develops." The president also realized the dangers of delivering too many radio Fireside Chats. Roosevelt acknowledged, "For the sake of not becoming a platitude to the public," he explained, "I ought not to appear oftener than once every five or six weeks. I am inclined to think that in England (Prime Minister Winston) Churchill, for a while, talked too much, and I don't want to do that." Roosevelt urged Norton to continue battling the conservative coalition, counseling her, "Do your best to stop the lions and tigers from roaring!" Norton, reassured by the president's words, replied, "I . . . believe he has the problem well in hand." Nevertheless, ongoing tensions between labor and management and fears that the legislative branch still might weaken

New Deal labor measures still worried her. "Congress," Norton detected, "is certainly 'jittery.' I believe a 'cooling off' process of a few weeks is in order."[26]

In April 1942, Norton again clashed with Rules Committee member Smith over labor policies on NBC radio in Washington, D.C. Smith advocated removing the forty-hour week clause because it allegedly hindered American defense production and erroneously charged that the National Labor Relations Act made it illegal for anyone to work over forty hours a week on government contracts. "This libel," Norton countered, "has been cunningly and widely spread by certain groups who would deprive underprivileged workers of a living wage." Most employers, she argued, did not object to paying overtime wages. "But there are always a few," she conceded, "who can kick up a fuss and get a sympathetic hearing from antilabor members of Congress."[27]

If Congress suspended the forty-hour work week provision, Norton feared that American war production would decline dramatically. She counseled, "With feeling running high and a great tendency to hysteria and exaggeration, it is to our great advantage to 'stop, look, and listen' before passing legislation which may have very serious consequences to our war production." Employers, Norton asserted, were making the forty-hour week a scapegoat for industrial problems. "Why dare to blame the 40-hour week," she asked, "for the short-sighted stupidity of those who should have known better and are not attempting to shift their responsibility to the workers of America?"[28]

Radio listeners sided with Norton, but the conservative coalition rejected her arguments. "The response from all over the country has been amazing," she gloated. "I have received letters from many, many people and with about three exceptions, they have all been most favorable." Republican Clare Hoffman of Michigan, however, accused Norton of using "the woman's prerogative of scolding and verbally spanking those who are near and dear to her." Rules Committee conservatives and anti–New Deal newspapers, Norton suspected, had sparked the rising antilabor sentiment. Norton pledged to continue her battle to maintain the forty-hour week provision and claimed, "The average American feels as I do about the labor situation." New Dealers ultimately blocked the House conservative coalition from altering the forty-hour week section in 1942.[29]

The same year, Norton also became embroiled in a tempestuous political controversy over a judicial appointment. President Roosevelt on May 4 nominated Thomas Meaney, a former Hudson County judge and counsel for the New Jersey State Banking and Insurance Commission, to fill a vacancy in the Federal District Court in northern New Jersey. Roosevelt stirred protests by sending the nomination request to Mayor Hague rather than Governor Charles Edison. Edison, a Democrat, was the son of renowned inventor Thomas Edison from Menlo Park. The U.S. Senate needed to confirm Meaney's nomination. Norton testified on Meaney's behalf at the Senate Judiciary Committee hearings, lauding him as "a gentleman, of great ability and integrity."

Edison, however, claimed that Meaney had demonstrated questionable behavior as a court-appointed counsel in the liquidation of a large Jersey City bank and had fired him because he had accepted a large fee from a special group to work against the interests of the general depositors. "The people," asserted Edison, "will always be dubious of the qualities of justice obtainable from a judge who all his life has been a part of, and obligated to, a sordid political machine." Edison's resistance stemmed partly from a political power struggle with Hague. "What he said," Norton recalled, "had all the earmarks of vindictive spite against Frank Hague, apparently overlooking the fact that the welfare and reputation of Tom Meaney, whom he admitted he did not know, were at stake." She concluded, "It was a cowardly thing to do to Tom Meaney."[30]

Norton bristled when she heard Edison's testimony. "As I sat there listening," she recollected, "I could almost feel my blood pressure rising!" Edison, Norton speculated, "evidently had great ambition to become the state leader." As Edison continued denouncing Meaney, Norton confessed, "I was blazing with anger." After all, Norton, Hague, and the Democratic State Committee had worked hard to get Edison elected as governor in 1940. Edison had campaigned throughout the state that fall, commending Hague and the Democratic State organization at a Sea Girt rally. When Norton asked Edison why he had changed his mind about Hague, the governor denied that he had. She interjected, "Then I think you are the most arrogant hypocrite that ever walked in New Jersey!" The incident stirred quite a commotion, receiving widespread newspaper publicity.[31]

Edison often had clashed with Hague after assuming the governorship and boasted publicly that "he was independent of any one's influence," keeping "Hague at a safe distance." He angered Hague by forgiving the railroads "millions of dollars in back taxes" and proposing "a state tax on municipalities where they operated." To the mayor's dismay, "the railroad lobby controlled the state legislature, the branch of state government Hague could not penetrate."[32]

Hague, embittered by Edison's actions, defended Norton and intensified his campaign to secure Meaney's confirmation. "You demonstrated to the Governor what true loyalty to the principles of the Democratic Party means," Hague wrote Norton, "and I feel sure your reminder to him at such a public gathering as that Committee room, about the sentiments he expressed to you after the Sea Girt meeting must have proved quite a shock." Hague concluded, "At any rate, he must know that you were expressing the sentiment of the rank and file of the Democratic Party and that he has not succeeded in fooling any of it members." At Hague's request, Norton assured Roosevelt that Meaney possessed outstanding legal credentials despite Edison's charges. Roosevelt wrote her, "You are a grand girl!" Edison's comments irritated the president, who requested his assistants to lobby on Capitol Hill for Meaney's confirmation. Harry Moore, who had served in the U.S. Senate, also visited former Senate colleagues pleading Meaney's case. The Senate on July 1 narrowly approved Meaney's nomination to the federal bench. Meaney served as a U.S. federal judge from July 3 until his death in May 1968.[33]

Although the Hague-Edison conflict continued to simmer, Norton easily won reelection. Governor Edison demanded publicly that Norton resign her House seat and Democratic State Committee chairmanship. At the next Democratic State Committee meeting, he did not support her renomination as head. The Democratic State Committee, though, ignored Edison's request, unanimously reelecting Norton. "Charles Edison," Norton sighed, "never realized his ambition to oust Frank Hague and become the Democratic leader in New Jersey." Norton's Thirteenth District constituents reelected her to a tenth consecutive House term that November. Norton trounced Republican Raymond Cuddy, 73,766 to 18,194, amassing nearly 80 percent of the popular vote and maintaining her broad base of political support. Republicans, however, made significant inroads across the state and nation, taking eleven of the fourteen New Jersey congressional seats and gaining forty-seven House seats. New Jersey Democrats Edward Hart and Elmer Wene retained their House positions, but William Sutphin lost his bid for reelection. Democrats, though, still wielded a narrow 222 to 209 majority in the House.[34]

Mayor Hague, meanwhile, designated August 26 as Mary Norton Day in Jersey City. He phoned Norton at her sister Loretta's summer Long Island home and asked her to be in Jersey City on August 26, but did not tell her why. Although Norton was reluctant to shorten her summer break, Hague persuaded her to return to her Jersey City apartment and stop by City Hall on August 26. He asked Norton, who was not a baseball enthusiast, to attend the Jersey City-Baltimore game at Roosevelt Stadium with Moore and him that afternoon. Hague had arranged with Jersey City baseball officials for that game to be ladies day, honoring Norton "for her loyalty to the President and the people." Norton reflected, "But never in my life have I had a more difficult time keeping from showing any emotion than I had that afternoon when I walked into Roosevelt Stadium."[35]

Nearly 26,000 women packed the brightly decorated stands at Roosevelt Stadium and cheered when Norton and Hague went to home plate. Hague lauded Norton and gave her a beautiful wrist watch, engraved on the back, "Presented to Mary T. Norton by Frank Hague in appreciation of her loyalty - 1942." Norton, who sat with Hague and his daughter, Peggy, in a special box, remembered little about the game, but treasured the experience. "I think almost everyone I had ever known since I entered politics came up to the box to greet me," she recollected. "I saw old and dear friends whom I had not seen in years. That was a red letter day for me, a wonderful, heart-warming experience."[36]

Majority Leader McCormack of Massachusetts and Secretary of Labor Perkins both telegrammed, eulogizing her congressional achievements. McCormack praised her record as a House member and Labor Committee chair and commended her dedicated loyalty to President Roosevelt, Speaker Rayburn, and to him. "You," he wired, "have courageously fought for the passage of humane and progressive legislation so essential (to) domestic welfare of our people." McCormack added, "You have honored them (Jersey City constituents) by the able and courageous manner in which you have represented them in the halls of Congress." Secretary Perkins cited Norton's "notable record as Chairman of the House Labor Committee" and "very real achievements in the interest of American wage earners."[37]

During World War II, Norton often refused to summon the House Labor Committee to consider antilabor measures. She feared that consideration of antilabor measures would "start a wave of destructive legislation aimed at destroying laws already enacted" and concluded, "The logical course for the Labor Committee was not to report out any bills." Conservative Representatives assailed Norton for not convening Labor Committee meetings to consider bills introduced by anti–New Dealers. Norton warned that, "Anything could happen if we let any labor legislation get out onto the floor. It seemed the wiser course to sit tight and try to hold onto the gains that had been made."

When Norton entered the House chambers one morning, conservative Republican Hoffman of Michigan, a Labor Committee member, chided her tactics. "We have a sit-down chairman of our committee," he complained. Norton, however, smiled at Hoffman. "I think he expected I would blow up and answer him!" she recollected. "I knew I had been a 'sit-down chairman,'" Norton conceded, "but I believed that to be the only way I could prevent bad legislation from being reported out in the name of war expediency."[38] Despite Norton's tactics, however, Congress started retracting the New Deal labor policies anyway. Public discontent with wartime strikes and its erroneous conception that the federal government was granting labor preferential treatment, coupled with Republican gains in the 1942 congressional elections, triggered an onslaught of antilabor moves.[39]

Anti–New Dealers, therefore, began bypassing Norton's Labor Committee with their antilabor measures. The House Judiciary Committee, Military Affairs Committee, and especially the Naval Affairs Committee, all chaired by Southern Democrats, increasingly seized jurisdiction over labor-related legislation. "Norton found much of her experience as Labor Committee chair in wartime frustrating because of encroachments on the panel's oversight." *Collier's* reported that Norton had "as little say on labor as Mrs. Perkins" and labeled her Labor Committee "ineffectual."

The conservative coalition, one writer observed, "made her blood boil! So she was constantly getting her blood pressure checked and muttering about her B. P., although she continued to work incredibly long hours for a woman of sixty-seven." Moreover, the War Labor Board and the War Manpower Commission, not the House Labor Committee, increasingly determined work policies.[40]

In 1943, the Labor Committee and the Naval Affairs Committee both claimed jurisdiction over legislation involving absenteeism in defense plants. When newspaper articles surfaced criticizing absenteeism among defense workers, Vinson's Naval Affairs Committee bypassed the Labor Committee, launching its own probe of absenteeism in shipyards and debating measures to curb the supposed growing absentee rate.[41] Democrat Lyndon Johnson of Texas, without consulting Norton, introduced in February an amendment to a Navy Department bill requiring shipyards to file quarterly reports on absenteeism with local draft boards. In January, *Time* disclosed that absenteeism in American factories and shipyards seriously impeded the nation's production of planes, ships, tanks, and munitions. Johnson found absenteeism "a serious problem needing corrective legislation," noting that no-shows at Navy yards had increased to 9.4 percent of the total workforce.

In March, the Naval Affairs Committee broadened the Johnson amendment to compel reports on absenteeism from all war-related industries. A record of no shows had to accompany any request made to a draft board for deferment by an employee deemed an essential worker. The Selective Service Act had required a renewal of all deferments every six months. Johnson's amendment would have curbed absenteeism in war plants by requiring "the immediate drafting of any worker absent from the job too often."

The Johnson proposal, which should have gone through the Labor Committee because it dealt primarily with labor, upset both labor leaders and Norton. Labor leaders warned it "would violate the Constitution by establishing involuntary servitude, convert the military service into a penal institution, give employers the power to inflict distasteful working conditions on labor by threatening to report them for absenteeism should they strike, and generate resentment and demoralization among war workers."

Norton, who did not learn about the Johnson amendment until after the Naval Affairs Committee had adopted it, claimed that the Labor Committee held proper jurisdiction over absenteeism and insisted that Vinson's Committee stop usurping her committee's rights and duties. She "angrily confronted" Vinson, who admitted "in embarrassment that he had incorrectly assumed that the Labor Committee had surrendered jurisdiction." Since Norton could not gain jurisdiction over the Johnson amendment, she insisted that the Rules Committee block it from reaching the House floor. The Rules Committee tabled the Johnson amendment, but the episode convinced Norton that it would take considerable time for women to achieve equitable treatment in Congress. [42]

Norton told the media that the Naval Affairs Committee had stepped on her committee's turf, recounting Vinson's deliberate evasion of her Labor Committee. "Mr. Vinson's committee is infringing on labor legislation," she protested. "Labor bills have been coming out of the Judiciary, Naval Affairs and other committees. There is no doubt of it, and I believe, no excuse for it." Norton claimed that Vinson circumvented the Labor Committee partly because a woman headed it. The Labor Committee approved a motion by Republican Richard Welch of California that the Naval Affairs Committee cease further action on absenteeism legislation until Norton's group had heard testimony and made recommendations to Congress. The Naval Affairs Committee promptly dropped its investigation of absenteeism in defense plants. Vinson told Norton, "You can have it. It's a hot potato." [43]

The Labor Committee conducted extensive hearings from March 12 to March 30 on absenteeism in defense plants. Witnesses reported relatively few willful absentees in defense plants and concluded that most workers had given their entire energies to war production. They testified that most absentees were women, who could not work full time because they encountered difficulty in finding care for their children. Norton's committee blamed inadequate child care facilities for the absentee problems among women in defense factories and admonished defense plants to help those employees resolve those issues. On May 4, it easily approved Norton's measure authorizing the U.S. Department of Labor to determine the extent and causes of absenteeism and ways of reducing the rates in certain plants. The bill asked the U.S. Department of Labor, War Manpower Commission, War Production Board, and Office of War Information to educate Americans about the absenteeism problem and "to clear up false impression now current that American workers are slackers."

In addition, labor strikes irked anti–New Dealers. Organized labor representatives in December 1941 had pledged not to strike for the duration of World War II. United Mine Workers (UMW) President John L. Lewis, however, did not consider the agreement binding and in May 1943 ordered 500,000 underpaid miners to strike, causing coal supplies to dwindle. The UMW strikes alienated a majority of the American people, who disapproved of work stoppages in vital war industries.

Democratic Senator Tom Connally of Texas introduced legislation authorizing the federal government seizure of strike-bound plants and mines and containing stringent penalties for interference with war production. By a decisive 63 to 16 margin, the Senate on May 5 adopted the Connally war labor dispute measure. Speaker Rayburn quickly referred the Connally bill to the House Military Affairs Committee, bypassing the Labor Committee.

Representative Smith of Virginia proposed even harsher antistrike legislation, placing legal restrictions on the economic and political activities of organized labor and banning political contributions by labor unions. The House on June 4 adopted Smith's bill by a 233 to 141 margin, with 100 Democrats, including 80 Southerners, and 133 Republicans voting affirmative. Norton aligned with 87 other Democrats, including five Southerners, 49 Republicans, and four third party members against the Smith bill.[44]

House and Senate conferees compromised between the Smith and Connally versions. The final terms required strikers in private plants to give a thirty-day notice and conduct a strike referendum, administered by the National Labor Relations Board. Strikes in government-seized plants or mines and political contributions by unions were banned. Although opposed to strikes in wartime, Roosevelt on June 25 vetoed the Smith-Connally measure and warned that strike votes would promote labor unrest. The president sternly criticized the outlawing of union political contributions in wartime, "a transparent effort to slap at Roosevelt and stem the growth in labor's political influence that the New Deal had fostered." The House and Senate, however, both overrode Roosevelt's veto later that day. The outcome signified "another important reminder of Roosevelt's loss of control over the Congress and the anti-labor swing in public sentiment since the reforming heyday of the Depression years." Roosevelt lamented, "I think the country has forgotten we ever lived through the 1930s."

The Smith-Connally War Labor Dispute Act, "ostensibly a war measure," really "dealt the labor movement a blow that conservatives had been itching to land since the passage of the Wagner Act in 1935." Conservatives "took their revenge for nearly a decade's worth of labor gains." The legislation erroneously assumed that irresponsible labor union leaders had forced reluctant workers to strike, but labor union leaders largely had restrained their members from striking. The Smith-Connally Act ironically sparked more strikes than it prevented. Employees in the automobile, rubber, and shipbuilding industries soon engaged in work stoppages.[45]

During the World War II era, Norton had enjoyed less success as Labor Committee chairperson. "She found much of her experience as Labor Committee chair in wartime frustrating because of encroachments on the panel's oversight and the bleak prospects of women's place in the post-war work-force." Other committees had assumed legislative authority that infringed on the jurisdiction of her committee, while the War Labor Board and the War Manpower Commission increasingly decided national World War II labor policies. Norton, however, had thwarted attempts by conservatives to emasculate the Wagner Act of 1935. "When amendments were offered in the House to practically destroy the statute, Mrs. Norton was almost alone responsible in blocking their passage. That the act remained intact through all her years as Chairman of the Labor Committee is evidence of her astute, keen and powerful leadership in behalf of labor."[46] The dauntless Norton soon plunged into her biggest legislative battle since the Fair Labor Standards Act of 1938.

NOTES

1. Mary T. Norton, "Madam Congressman: The Memoirs of Mary T. Norton of New Jersey," (Hereafter cited as Memoirs), Mary T. Norton MSS, New Jersey Collection, Archibald Stevens Alexander Library, Rutgers, The State University of New Jersey, p. 170; "A Congress to Win the War," *New Republic* 106 (May 18, 1942), pp. 700, 703. For the role of Congress on isolationist and internationalist issues, see Robert A. Divine, *The Illusion of Neutrality* (Chicago, IL: University of Chicago Press, 1962); Wayne Cole, *Roosevelt and the Isolationists* (Lincoln, NE: University of Nebraska Press, 1983); and David L. Porter, *The Seventy-sixth Congress and World War II* (Columbia, MO: University of Missouri Press, 1979).

2. Norton, "Memoirs," p. 175.

3. Mary T. Norton to Franklin D. Roosevelt, January 2, 1941, Franklin D. Roosevelt MSS, President's Personal File 5418, Norton; Mary T. Norton to Eleanor Roosevelt, January 21, 1941, FDR MSS, President's Secretary's File, Container 140, Congress, 1941; Mary T. Norton to Franklin D. Roosevelt, March 4, 1941, FDR MSS, Official File 4193; Mary T. Norton to Franklin D. Roosevelt, March 15, 1941, FDR MSS, PPF 5418, Norton; Mary T. Norton to Dr. S. A. Cosgrove, May 5, 1941, Norton MSS, Box 1, General Correspondence, 1941; "Congress to Win," *New Republic*, May 18, 1942, pp. 700, 703; Mary T. Norton to Franklin D. Roosevelt, May 27, 1941, FDR MSS, PPF 5418, Norton; Mary T. Norton to Franklin D. Roosevelt, May 28, 1941, FDR MSS, PPF 5418, Norton.

4. Franklin D. Roosevelt to Mary T. Norton, January 6, 1941, FDR MSS, PPF 5418, Norton; Franklin D. Roosevelt to Mary T. Norton, March 18, 1941, FDR MSS, PPF 5418, Norton; Franklin D. Roosevelt to Mary T. Norton, April 21, 1941, Norton MSS, Box 2, Corr., Franklin D. Roosevelt, 1928–1945; Franklin D. Roosevelt to Mary T. Norton, June 5, 1941, FDR MSS, PPF 5418, Norton.

5. Robert Dallek, *Lone Star Rising: Lyndon Johnson and His Times, 1908–1960* (New York: Oxford University Press, 1991), p. 226; Mary T. Norton, "Selective Service," Speech, Washington, D.C., August 12, 1941, FDR MSS, PPF 5418, Norton.

6. Dallek, *Lone Star Rising*, p. 227; "Congress to Win," *New Republic*, May 18, 1942, pp. 700, 703; Norton, "Memoirs," p. 176; Franklin D. Roosevelt to Mary T. Norton, September 15, 1941, FDR MSS, PPF 5418, Norton; Porter, *Seventy-sixth Congress*, p. 170.

7. Norton, "Selective Service," Speech, Aug. 12, 1941; Franklin D. Roosevelt to Mary T. Norton, September 15, 1941, FDR MSS, PPF 5418, Norton; "Congress to Win," *New Republic*, May 18, 1942, pp. 700–3.

8. *Washington Evening Star*, April 24, 1941; Mary T. Norton to Lorena Hickok, April 27, 1941, Lorena Hickok MSS, Box 16, Corr., Norton, 1941–1945.

9. Norton to Hickok, Apr. 27, 1941; Edwin Watson Memorandum for Franklin D. Roosevelt, April 29, 1941, FDR MSS, PPF 5901, Carl Vinson.

10. Mary T. Norton to Lorena Hickok, March 26, 1941, Hickok MSS, Box 16, Corr., Norton, 1941–1945.

11. Norton to Hickok, Apr. 27, 1941; *New York Times*, March 21, 1941; Norton, "Memoirs," p. 177; *Jersey City Journal*, March 3, 1941.

12. Emily A. Geer, "A Study of the Activities of Women in Congress with Special Reference to the Congressional Careers of Margaret Chase Smith, Mary T. Norton, and Edith Nourse Rogers," (Masters thesis: Bowling Green State University, 1952), pp. 133–34; Angeline Bogucki, "Summary of the Legislative Career of Representative Mary T. Norton," Legislative Reference Service, Library of Congress, Washington D.C., November 3, 1950; Mary T. Norton, "The Defense of America," Speech, Regional

Conference of Democratic Women, Los Angeles, CA, September 13, 1941, Norton MSS, Box 5, Speeches, 1941.

13. Norton, "Memoirs," pp. 178–79.

14. Norton, "Memoirs," pp. 179–80.

15. Mary T. Norton to Lorena Hickok, October 27, 1941, Hickok MSS, Box 16, Corr., Norton; Mary T. Norton to Lorena Hickok, November 20, 1941, Hickok MSS, Box 16, Corr., Norton; *New York Times*, December 4, 1941, pp. 1, 22; "House Vote #73 (Dec. 3, 1941)" in http://www.govtrack.us/congress/vote.xpd?vote=h1941–73.

16. Norton, "Memoirs," pp. 180–81.

17. Norton, "Memoirs," p. 181.

18. Norton, "Memoirs," pp. 181–82.

19. Norton, "Memoirs," p. 180.

20. Norton, "Memoirs," p. 182; Mary T. Norton to Lorena Hickok, December 31, 1941, Hickok MSS, Box 16, Corr., Norton.

21. Norton, "Memoirs," p. 183.

22. Norton, "Memoirs," pp. 185–86.

23. Norton, "Memoirs," p. 187.

24. National Women's History Museum, "Women Wielding Power: Pioneer Female State Legislators: New Jersey," http://www.nwhm.org; Norton, "Memoirs," p. 188.

25. Mary T. Norton to Franklin D. Roosevelt, March 23, 1942, FDR MSS, PSF, Container 140, Congress; Norton, "Memoirs," p. 190; Richard N. Chapman, *Contours of Public Policy, 1939–1945* (New York: Garland Publishing Company, 1981), p. 177.

26. Franklin D. Roosevelt to Mary T. Norton, March 24, 1942, Norton MSS, Box 2, Corr., Franklin D. Roosevelt, 1928–1945; Mary T. Norton to Grace Tully, May 1, 1942, FDR MSS, PPF 5418, Norton; Chapman, *Contours of Public Policy*, p. 177.

27. Mary T. Norton, "The 40-Hour Week," Speech, NBC, Washington, D.C., April 20, 1942, Norton MSS, Box 5, Speeches, Miscellaneous; Norton, "Memoirs," p. 190.

28. Norton, "40-Hour Week," Speech, Apr. 20, 1942.

29. Norton, "Memoirs," p. 190; Mary T. Norton to John H. Gavin, April 22, 1942, Norton MSS, Box 1, Gen. Corr., 1942.

30. Norton, "Memoirs," pp. 197–98; Alfred Steinberg, *The Bosses* (New York: Macmillan Publishing Company, 1972), pp. 65–66; Bogucki, "Summary."

31. Norton, "Memoirs," pp. 198–200.

32. Carmela Karnoutsos, "Frank Hague, 1876–1956," *Jersey City Past and Present Home Page*, New Jersey State Historical Commission, http://www.njcu.edu; Bogucki, "Summary."

33. Frank Hague to Mary T. Norton, May 29, 1944, Norton MSS, Box 1, Gen. Corr., 1944.; Steinberg, *The Bosses*, p. 66; Norton, "Memoirs," p. 20; Marion McDonagh Burke, Interview with Author, August 7, 1981.

34. Norton, "Memoirs," p. 200; "Congressional Election Statistics, November 3, 1942," (Washington, D.C.: U.S. Government Printing Office, 1943), p. 19.

35. Norton, "Memoirs," p. 201.

36. Norton, "Memoirs," p. 202.

37. John W. McCormack to Mary T. Norton, August 25, 1942, Norton MSS, Box 1, Gen. Corr., 1942; Frances Perkins to Mary T. Norton, August 25, 1942, Norton MSS, Box 1, Gen. Corr., 1942.

38. Norton, "Memoirs," pp. 167–68.

39. Harry A. Millis and Emily Clark Brown, *From the Wagner Act to Taft-Hartley* (Chicago, IL: University of Chicago Press, 1950), pp. 294, 332–334, 346–354; Roland A. Young, *Congressional Politics During the Second World War* (New York: Columbia University Press, 1956), pp. 57–58; Chapman, *Contours of Public Policy*, p. 229; Kennedy, *Freedom from Fear*, p. 643.

40. Featured House Publications, *Women in Congress, 1917–2006*, April 27, 2007, 108th Cong., 1st Sess., H. Doc. 108–223, http://www.gpo.gov; "Mary T. Norton, 1875–1959," http://womenincongress.house.gov/member-profiles; Amy Porter, "Ladies of Congress," *Collier's* 112 (August 28, 1943), p. 22; "Mary T. Norton," *Current*

Biography 5 (1944), p. 502; Doris Faber, *The Life of Lorena Hickok: E.R.'s Best Friend* (New York: William Morrow & Company, 1980), p. 297.

41. "Mary T. Norton," *Current Biography*, 1944, p. 502.

42. "Mary T. Norton," *Current Biography*, p. 502; "Labor: Absent Without Leave," *Time* 61 (January 11, 1943); Dallek, *Lone Star Rising*, p. 255; Robert A. Caro, *The Years of Lyndon Johnson: Means of Ascent* (New York: Alfred A. Knopf, 1990), p. 78.

43. Norton, "Memoirs," p. 192; U.S. Congress, House, Committee on Labor, "Directing the Secretary of Labor to Make an Investigation and Study of Causes of Absenteeism," *Reports*, no. 205, May 4, 1943; "Mary T. Norton," *Current Biography*, p. 502.

44. Marcy Kaptur, *Women of Congress: A Twentieth Century Odyssey* (Washington, D.C.: Congressional Quarterly, 1996), p. 46; "Summary of Legislation reported by Labor Committee during Chairmanship of Mrs. Norton," Norton MSS, Box 4, Personal Biographical Material; Millis, *Wagner Act to Taft-Hartley*, pp. 298, 354–55; Young, *Congressional Politics*, pp. 63–65; *Congressional Record*, 78th Cong., 1st Sess., pp. 3983, 3993, 5391–92; Chapman, *Contours of Public Policy*, pp. 229–32.

45. Samuel I. Rosenman, ed., *The Public Papers and Addresses of Franklin D. Roosevelt*, Vol. 12 (New York: Macmillan, 1950), pp. 268–72; Richard Polenberg, *War and Society: The United States, 1941–1945* (Philadelphia, PA: J. B. Lippincott, 1972), pp. 167–70; *Congressional Record*, 77th Cong., 1st Sess., pp. 6489, 6548–49; Millis and Brown, *From the Wagner Act to Taft-Hartley*, pp. 298–99, 353, 356; Chapman, *Contours of Public Policy*, pp. 232–33; Kennedy, *Freedom from Fear*, pp. 641–42; Doris Kearns Goodwin, *No Ordinary Time: Franklin and Eleanor Roosevelt: The Home Front in World War II* (New York: Simon and Schuster, 1994), p. 443.

46. "Mary T. Norton," *Current Biography*, p. 502; Mary T. Norton Labor Record, Norton MSS, Box 4, Personal Biographical Material. See also John Whiteclay Chambers II, "Mary Teresa Hopkins Norton," *Dictionary of American Biography*, Supp. 6 (New York: Charles Scribner's Sons, 1981), p. 480.

SEVEN

The Fair Employment Practices Committee and Beyond

During World War II, Norton battled vigorously to ensure fair employment practices for women workers. Over 50 million American civilians were employed on the home front by 1945. The number of women workers rose from 13 million to 19 million between 1941 and 1945, comprising a then record 36 percent of the American work force. Although two million women worked in defense-related industries, around 95 percent of female employees held unskilled jobs as secretaries or clerks.

President Franklin Roosevelt in June 1941 issued Executive Order 8802 banning discrimination in the hiring of defense industry or government workers because of "race, creed, color, or national origin." His administration established the Fair Employment Practices Committee (FEPC) to investigate complaints involving racial discrimination in all industries under contract to the federal government and to eliminate such discrimination. Roosevelt issued the executive order to avert a threatened civil rights March on Washington, being organized by A. Philip Randolph, head of the Brotherhood of Sleeping Car Porters Union. African-American workers envisioned the FEPC supporting their right to equal job opportunity.[1]

Norton, an FEPC backer who deplored job discrimination because of gender, race, or color, encouraged the hiring of women and minorities. She argued that the FEPC would prevent racial and gender discrimination in hiring and believed, "No man should be denied the right to find a job, support his family, and get ahead economically as far as his capabilities carry him." Monsignor Francis Haas, professor of philosophy and political science at Catholic University in Washington, D.C., and a close friend of Norton, administered the FEPC. "I have never known anyone," Norton affirmed, "who could inspire me, build up my confidence in myself and my faith in God more than he could."[2] Haas, who had written and lectured extensively on labor problems, had encouraged Norton during her battles on the Fair Labor Standards Act.

In 1943, Roosevelt greatly strengthened the FEPC with new Executive Order 9346, which prohibited job discrimination by any federal agency, war plant, government contractor, or labor union because of race, creed, color, and national origin. The FEPC, the temporary executive agency enforcing the order, lacked sufficient funds and personnel, however, and consequently resolved only one-third of the 8,000 complaints it heard. Norton in 1944 aligned with the New Dealers to narrowly approve the FEPC appropriations, 123 to 119, as Republicans and conservative Democrats nearly denied the agency funds.[3]

In 1944, Norton strove to make the FEPC permanent. Monsignor Haas quit as FEPC administrator to become Bishop of Grand Rapids, Michigan. During the summer, Norton invited Eleanor Roosevelt to address top women government leaders about job discrimination at a luncheon in the House Speaker's dining room. Roosevelt warned that the Axis powers were resorting to racial discrimination in the United States for propaganda purposes. Roosevelt's address inspired Norton to introduce legislation establishing a permanent FEPC to combat discrimination in employment because of race, gender, creed, color, and national origin. "The chances for a permanent FEPC did not look hopeful," Norton conceded, "but I decided that night to go ahead and see what I could do. I was 69 years old and starting out on the second big fight of my career." The House Labor Committee held extensive hearings on Norton's measure and approved sending it to the House floor. The House Rules Committee, however, took no action on the FEPC bill, preventing floor debate in 1944.[4]

In January 1945, Norton again offered a measure to establish a permanent FEPC. The House Labor Committee approved her legislation on February 20. Three days later, she asked the House Rules Committee for a special rule to bring the bill to the House floor for debate. On March 8, the morning after her seventieth birthday, Norton testified before the Rules Committee. "I knew I was in for a tussle with the Rules Committee,"[5] she admitted. Conservative Southern Democrats, including Edward Cox of Georgia, Howard Smith of Virginia, William Colmer of Mississippi, and J. Bayard Clark of North Carolina, controlled that committee. "My bill," Norton told committee members, "proposes a great reform that will appeal to every fair-minded member of Congress." Tension mounted in the Rules Committee room. Norton, unperturbed, cited the benefits of making the FEPC permanent. Rules Committee Chairman Abe Sabath of Illinois agreed with Norton's FEPC request but warned that granting a special rule required considerable deliberation and asked if Smith of Virginia wanted to challenge Norton's assessment. Smith spoke briefly before the committee adjourned, but no committee member made a motion on her request. Norton, therefore, realized that the Rules Committee did not intend to act speedily on her proposal.[6]

The House Rules Committee resorted to several complicated delaying tactics. Sabath's committee did not reconvene again until April 19, a week after Roosevelt's death and Harry Truman's ascension to the presidency. Roosevelt had died suddenly on April 12 of a massive cerebral hemorrhage at Warm Springs, Georgia. Shortly before Roosevelt's death, his Secretary Grace Tully had called Sabath relaying the president's request that the Chairman "do everything in his power to endeavor to bring about the adoption of a rule for this legislation."[7]

Norton on April 19 pleaded with the House Rules Committee to expedite action on her measure but again encountered staunch resistance from conservative members. During her testimony, Norton engaged in a heated exchange with Cox. "There are certain groups," Norton testified, "who have been greatly discriminated against." When Cox asked, "Who?" Norton replied, "You can't be serious! The Negro, of course." Cox queried, "Where?" Norton snapped, "Everywhere." Chairman Sabath banged his gavel in an attempt to stop the shouting match. "Wait a minute, Mr. Chairman," Cox yelled. "Wait a minute yourself, Mr. Cox," Norton interjected. "I told you exactly what I thought was fair, and don't intend to answer questions you've already asked me five times. Aside from your prejudice, I am very fond of you." "Thank you, ma'am," Cox interrupted. "But this bill is against our Jim Crow laws." "The sooner you get rid of them," Norton retorted, "the better the South will be off."[8]

Other House Rules Committee conservatives likewise interrogated Norton. Republican Charles Halleck of Indiana started questioning Norton, assuring her that he was not trying to embarrass her. "I am not easily embarrassed," Norton quipped. "I have been chairman of the Labor Committee for a long time," she added. "I think the Rules Committee has been most unfair to the Labor Committee." Norton then asked, "Why are you gentlemen so determined to be unfair?" Republican Clarence Brown of Ohio asked, "Are you speaking of the committee collectively?" "Individually," Norton conceded, "some of you are fine. I'm not the smartest person in the world," she admitted, "but I am sincere. Collectively, I think you fall short of that." Her reprimand startled the conservative Rules Committee members. Colmer of Mississippi interjected, "I don't think your law will work. In my section we feel kindly toward the Negro." Norton interrupted, "What have you done for him in over 200 years?" "Fed him when he was hungry and clothed him when he was naked," Colmer countered. Norton, in disbelief, snorted, "Humph!" Colmer abruptly quit the exchange, remarking "Mrs. Norton, I give you round one, hands down."[9]

In late April, Norton thrice asked the House Rules Committee to grant a special rule to send her measure to the House floor for debate. Despite her valiant efforts, the Rules Committee did not report her FEPC legislation for the remainder of the Seventy-ninth Congress. Norton, therefore, resorted to the same discharge petition strategy she had employed on the Fair Labor Standards Act. She on April 27 placed a petition on Speaker Rayburn's desk to discharge her FEPC bill from the Rules Committee and bring it to the House floor for debate. Norton told House members, "The Rules Committee has continually since 1937, when I made my first request to that body as chairman of the Labor Committee refused to grant rules to bring constructive labor legislation to the floor of the House."[10] Her discharge petition, however, died because only 125 of the required 218 members signed by late summer 1945.

The House Appropriations Committee also discouraged Norton by eliminating funding for the temporary FEPC from the war agencies appropriations bill. Democrat Clarence Cannon of Missouri, the committee chairman, omitted the FEPC appropriation because Congress was considering Norton's proposal to establish a permanent and statutory FEPC and Congress had not yet enacted FEPC into law. At a White House meeting, Norton told President Truman how the Rules Committee had blocked her measure from reaching the House floor for debate. "You've got a tough fight ahead of you," Truman agreed, "but I think you'll win out eventually."

President Truman appealed to the House Rules Committee to give quick clearance to Norton's FEPC measure. He on June 5 wrote Chairman Sabath protesting the deletion of FEPC funding from the war agencies appropriation bill and the Rules Committee refusal to act on Norton's legislation. "Unless it (Norton's bill) is sent to the floor," he warned Sabath, "the members of the House will have no opportunity to vote on it. The result will be that on July 1 next the principle of fair employment practices will have been abandoned by the House of Representatives. I therefore urge the Rules Committee to adopt a rule permitting this legislation to be voted upon by members of the House as quickly as possible." Sabath read Truman's letter to his House colleagues and also conveyed former President Roosevelt's last wishes to continue the FEPC. Norton recollected, "It was wonderful support of my fight."[11]

The war agencies' appropriations bill sparked animated floor debate on June 7. At the outset, Colmer asked, "Mr. Speaker, reserving the right to object, is there any appropriation made in this bill for continuation of the so-called FEPC?" Cannon, who conducted the floor debate, replied that the war agencies' appropriations bill did not include FEPC funding. Another House colleague wondered why. Cannon explained that no appropriation could be included without House authorization. Any resolution granting the FEPC allocation would have to be introduced on the House floor, traverse through the Rules Committee, and be approved by the House before it could be included in the bill. Cannon added that Norton had introduced a measure to make the FEPC permanent. The Appropriations Committee had deferred action on continuation of the

FEPC pending House Rules Committee action on Norton's bill. "The appropriation," Cannon stressed, "has not been rejected, only deferred." [12]

Norton reminded Cannon that the House Rules Committee had procrastinated on her FEPC measure. Unless the House allocated money for continuation of the FEPC by June 30, the end of the fiscal year, the agency would expire. She claimed, "It is practically impossible to get that bill through by June 30." Cannon concurred with Norton's assessment and explained, "There are only two ways in which such a provision could be brought to the floor of the House." The Rules Committee either could report her legislation out or approve an amendment to the appropriations measure including the wartime FEPC. Norton asked pointedly if Cannon believed that "the Committee on Rules would do any such thing? They have refused since February 23 to give us a rule on a permanent FEPC." Cannon explained, "The Committee on Appropriations cannot appropriate a single dollar without authorization." When Norton countered that the 1944 bill had included an appropriation for the wartime FEPC, Cannon retorted that both parties had agreed to implement a special procedure on that occasion. "Such procedure," he indicated, "is not possible this year and therefore the Committee on Appropriations is helpless." When questioned why the FEPC appropriation was excluded, Cannon responded, "We are told if certain agencies are included in the bill, no rule will be forthcoming from the Rules Committee. What recourse have we but to eliminate such items?" [13]

Tension built on the House floor. When one congressman asked which Rules Committee member was "pointing a legislative gun" at the Appropriations Committee, a Republican Rules Committee member denied the accusation and countered, "The gentleman should know something about his facts before he comes on the floor and makes assertions like that." Norton asked "Who is the controlling factor in the Committee on Rules who would dare do such a thing?" "I am certain," Cannon interjected, "the lady exerts just as effective an influence and certainly a more persuasive influence with the Rules Committee than I do." Norton struck back, "We all know the facts, we all know why FEPC was omitted, but it took a lot of courage to come before this House and tell us that the Rules Committee, or a few members of the Rules Committee, were running the entire House!" [14]

Norton's quest to make the FEPC permanent did not succeed. Norton on June 12 reminded House colleagues that the House Rules Committee still had not granted a rule on her measure, denouncing its "arbitrary and tyrannical" tactics. She suggested that the House needed an FEPC of its own to ensure that it "shall not be prevented by less than 12 members from performing its duty." Her discharge petition fell far short of securing 218 signatures, and Congress halved the FEPC's wartime budget in 1945. Norton noted, "We fought hard to save the wartime FEPC, but failed." [15] Eleanor Roosevelt lauded Norton's valiant battle. In July 1945, she wrote Norton, "I admire your courage in the splendid fight you are making for the Fair Employment Practices Bill. I know that nothing would have come out of it, if it had not been for your work. I know you feel as I do, that what was finally accomplished, while not what we wanted, is better than one could hope for, for a while."[16]

Congress dissolved the FEPC within one year, eliminating the only federal forum for airing charges of discriminatory hiring practices. Norton had lost what she termed "the second biggest fight of my career in Congress," a stark contrast to her monumental success on the Fair Labor Standards Act of 1938. She refused to give up the battle, however, relentlessly introducing legislation for a permanent FEPC at every congressional session until her retirement in 1951.

Republicans, meanwhile, won the race for governor in New Jersey. In November 1943, Republican Walter Edge defeated Democrat Vincent Murphy to replace Charles Edison as governor. Edge, who had served as governor from 1917 to 1919 and as U.S. senator from 1919 to 1929, capitalized on the continued split between the American Federation of Labor (AFL) and Congress of Industrial Organizations (CIO). Edge, an advocate of streamlined state government and a new state constitution, denounced Hague's power and argued that a vote for Newark Mayor Murphy was a tally for the domination of "labor leaders, communists, and Hagueism." Hudson County delivered a 98,000-vote majority for Murphy, bolstered by the CIO rank and file, but the AFL gave him only lukewarm support. Norton complained to President Roosevelt that the AFL leaders "played the same kind of a game they played with me when they tried to defeat the 'Wage & Hour bill.'" One AFL leader, whom she tried to convince to support Murphy, told her, "We don't support any labor candidate. If he loses it will reflect on our organization." Norton lamented that Governor Edison "lost interest in him (Murphy)—if he ever had any" after initially endorsing him. She concluded, "We worked hard to elect our candidate but the cards were stacked against us."[17]

Norton continued to admire President Roosevelt's astute wartime leadership in helping the nation handle the "greatest danger of its history" and often encouraged him. In April 1942, she wired Roosevelt, "God bless and keep you to continue to direct our beloved America. We shall keep faith with you and celebrate with justice some day." A month later, Norton reassured the president, "You may always count on my loyalty and devotion to you and to the principles you hold to be right and just." In January 1943, she telegrammed him, lauding his "great record of progressive government to benefit humanity particularly during the past ten years" and added, "May God bless and keep you to continue your work for all the peoples of the world." That fall, Norton wrote Roosevelt, "I am one Democrat who believes you are the greatest exponent of Justice and a square deal in all the world today. It may be history will record that your recognition of human values will live and serve generations of unborn

Americans." Her messages inspired the president. "It is characteristic of your generosity and loyalty and made me very happy," Roosevelt reflected. "I appreciate it more than I can say."[18]

At the 1944 Democratic National Convention in Chicago, Illinois, Norton wholeheartedly backed Roosevelt's quest for an unprecedented fourth term as president. The delegates nominated Roosevelt by acclamation. American troops still were fighting hard to defeat Germany on the Western European front and Japan in the Pacific theatre. "It would have seemed foolhardy in the extreme," Norton contended, "to change leadership at this point."[19]

Truman of Missouri, who had served in the U.S. Senate since January 1935, was selected as Roosevelt's running mate. He had helped frame the Transportation Act of 1940 and had headed a committee investigating American defense industries during World War II. Truman initially did not want to be considered for the vice presidency. The night before the convention opened, Norton and Truman were waiting for a Platform Committee meeting to begin. She half jokingly remarked to him, "Well, it looks as though you're going to be Vice-President." Truman, who looked perturbed, told her, "I don't want to be Vice-President. I want to stay right where I am and finish the job I'm doing." An aide then notified Truman that he had a telephone call. "There, you see!" Norton said laughingly. "He shook his head and followed the boy out of the room, looking very unhappy," she observed. "He did not return." The telephone call came from Roosevelt, who asked him to be the vice presidential nominee. Truman reluctantly accepted the invitation, replacing Henry Wallace. Norton joined the entire New Jersey delegation in supporting Truman's nomination. She admired the Missouri senator's performance in directing the Truman Committee investigating American defense industries and deemed him "a strong, steady sort of man, capable and trustworthy," qualities that would make him an effective vice president.[20]

Norton still remained heavily involved in national Democratic Party affairs. Besides being selected to the Democratic National Committee, she became the first woman to cochair a party Platform Committee, sharing responsibilities with Democrat John McCormack of Massachusetts. Norton, though, resigned in 1944 as chairman of the New Jersey Democratic State Committee after a decade of service. "I could no longer give the job the time it required," she explained. Besides being elected as national committeewoman from New Jersey, Norton stressed, "My work in the House had become exceedingly heavy." She was battling to secure House adoption of her bill to make the FEPC permanent.[21]

The 1944 presidential campaign proved anticlimactic. Roosevelt faced Republican Governor Thomas Dewey of New York in the November election. "It had little of the fire and drama of the Roosevelt-Willkie battle in 1940," Norton recollected. "Roosevelt supporters," she observed, "were very much heartened by a superb demonstration of courage and stamina he gave toward the end, when he toured the New York Metropolitan area all one forenoon in an open car on one of the coldest, wettest days (October 21) I can remember, and that night made one of his greatest foreign policy speeches." At the Foreign Policy Association in New York, Roosevelt called for an American commitment to use its troops to back up postwar peacekeeping. "Peace, like war," he maintained, "can succeed only where there is a will to enforce it, and where there is available power to enforce it." [22]

Norton urged Roosevelt's reelection because of his "unmatched experience both nationally and internationally" and his being "the greatest humanitarian the nation has ever produced." She pictured the president as "a world citizen, a statesman, a diplomat . . . respected, loved and admired by our Allies and feared by our enemies." Norton especially praised Roosevelt's radio speeches. "They were a real inspiration to me, particularly when the going was a bit rough," she wrote the commander in chief in early November. Although aware of the heavy physical burden of another presidential term, Norton assured him, "I know no other American could do it quite so well." The president called Norton's letter "a real inspiration." "The burdens ahead are heavy," he acknowledged, "but the load is lighter when I know that I have the confidence of such good friends as yourself." [23]

President Roosevelt was reelected to an unprecedented fourth term in November, capturing over 53 percent of the popular vote and trouncing Dewey, 432 to 99, in the electoral college. The Democrats still controlled Congress, gaining 20 House seats for a 242 to 192 advantage over Republicans and retaining 57 of the 96 Senate seats. Norton kept her Thirteenth District Congressional seat, routing Republican Frank Gimino, 89,736 to 38,336. She tallied nearly 70 percent of the popular vote, the second highest numerical total among the New Jersey delegation. Her quest to make the FEPC permanent appealed to women constituents. The Republicans, however, gained one House seat in New Jersey, solidifying their control of the state's delegation. Edward Hart was the only other New Jersey Democrat to prevail in the House.

Norton welcomed the election of Democrats Helen Gahagan Douglas of California, Chase Woodhouse of Connecticut, and Emily Douglas of Illinois to the House. After the departures of Representatives Katherine Byron of Maryland and Veronica Boland of Pennsylvania in January 1943, Norton was the only woman from the Democratic Party still in the U.S. Congress. Norton wrote Douglas of California, "I have really been lonesome all by myself on the Democratic side and I shall be happy to have some companions. It is wonderful that you will be here serving with me and I sincerely hope that for you it will be the beginning of a career you will enjoy as much, if not more, than the successful career you have had." [24]

The House Democrats on January 2 unanimously pledged support to Roosevelt at their first caucus meeting of Seventy-ninth Congress. Norton, as secretary of the party caucus, notified the president about the resolution, adding "with best wishes for your continued good health and success." Roosevelt replied, "I am deeply touched by the resolution of confidence." He added, "I am strengthened and encouraged by the pledge of support and am also delighted to have the resolution forwarded to me by so good and loyal a friend as you."

On a cold, snowy afternoon, Norton attended the inauguration ceremonies for President Roosevelt on January 20, 1945, at the South Portico of the White House. At the presidential reception in the Red Room of the White House, she observed that Roosevelt "was smiling and happy when he came in in his wheelchair." Norton discerned, however, that he looked frail and older. "The years of hard work and anxiety had taken their toll," she detected, "but the same cheerful spirit was there." [25]

The Yalta Conference of February 1945 further drained Roosevelt's physical strength. The president conferred with British Prime Minister Winston Churchill and Soviet leader Joseph Stalin for the last time, making critical decisions regarding the future of the postwar world. After sailing back to the United States, he informed Congress what had transpired at the conference. "That speech," Norton wrote, "I shall never forget." She detected sadness in Roosevelt's voice when he reflected, "It was not all we wanted, but it was all we could get." The president compromised with Stalin over the future of Germany, Eastern Europe, the United Nations, and Japan. Norton never saw Roosevelt again. In early March, the president congratulated Norton upon her completion of two decades in Congress. "The country in this critical time," he stressed, "has need of the wise counsel which you can give out of your long experience in legislative affairs." [26]

On the fateful April 12, 1945, Norton visited Agnes Gorman, the daughter of a close friend, in Jersey City. Three of Gorman's sons served in the military overseas. When a boy delivering eggs rang the doorbell, Gorman answered. "Have you heard?" the boy inquired. "The President is dead." Gorman initially did not believe him. When the boy reiterated, "Mrs. Gorman, it's true!" she slammed the door in his face and muttered, "Why can't they leave the man alone." Jersey City residents, though, started gathering in the streets. Gorman turned on the radio and learned that the boy's sad news indeed was true. Roosevelt had died of a massive cerebral hemorrhage at Warm Springs, Georgia. "Mrs. Gorman and I," Norton recalled, "just sat there in front of the radio for some time, without speaking. I knew she was thinking of her boys and the effect on them. I felt completely desolate—as though one of own family had gone." Norton reflected, "It is difficult at this time to express the sorrow that is in my heart. Words seem so inadequate. With the majority of the world, I realize that the greatest humanitarian leader of all time has gone to his reward." She concluded, "Our job now is to carry on where he left off and make his realistic dreams of world peace and security come true."[27] Truman was sworn in as president shortly after Roosevelt's death.

Norton rode the train that night to Washington and wanted to be left alone to reminisce about Roosevelt's life. She detected, "Even his bitterest enemies had a good word for Franklin Roosevelt that night." Some senators and representatives attended a private funeral service at the White House. Norton joined the Roosevelt family, cabinet members, and close friends on the funeral train from Washington to Hyde Park, New York, where the president had resided. As the train moved northward that night, teary-eyed crowds gathered at every station. Norton realized, though, Roosevelt "had not suffered at the end" and "had gone out as he would have liked to go."[28]

Hyde Park residents paid their last respects to Roosevelt as the funeral train stopped below the president's home, high on a bluff overlooking the town. According to Norton, "There was a long wait, while the flag-draped casket was borne up the long, steep road from the (Hudson) river on a gun caisson, drawn by black horses." At the Episcopal burial service, Norton reflected, "His soul, I knew was with the God he had served so well." She added, "This will always be a shrine."[29]

Norton, meanwhile, continued stirring the consciousness of women about sex discrimination in employment and gender pay inequities. She often coordinated weekly luncheons for congressional women, sponsored periodic lunchtime seminars for prominent Washington women, and spoke frequently at Democratic Party women's division meetings. Norton relished the significant wartime economic gains made by women entering the professions or trades, working in war-related factories, and serving in the armed forces. She boasted, "They have excelled in all the tasks assigned to them. They have amazed their employers, and probably themselves. They have gained the respect and confidence of the public.[30]

Norton still championed eliminating sex discrimination in employment and proposed legislation mandating equal pay for women, but met formidable resistance on both scores. Although the Fair Labor Standards Act of 1938 had fixed minimum pay rates regardless of gender, she protested that business employers continued paying women lower wages for similar tasks. Norton insisted that males and females should be treated equitably as workers regardless of sex and be compensated on their "ability to fill the jobs, not because of sex." Norton's Labor Committee approved her gender equity measures in 1944 and 1945, but the House did not follow suit either time. The U.S. Chamber of Commerce and other business groups stymied Norton's legislation.[31]

Although hoping women would sustain their economic gains following World War II, Norton feared instead that women would lose the professional and industrial jobs they had performed so capably when soldiers returned home from military service. Businesses were reluctant to train women who they regarded as just temporary employees and had informed them their employment would terminate when the men returned from overseas. Norton implored women to remain in the work force after World War II and wanted legislative protection given to all females desiring to retain their jobs in the professions, trades, and factories. "This is the time for women everywhere to prove that they appreciate the responsibility they have been given," she affirmed in 1945. Norton warned how industries and labor unions were pressuring women to let returning veterans seeking employment have their jobs. "Women are going to be pushed into a corner," she suspected, "and very soon at that." If that occurred, it would be a "heartbreaking setback" for women. Norton's concerns were warranted. By 1947, women's participation in the workforce had declined from 36 percent to 28 percent.[32]

Norton also grieved that women had not organized as an effective political bloc and urged them to become more involved politically. Women, she counseled, should unite to better fulfill their job aspirations and terminate sex discrimination. Norton campaigned for "the full participation by women as voters, party members, and candidates for office, and at all levels of government." To Norton, "women's political activism was not an issue of women's rights but of women's rightful place in American democracy." Women too often, she suspected, were denied political offices commensurate with their abilities. They held just one cabinet position, one U.S. Senate post, nine U.S. House seats, and no U.S. Supreme Court justiceships, although serving as heads of military branches, collectors of customs, postmasters, and labor conciliators and belonging to the Social Security Board and Civil Service Commission.

Norton complained that too few women even exhibited interest in politics, instead remaining "content as 'Sitting-Room Sarahs or Kitchen Katies.'" "We won't see a dozen women in Congress in our time," she prophesied, "because women won't vote for women." Norton sought more active participation by women as voters, party members, and candidates. Women, she claimed, wielded the balance of power numerically and stood "on the threshold of a glorious future." If females organized politically, Norton predicted that they could "do anything they want to." "We could do as great a job in politics as we are doing in industry and the door is wide open," she insisted. "We could elect more women to office."[33] Norton's hopes, though, largely went unfilled. Women consistently comprised less than 5 percent of the House membership until the mid-1980s.

Norton wanted women to play a more crucial role in building a stable world peace in the Cold War era but opposed the Equal Rights Amendment. She urged women to become involved in the peace movement and "to demand the end of wars." "This would seem to be," Norton believed, "the most constructive and finest contribution women could make to a postwar world."[34] Feminist groups renewed their campaign of an Equal

Rights Amendment because women had made many significant contributions to the World War II effort. Republican Representatives Winifred Stanley of New York and Margaret Chase Smith of Maine pushed in 1943 for passage of the Equal Rights Amendment to commemorate the twentieth anniversary of its introduction to Congress. Norton, though, rejected the Equal Rights Amendment largely because "it would nullify state laws that protected women in industry." She favored instead legislation mandating equal pay to protect women in industrial occupations and in 1947 coauthored a measure "declaring it national legislative policy to make no distinction on the basis of sex." [35]

Norton focused increasingly on gender equity employment issues. During World War II, over two million women worked in munitions plants. They either were the wives of servicemen who needed to work to support their families or single women who wanted to do their part to back the war effort. The War Manpower Commission conducted an extensive national "Rosie the Riveter" campaign to recruit women into the workforce. "Posters of Rosie's muscular, can-do image as a production line worker at an armaments plant projected an unconventional image of women as a source of physical strength." [36]

In 1942, a bipartisan group of eight congresswomen, headed by Norton, sought to add federal financing for nurseries to a Works Progress Administration (WPA) bill in the Appropriations Committee. The octet included Democrats Norton, Veronica Boland of Pennsylvania, Katharine Byron of Maryland, and Caroline O'Day of New York, and Republicans Frances Payne Bolton of Ohio, Jeannette Rankin of Montana, Edith Nourse Rogers of Massachusetts, and Margaret Chase Smith of Maine. Conservative Republican Jessie Sumner of Illinois, who was single, was the lone congresswoman opposing the federal financing for nurseries.

The octet attended an Appropriations Committee meeting. The Appropriations Committee already had completed action on the WPA bill and was ready to adjourn, but Chairman Clarence Cannon of Missouri and several other committee members agreed to listen to the octet's request. "The committee members were sympathetic," Norton recollected, but Cannon told them, "I'm sorry, but it's too late." Cannon added that the House would debate the WPA appropriations bill in a few days. Norton replied, "Don't forget—I'm a committee chairman, too. I know how these things work." She admitted, "We were terribly disappointed of course" and notified Cannon, "If the committee did not oppose me, I would offer an amendment when the bill was being debated on the floor." [37] Cannon promised not to oppose her amendment.

When the House debated the WPA appropriations measure, Norton proposed her amendment designating $6 million to support day nursery care for children whose mothers worked in defense industries. She deemed day care facilities essential to curtailing absenteeism among women defense workers, recounting her own experience in Jersey City during World War I. "I felt the amendment was safe," Norton thought, "when to my surprise the chairman of the Appropriations Committee opposed it." Her amendment lost on a standing vote. Cannon followed a House tradition that committee chairman opposed any legislation that it had not reported out. Norton quickly requested a teller vote. Cannon, having fulfilled his committee obligation on the previous tally, supported Norton's amendment this time. Cannon's switch enabled her amendment to squeak through narrowly, 71 to 70. Norton termed the outcome "a close shave" and was relieved "Chairman Cannon had kept his promise to me." Nursery day care facilities were constructed wherever women defense workers were needed. The federal funding for these facilities eventually rose to $75 million.[38]

Norton, who joined the House Education Committee in 1943, intensified her campaign for government-funded child nurseries. She was "the leading proponent in the House of appropriations for nurseries, where children can be given adequate care while their mothers assume their places in industry." By 1943, child-care problems had reached critical proportions nationally. Only 16 of the 662 geographical areas needing child-care facilities had operating programs. To Norton's chagrin, Congress stopped federal funding for child care centers and left that responsibility to state and local governments. Norton sought to rectify the problem by broadening the Lanham Act of 1940 to include day care centers. The Lanham Act had permitted the use of federal funds to build public housing for defense industry workers and was "designed to construct buildings, not care for children."

The Roosevelt administration ruled in 1943 that Lanham Act funds could be used to build and operate child care centers. Democrat Fritz Lanham of Texas, who had sponsored the 1940 legislation, disapproved of using federal funds for building and operating day care centers and "repeatedly interfered to stop the use of federal funds for child-care projects, especially those administered by welfare agencies." Norton, a staunch advocate of day care centers, sponsored an amendment to the Lanham Act in 1943. Her amendment sought federal allocations for constructing and running day care centers for the children of working mothers to be administered by the Federal Works Administration.

In the fall of 1943, Congress adopted Norton's amendment. Norton's proposal improved the child care situation moderately. The government constructed and managed around 2,800 child care centers, as the number of children enrolled in federally supported facilities increased from under 66,000 in February 1944 to 100,000 one year later. Nevertheless, "the number of children receiving supervision in federal centers represented less than 10 percent of those needing it." According to historian Richard Polenberg, "The majority of working mothers did not use them." The Women's Bureau found that "only one out of ten working mothers with children sent them to a day-care center."

Jersey City did not even apply initially for federal child care center funding. Mrs. Richard Henke, Secretary of the Council of Social Agencies, apprised Norton of the dire situation facing the Jersey City day care facilities. In November 1943, Norton urged Mayor Hague to seek federal child care center funding. "The need for day care for the children of working mothers in the Jersey City area is very great and cannot be met under the existing facilities." She affirmed, "I feel sure that if an application were filed for assistance, it would probably be granted because of the great need." Norton wrote Hague, "I dislike having the City fall down on any responsibility and feel sure that you have been so busy that you have not had the time to consider this grave problem."

Several problems beset child care centers nationally. Facilities often were not available for use when and where they were needed. Communities seeking assistance frequently struggled through red tape, vying for funds with other types of facilities. One government official observed, "There is a positive aversion to group care of children in the minds of working women. To some it connotes an inability to care for one's own; to some it has a vague incompatibility with the traditional idea of the American home; to others it has a tint of socialism." Mothers instead left their children in the care of a neighbor or an older sibling.

President Truman planned to let federal allocations for child care centers expire on October 31, 1945. In August 1945, the Federal Works Administration announced, "Grants under the Lanham Act would end as soon as the war crisis was over." Most authorities argued that "the large number of mothers in the labor force made a continuation of such facilities essential," but "entreaties for help received little encouragement from administration officials." Norton implored Truman and Congress to grant a six-month extension. She wrote the president in September 1945, "The Child Care Program is just as important now as it was before the victory" and asked him to issue an executive order to maintain it. Many women needed to work because they provided principal family support but could not continue their jobs without having day care facilities. "There are still a great many mothers," Norton stressed, "who must continue their employment." She pointed out, "Wives of servicemen still overseas and widows of servicemen find that without employment they cannot maintain their families." Women needed more time to make alternative arrangements for their children, while large, overcrowded cities required time to establish more local day care centers. Norton received "hundreds of pathetic letters" from working mothers pleading for continuation of federal support for day care centers. "I do not feel," she concluded, "that we can afford to neglect our children." At President Truman's request, Congress authorized $7 million for the day care centers to continue through March 1, 1946. The responsibility for the child-care centers thereafter rested with the states.

Democrats Norton and Augustine Kelley of Pennsylvania cosponsored the Maternal and Child Welfare Act of 1945 as an amendment to the Social Security Act. Congress approved the amendment, which provided $22 million, through the U.S. Children's Bureau, to the states for maternal and child health, child welfare services, and services to crippled children. The allocation enabled states "to expand their present services and to develop new ones—particularly to help children whose problems are so serious as to demand immediate and special attention." The measure enabled many communities to provide individual guidance and social services for children in their own homes by child welfare workers, temporary child care in foster homes, day care services, and services aimed at improving existing conditions.[39]

Following World War II, Norton proposed other maternal and child welfare bills. The Truman administration, women's organizations, and labor unions typically backed these measures, but the legislation encountered insurmountable resistance from Republicans and conservative Democrats. The nation still seemed largely ambivalent to the concerns of working mothers. In 1947, Norton commented, "I regret that many of these nurseries are not being continued. Although peace has come, we seem to have lost the urge and are not placing emphasis on the need for child protection and child health." She stressed, "The necessity is still very great."[40]

During the latter stages of World War II, Norton continued to experience setbacks as House Labor Committee chairman. Her yeoman efforts to make the FEPC permanent, establish gender equity in hiring and pay scales, and provide federal funding for child care centers for working mothers met formidable resistance from conservative colleagues. "She found much of her experience as Labor Committee chair in wartime frustrating" partly because of "the bleak prospects of women's place in the post-war work-force" and since women would be forced out of their jobs "to make way for demobilized GIs seeking employment."[41] Norton soon witnessed the Labor Committee sharply curtail New Deal legislation and left that turbulent group for the calmer Administration Committee while turning attention to a myriad of challenging postwar domestic and foreign policy issues.

NOTES

1. Richard Polenberg, *War and Society: The United States, 1941–1945* (Philadelphia, PA: J. B. Lippincott Company, 1972), p. 146; David M. Kennedy, *Freedom from Fear: The American People in Depression and War, 1929–1945* (New York: Oxford University Press, 1999), p. 767; Barbara J. Tomlinson, "Making Their Way: A Study of New Jersey Congresswomen, 1924–1994," (Ph.D. dissertation: Rutgers: The State University of New Jersey, 1996), p. 40. For employment patterns, see also Alice Kessler-Harris, *Out to Work: A History of Wage-Earning in the United States* (New York: Oxford University Press, 1982), pp. 276–77, 294.

2. Mary T. Norton, "Madam Congressman: The Memoirs of Mary T. Norton of New Jersey," (Hereafter cited as "Memoirs") Mary T. Norton MSS, New Jersey Collection, Archibald Stevens Alexander Library, Rutgers, The State University of New Jersey, p. 212; National Women's History Museum, "Women Wielding Power: Pioneer Female State Legislators: New Jersey," http://www/nwhm.org; Featured House Publications, *Women in Congress, 1917–2006*, April 27, 2007, 108th Cong., 1st Sess., H. Doc. 108–223, http://www.gpo.gov; "Mary T. Norton 1875–1959," in http://womenincongress.house.gov/member-profiles.

3. Polenberg, *War and Society*, p. 119.

4. Norton, "Memoirs," pp. 214–15; 'History of legislation reported by Labor Committee during Chairmanship of Mrs. Norton," Norton MSS, Box 4, Personal Biographical Material.

5. Marcy Kaptur, *Women of Congress: A Twentieth Century Odyssey* (Washington, D.C.: Congressional Quarterly, 1996), p. 47; Norton, "Memoirs," pp. 214–15; Mary T. Norton Labor Record, circa 1949, Norton MSS, Box 4, Personal Biographical File; "History of legislation,"

6. *Atlanta Journal*, March 9, 1945; Norton Labor Record.

7. Emily A. Geer, "A Study of the Activities of Women in Congress With Special Reference to the Congressional Careers of Margaret Chase Smith, Mary T. Norton, and Edith Nourse Rogers," (Masters thesis: Bowling Green State University, 1952), p. 134; Norton, "Memoirs," p. 222.

8. *Washington Times-Herald*, April 20, 1945.

9. *Washington Times-Herald*, Apr. 20, 1945.

10. *Washington Times-Herald*, Apr. 20, 1945; "History of legislation."

11. Norton, "Memoirs," pp. 221–22.

12. Norton, "Memoirs," p. 223.

13. Norton, "Memoirs," pp. 223–24.

14. Norton, "Memoirs," p. 225; Helen Gahagan Douglas to Mary T. Norton, September 23, 1941, Norton MSS, Box 1, General Correspondence, 1941.

15. Norton, "Memoirs," p. 221; Tomlinson, "Making Their Way," p. 40.

16. Eleanor Roosevelt to Mary T. Norton, July 21, 1945, Norton MSS, Box 2, Corr., Franklin D. Roosevelt, 1928–1945.

17. Norton Labor Record; Norton, "Memoirs," p. 201; Joseph F. Mahoney, "Walter Evans Edge," in Paul A. Stelhorn and Michael J. Belkner, eds., *The Governors of New Jersey, 1664–1974* (Trenton, NJ: New Jersey Historical Commission, 1982).

18. Mary T. Norton to Hugo Bermann, July 17, 1942, Norton MSS, Box 1, Gen. Corr., 1942; Mary T. Norton to Franklin D. Roosevelt, April 28, 1942, Franklin D. Roosevelt MSS, President's Personal File 5418, Norton; Mary T. Norton to Franklin D. Roosevelt, May 29, 1942, FDR MSS, PPF 5418, Norton; Mary T. Norton to Franklin D. Roosevelt, March 4, 1943, FDR MSS, PPF 5418, Norton; Mary T. Norton to Franklin D. Roosevelt, November 3, 1943, FDR MSS, PPF 5418, Norton.

19. Norton, "Memoirs," p. 202.

20. Norton, "Memoirs," pp. 203–4.

21. Norton, "Memoirs," p. 201.

22. Norton, "Memoirs," p. 204; George McJimsey, *The Presidency of Franklin D. Roosevelt* (Lawrence, KS: University Press of Kansas, 2000), p. 256; Franklin D. Roosevelt, Radio Address, Foreign Policy Association, New York City, October 21, 1944, http://www.presidency.ucsb.edu.

23. Mary T. Norton, "Election of 1944," October 1944, Norton MSS, Box 1, Gen. Corr., 1944; Mary T. Norton to Franklin D. Roosevelt, November 5, 1944, FDR MSS, PPF 5418, Norton.

24. "Statistics of the Presidential and Congressional Election of November 7, 1944," (Washington, D.C.: U.S. Government Printing Office, 1945), p. 25; Mary T. Norton to Helen Gahagan Douglas, November 27, 1944, Norton MSS, Box 1, Gen. Corr., 1944.

25. Mary T. Norton to Franklin D. Roosevelt, January 3, 1945, FDR MSS, Box 1, Gen. Corr., 1945; Franklin D. Roosevelt to Mary T. Norton, January 11, 1945, Norton MSS, Box 1, Gen. Corr., 1945; Norton, "Memoirs," p. 205.

26. Norton, "Memoirs," p. 205; Franklin D. Roosevelt to Mary T. Norton, March 5, 1945, FDR MSS, PPF 5418, Norton.

27. Norton, "Memoirs," p. 207; Mary T. Norton to Ronald V. Cochran, April 14, 1945, Norton MSS, Box 1, Gen. Corr., 1945.

28. Norton, "Memoirs," p. 208.

29. Norton, "Memoirs," p. 209.

30. Marian McDonagh Burke, Interview with Author, August 7, 1981; Mary T. Norton, "Democratic Women's Part in the World Today," Speech, NBC, September 27, 1943, Norton MSS, Box 1, Gen. Corr., 1943; Mary T. Norton, "We Must Hold Our Ground," *Newsweek* Symposium of the Role Women Will Play in Business and Industry, New York City, 1943, Norton MSS, Box 3, Political Writings.

31. Norton, "We Must Hold," *Newsweek* Symposium, 1943; Kaptur, *Women of Congress*, p. 46; *Congressional Record*, 79th Cong., 1st Sess., p. 27; Malcolm Muir, Jr., *The Human Tradition in the World War II Era* (Wilmington, DE: Scholarly Resources Books, 2001), p. 129.

32. Tomlinson, "Making Their Way," p. 40; "Mary T. Norton," *Current Biography* 5 (1944), p. 502; Annabel Paxton, *Women in Congress* (Richmond, VA: Dietz Press, 1945), p. 37; Featured House Publications, *Women in Congress, 1917–2006*; "Mary T. Norton 1875–1959," http://www.womenincongress.house.

33. Carmela Ascolese Karnoutsos, "Mary Teresa Norton, 1875–1959" in Joan N. Burstyn, ed., *Past and Present: Lives of New Jersey Women* (Syracuse, NY: Syracuse University Press, 1997), pp. 368–70; Amy Porter, "Ladies of Congress," *Collier's* 123 (August 28, 1943), pp. 22–23; Paxton, *Women in Congress*, pp. 37, 35; Norton, "We Must Hold," *Newsweek* Symposium, 1943.

34. Norton, "Democratic Women's Part," Speech, Sept. 27, 1943; Norton, "We Must Hold," *Newsweek* Symposium, 1943.

35. Kaptur, *Women of Congress,* p. 46; National Women's History Museum, "Women Wielding Power"; Karnoutsos, "Mary Teresa Norton."

36. Norton, "Memoirs," p. 194; David M. Kennedy, *Freedom from Fear: The American People in Depression and War, 1929–45* (New York: Oxford University Press, 1999), pp. 776–82. For the problems faced by women workers, see Phillip S. Foner, *Women and the American Labor Movement from World War I to the Present* (New York: The Free Press, 1980); Alice Kessler-Harris, *Out to Work: A History of Wage-Earning Women in the United States* (New York: Oxford University Press, 1982), pp. 276–77; and Rosalind Rosenburg, *Divided Lives: American Women in the Twentieth Century* (New York: Hill and Wang, 1992).

37. Norton, "Memoirs," p. 194.

38. Norton, "Memoirs," pp. 194–95.

39. Norton Labor Record; National History Museum, "Women Wielding Power"; Karnoutsos, "Mary Teresa Norton"; William H. Chafe, *The Paradox of Change: American Women in the 20th Century* (New York: Oxford University Press, 1991), pp. 150–51, 164–65; Polenberg, *War and Society*, pp. 148–49; Mary T. Norton to Harry S. Truman, September 28, 1945, Norton MSS, Box 1, Gen. Corr., 1945; Matthew J. Connelly to Mary T. Norton, October 11, 1945, Norton MSS, Box 1, Gen. Corr., 1945; Dorothy M. Lewis, "The Listening Post/ More Federal Aid for Mothers and Children," *Educational Leadership* 4 (December 1946), p. 203.

40. Kessler-Harris, *Out of Work*, p. 298; Cynthia Harrison, *On Account of Sex: The Politics of Women's Issues, 1945–1968* (Berkeley, CA: University of California Press, 1988), p. 43; Tomlinson, "Making Their Way," p. 40; Mary T. Norton, Radio Interview, WOL, Washington, D.C., January 22, 1947, Norton MSS, Box 5, Speeches, Labor, 1937–1949.

41. "Mary T. Norton," *Current Biography*, p. 502. See also John Whiteclay Chambers II, "Mary Teresa Hopkins Norton," *Dictionary of American Biography*, Supp. 6, 1956–1960 (New York: Charles Scribner's Sons, 1981), p. 480.

EIGHT

The Postwar Years

After World War II, Norton became more directly involved in international affairs. During her first two decades in Congress, she largely had focused on domestic issues and remained inside the continental United States. In October 1945, an opportunity opened up for her to travel to Europe. President Harry Truman invited seventy-one-year old Norton to attend the International Labor Conference in Paris, France, as an adviser and alternate delegate. The conclave marked the first major post–World War II international labor meeting held in battle-ravaged Europe. The American delegation also included Mrs. Clara Beyer of the U.S. Labor Department, Dr. Ralph Bunche of the U.S. State Department, several other U.S. State Department staff members, and Democrat Elbert Thomas of Utah, chairman of the Senate Labor Committee.

The American delegation left New York City aboard the Queen Mary, a troopship, on October 1 and arrived in Southampton, England, five days later. After stopping in London, England, they boarded a ship crowded with soldiers from New Haven, England, and traveled to Dieppe, France. "I got my first view of what war really can do to a city the next morning when we arrived at Dieppe."[1] Norton recollected. A representative from the American embassy in Paris, France, drove the delegation to their quarters at the California Hotel in Paris.

The International Labor Conference delegates met at the unheated Sorbonne on the University of Paris campus. "It was like entering a damp cellar that had been closed for years," Norton recalled, "and we sat through the meetings in heavy coats and furs." Norton contracted a virus infection that settled in her leg for several months. She heard delegates from the Netherlands, Belgium, Poland, Greece, and other countries overrun by the Nazi armies relate agonizing stories about widespread suffering from malnutrition, starvation, and inadequate clothing. The delegates described families separated by death or deportation into German concentration camps and told about the destruction of homes, schools, and public buildings; disruption of transportation facilities; and inflated currencies. Heart-rending stories about homeless people, including 500,000 in Poland, over one million in Greece, and eight million in Italy, were recounted. One-sixth of the Belgian workers were forced into German labor camps.[2]

Norton also witnessed the enormous devastation inflicted by modern warfare upon western Europe and realized the Europeans desperately needed American economic assistance. "No experience in my whole life," she declared, "made a deeper impression on me." Norton termed "the destruction visible outside Paris" and "the evidences of suffering in the tired faces, undernourished bodies and shabby clothing of the people were appalling." She met one hotel headwaiter whose wife had no access to a bar of soap for five years. Women made dresses out of bedspreads and curtains. "If Americans knew the facts of the intense suffering in Europe, of the total destruction of factories and fields," Norton insisted, "they would gladly share their food, their clothes, and their money." She urged Americans to collect money and donate supplies to European relief and recovery "if civilization is to be saved." "Wake up America before it is too late," Norton warned. "The war is not over."

Norton voiced one major regret about her European trip. The devout Roman Catholic had hoped to meet Pope Pius XII at the Vatican. Norton had planned to fly to Rome, Italy, with Senator Thomas, a Mormon from Utah and child welfare advocate, for a private audience with the Pope. Her virus infection unfortunately dashed those plans. The throbbing pain in her leg even made walking very difficult.[3]

Norton's described her agonizing return voyage to New York City as "one of the most trying I ever experienced." The American delegation had intended to fly from Paris to London, England, but dense fog grounded all planes. They crossed the English Channel by boat instead and were driven by an American embassy official to Southampton, England. "We were half starved," she complained, "having had nothing to eat all day." The American delegation finally boarded the Queen Mary after "hours of misery." A doctor assigned Norton to the stateroom to help her rest easier. "The Queen Mary," she remembered, "was so crowded with our returning troops that soldiers slept in bathtubs. I doubt if my mother was any happier seeing land after that terrible voyage many years ago than I was the morning we docked in New York."

Norton's sisters, Anne Hopkins and Loretta McDonagh; Joseph McDonagh, Loretta's husband; and several friends greeted her at the New York City harbor. Norton temporarily felt better than she had for several weeks, but the arduous boat trip weakened her health. She spent the remainder of 1945 and nearly all of 1946 in hospitals, at home with nurses, or under the care of Dr. Thomas White, often preventing her from attending House floor sessions and fulfilling her Labor Committee responsibilities. "Mrs. Norton is still not feeling well and she has secured a leave of absence from the House until January 3rd," Lucille McDonagh Considine, Norton's niece and secretary, wrote in late November 1945. "Her doctor feels that she really needs a complete rest." Norton recuperated in January 1946 at the Key Biscayne, Florida, winter home of Jersey City Mayor Frank Hague. Marion McDonagh Burke, another Norton niece, later recalled, "Mary was sick and too heavy and never felt well after her European trip."[4] To make matters worse, Joseph McDonagh suffered a fatal heart attack in the autumn of 1946 at his New York City apartment. "It was a terrible blow to all of us," Norton lamented. His generosity, warm hospitality, and zest for life had invigorated her.[5]

After World War II, Norton rallied behind Truman's foreign policies to contain the spread of Communism in Europe, Asia, and elsewhere. The Soviets occupied militarily virtually every Eastern European nation after World War II, installing pliant communist governments in Poland, East Germany, Albania, Bulgaria, Hungary, Rumania, and Czechoslovakia. The Truman administration tried to curb the expansion of Communism by military and economic means. Norton in 1947 supported the Truman Doctrine, authorizing $400 million in military and economic assistance to Greece and Turkey. Communist insurgents from Albania, Bulgaria, and Yugoslavia had threatened to overthrow the pro-Western Greek government. In a display of bipartisanship, the House overwhelmingly approved the Greek assistance, 287 to 107, on May 9. In 1948 Norton backed the Marshall Plan, granting $17 billion in economic aid to help ravaged Western European nations recover from poverty, hunger, desperation, and chaos. The House resoundingly approved the Marshall Plan, 329 to 74, on March 31. The Greek assistance measure and the Marshall Plan both became law. In 1949, Norton supported the North Atlantic Treaty Organization (NATO), a regional military alliance defending Western European nations. The U.S. Senate easily ratified the NATO treaty in July.[6]

On the domestic front, Norton continued to battle for working-class Americans. She, in September 1945, sponsored legislation to raise the minimum wage of workers from 40 cents to 65 cents an hour. Norton realized that the 40-cent per hour minimum wage "was far too small and completely out of line with rising living costs." In a message to Congress earlier that month, President Truman had proposed a twenty-one-point domestic program, including substantially increasing the minimum wage to eliminate "sub-standards of living." He concluded, "The goal of a 40-cent-per-hour minimum wage was inadequate when established. It had now become obsolete." The Seventy-ninth Congress, though, refused to raise the minimum wage. The conservative coalition "opposed any expansion of the minimum wage to workers in the agricultural industry, as it might throw farm prices and labor costs off balance." Many Republicans "were intent on overhauling New Deal labor policies."[7]

Congress adjourned in early August 1946 to allot for election campaigning. Norton reflected, "It has been a hectic session," but added, "They always are preceding an election." Dr. White curtailed Norton's campaign activities in 1946, when she sought reelection to a twelfth consecutive House term. Republican challenger John Jones repeatedly assailed Norton's inactivity, congressional absences, and missed roll calls. "It was hard to sit at home, read the newspapers, and do nothing about it," Norton conceded. "But Doctor White was adamant, and in the end it came out all right." The New Jersey campaign speakers' bureau filled in for Norton that fall. Although Jones proved a more formidable opponent, Norton still triumphed easily, 69,440 to 36,270. Norton's 64 percent vote total marked her lowest proportion since 1928, attributable to her forced absences from Congress and the campaign trail. She pointed out, "I was reelected to my twelfth term in Congress—without having made a single campaign speech!" Few congressional candidates in American history have won reelection without delivering a campaign speech. Republicans, though, retained twelve of the fourteen seats in the New Jersey delegation, with Hart the lone Democrat beside Norton.[8]

In the 1946 mid-term congressional elections, the Democrats did not fare nearly as well as Norton. The Republicans captured both the U.S. House and U.S. Senate for the first time since 1928, picking up fifty-five House seats to dominate the lower chamber by a 246 to 188 margin and gaining twelve Senate seats to control the upper chamber, 51 to 45. Truman's public approval rating had sunk to 32 percent over his handling of numerous postwar labor strikes and the unpopular wartime price controls for treating food and gasoline shortages.

Norton lost her prestigious House Labor Committee chairmanship when the Republicans seized control of the lower chamber and hoped that Richard Welch of California, ranking Republican committee member, would replace her. Welch, she recollected, "had always been in my corner and had given me wonderful support on every liberal measure we had before us." Republican House leaders, however, designated Welch as chairman of the Public Lands Committee instead. Republican Fred Hartley of New Jersey, the next ranking Republican member who had served nine consecutive House terms, was appointed chairman of the newly enlarged House Education and Labor Committee. The Reorganization Act of 1946 had merged the Education Committee with the Labor Committee.[9]

Norton clashed with Hartley, a staunch conservative and bitter foe of organized labor. In January 1947, she resigned from the House Education and Labor Committee because she "could not serve with a Chairman for whom I have no respect." Norton alleged that Hartley knew little about that committee. "Hartley," Norton contended, "has attended exactly six meetings of the committee in 10 years. I refuse to serve under him. It would be too hard on my blood pressure!" Norton protested, "The Labor Committee was in the hands of its enemies." Hartley, she charged, aligned "with the members of his party who resented every gain made by labor during the Roosevelt years and had fought, with every trick they could command, to 'put labor back in its place.'"[10]

Although leaving the House Education and Labor Committee, Norton still championed labor causes. She had belonged to the Labor Committee from 1925 to 1947 and had chaired it for a decade, espousing better wages, reduced hours, improved conditions, and wider benefits for the American worker. Norton had resisted all attempts to weaken the Wagner National Labor Relations Act of 1935 and the Fair Labor Standards Act of 1938. "My devotion to labor will continue unabated," she vowed. "I sincerely hope that in the interest of industry as well as labor, the progressive legislation enacted during the past 13 years under a Democratic administration will not be repealed." Above all, she did not want any punitive amendments weakening the New Deal labor laws.

During the contentious Eightieth Congress, however, the House Education and Labor Committee stymied Norton's measures to terminate sex discrimination in industry and raise the minimum hourly wage from 40 cents to 65 cents. Norton testified that the existing 40 cents minimum, enacted nearly a decade earlier, gave "no protection whatsoever" to millions of working people and called a 65 cent hourly wage a dire necessity to forestall the privation of workers. The Republicans and conservative Democrats, who controlled Hartley's Committee, rejected both Norton bills in 1947. In a January 1947 radio interview, Norton had conceded, "Any changes I might propose would not get very far in this Congress."[11]

The Education and Labor Committee drafted new legislation that curtailed or weakened many of the New Deal labor reforms. Hartley, in 1947, proposed sweeping changes in national labor policy, combining most of the antiunion bills that conservatives had introduced since 1938. His measure banned the closed shop requiring union membership and made the union shop a subject of collective bargaining only if the employer agreed. Secondary boycotts were outlawed, and unions were subjected to antitrust legislation. Hartley's bill permitted federal injunctions against strikes deemed harmful to public welfare and let employers seek injunctions in other cases. Three separate federal agencies were designated to handle administration, prosecution, and conciliation, replacing the National Labor Relations Board. Hartley's legislation also restricted internal union activity, excluded supervisory employers from coverage, and denied bargaining rights to unions with communist officers.[12]

The Education and Labor Committee on April 11 approved the Hartley measure. Four conservative southern Democrats aligned with the Republican majority backing the Hartley bill. They contended that the Hartley legislation would decrease industrial strife, equalize labor-management relations, and rescue the worker who had "for the past fourteen years, as a result of labor laws ill-conceived and disastrously executed . . . been deprived of his dignity as an individual." Six Democrats dissented, charging the Hartley measure was "designed to wreck the living standards of the American people" and would trigger industrial chaos.[13]

During House debate, Norton helped direct the unsuccessful battle against the Hartley bill. She denounced the attempt by conservatives to stifle labor and lobbied colleagues to defeat it. The lower chamber, however, on April 17, decisively rejected a motion to recommit the bill, 291 to 122, and overwhelmingly adopted the Hartley measure, 308 to 107. Ninety-three Democrats, including 79 Southerners, aligned with the Republican majority, while 84 Democrats, including Norton, 22 Republicans, and one American Laborite, disapproved.[14]

The Senate in May approved less stringent legislation, sponsored by Republican Robert Taft of Ohio. The Conference Committee ironed out differences between the House and Senate bills, mostly accepting the latter. The House dropped its insistence on banning industry-wide collective bargaining, limiting employers' contributions to welfare funds, virtually outlawing of the union shop, subjecting unions to the antitrust laws, authorizing injunctions and damage suits by employers, and abolishing the National Labor Relations Board. The Senate, on the other hand, accepted the House bans on strikes by government employees and on political contributions by unions.[15]

During House floor debate on the Conference Committee version, Norton on June 8 assailed the Taft-Hartley measure. Although conceding that the Wagner National Labor Relations Act could be improved upon, she adamantly backed collective bargaining between management and labor. When asked why she had resigned from the House Education and Labor Committee, Norton cited Chairman Hartley. The New Jersey Republican, Norton added, "had never previously shown any interest in working men." Hartley, visibly perturbed, showed House colleagues a 1941 letter from American Federation of Labor (AFL) President William Green lauding him for his votes on some labor legislation. Norton telegrammed Green inquiring about the authenticity of the 1941 letter and soliciting his opinion of Hartley. Green replied that Hartley's attitude had changed since 1941, now making him "labor's number one enemy."[16] Norton stressed that the Wagner Act protection given labor had increased industrial production and reminded colleagues how labor had contributed significantly to defeating the Axis powers in World War II. She accused anti—New Dealers of forgetting "the great war record of labor without which it would have been impossible to win the war." "The labor baiters and the labor haters," Norton lamented, "at long last are having a field day." She called the Taft-Hartley measure "a wholesale retreat to the days when labor had no rights." Her speech triggered "a crescendo of catcalls, cries of protest, and howls of political pain."[17] Congress ignored Norton's pleas, decisively adopting the Conference Committee terms in June.

President Truman on June 20 delivered a stinging veto of the Taft-Hartley Act. He denounced the measure as unworkable and unfair and feared that it would increase strikes, restrict the subjects for collective bargaining, and deprive workers of necessary protections. To Norton's dismay, the House resoundingly overrode Truman's veto, 331 to 83, the same day. Three days later, the Senate followed suit, 68 to 25, making the law operative. The Taft-Hartley legislation sharply curtailed the Wagner Act of 1935, enumerating unfair labor practices, outlawing the closed shop, limiting the ability of unions to strike, and authorizing the president to impose eighty-day cooling off periods before workers could strike. The measure diluted national labor standards by empowering individual states to limit organizing by workplace labor. Businesses argued the legislation balanced the power between management and unions, but labor unions condemned it as a move to control working men and women and to limit their rights to fair treatment. Southern plants experienced less pressure to raise their working standards and wages to Northern levels.[18]

Norton fought to repeal the Taft-Hartley Act and urged restoration of the Wagner Act. In December 1947, she charged that the measure placed labor unions in a "straight-jacket," unable to discipline their own members and warned that denying workers a decent living standard might facilitate the spread of Communism within the nation. According to Norton, "None profited more from protective labor legislation than the National Association of Manufacturers, that group of little men who wrote this bill for their own profit and found a subservient Republican Congress ready and anxious to do their bidding." Election year politics blocked House action on Norton's repeal pleas for the remainder of the Eightieth Congress. In March 1948, Norton detected, "There have been so many things in our country and throughout the world to upset us all but I think that some of them can be blamed on the fact that this is an election year. Some people just can't put the really big issues above politics."[19]

After the Democrats regained control of Congress in the 1948 elections, the Truman administration and labor unions renewed their campaigns to repeal the entire Taft-Hartley Act. In a radio address over the American Broadcasting Company on February 5, Norton denounced the Taft-Hartley Act as being "born out of desire for repression." The Taft-Hartley measure, she protested, was "not just a step backward—but a wholesale retreat to the days when labor had no rights under the laws." In April, Norton again trumpeted rescinding the Taft-Hartley law and defended collective bargaining. "Everything," she declared, "depends on whether one is really, honestly for or against collective bargaining. If we are sincere and want workers to organize and bargain through their own representatives, we will vote (to) terminate Taft-Hartley at once."

Although Hartley did not seek reelection in 1948, like-minded Democrat John Wood of Georgia proposed a bill resembling the Taft-Hartley Act. Taft introduced legislation altering his original act substantially. With Norton dissenting, the House on May 3 approved the Wood bill, 217 to 203. The following day, however, Norton aligned with the majority to send the Wood bill back to the Education and Labor Committee by a 212 to 209 vote. The Senate passed the Taft bill easily, but House Republicans and Southern Democrats still preferred the Wood bill. The Taft-Hartley Act remained intact, as Norton's pleas for outright repeal went unanswered.[20]

Government reorganization likewise drew Norton's attention. In May 1946, she urged President Truman to transfer the independent Children's Bureau to the Federal Security Administration to enable it to better help thousands of European orphans and homeless children. Truman agreed that the Children's Bureau belonged in the Federal Security Administration and pledged, "If we get cabinet rank for that organization, as I hope we will, you will find that we will have a Children's Bureau that will really function." Norton also secured House approval of her measure enlarging the U.S. Department of Labor to include an undersecretary and three assistants, thus improving its efficiency and expanding its operations.

When the House debated the Labor-Federal Security Agency appropriation in 1947, Norton opposed transferring the child labor and youth employment programs from the Division of Labor Standards to the Wage and Hour Division within the Labor Department. She viewed the Wage and Hour Division as "chiefly an enforcement agency" that was "not equipped to develop better state child labor standards by working with the states and various community organizations." To Norton's chagrin, the House approved the transfer without a roll call vote.

Norton also backed the Reorganization Act of 1946, which streamlined the cumbersome congressional committee system. The measure reduced the number of standing committees and carefully defined their jurisdiction, upgraded staff support for legislators, strengthened congressional oversight of executive agencies, and created an elaborate procedure to put congressional spending and taxation policies on a more rational basis. The House, however, disappointed Norton by not voting on the section establishing pensions for representatives. "I was amazed at some of the speeches in the Record against the reorganization bill," Norton wrote. "What hypocrites there are in the world," she charged. "Some of those who spoke against it—I mean the salary part & retirement provisions—were among those most anxious to have a bill go thru. They knew they were on safe ground." Norton, who had predicted there would not be a roll call vote, vowed, "I'm one, if I had been there who would have spoken in favor of it."[21]

Norton joined the newly formed House Administration Committee in January 1947. The Reorganization Act of 1946 had established the House Administration Committee, which combined the Accounts, Disposition of Executive Papers, Enrolled Bills, Library, Memorials, and Printing Committees. The Administration Committee managed the House operations, the auditing and paying of House bills, the travel allowances for members on official business, the printing of the *Congressional Record*, and the operation of the House stationary store. It also administered the Library of Congress, the House Library, Statutory Hall, and the Botanic Gardens, and handled federal election laws involving the president, vice president, and congressional members, contested elections, corrupt practices, and credentials and qualifications.

The Administration Committee meetings were held in a large, old-fashioned room with fireplaces in the old section of the Capitol under the dome. Pictures of former senators and representatives adorned the walls. Norton, who became ranking Minority Committee member in 1947 because of her House seniority, found this assignment much less tense, partisan, and physically demanding than the Labor Committee post. "Few controversial matters are handled by the Administration Committee," she learned, "and the members work together harmoniously, with a minimum of partisan politics." The lightened load gave Norton more time to concentrate on the needs and problems of her district constituents and New Jersey residents on other legislative issues. Since New Jersey Democrats had no senators and only two representatives in the House, her caseload greatly increased. Democrats throughout the state asked her to handle problems dealing with immigration, veterans, and other issues.[22]

Jersey City politics likewise changed. Hague, who had persuaded Norton to pursue a political career, retired in June 1947 at age 72 during his eighth term as Jersey City mayor after having served three decades. He remained chairman of the state and county Democratic parties and vice chairman of the Democratic National Committee until 1949. Jersey City had grown from a small town to a large industrial city during Hague's tenure, boasting one of the nation's finest hospitals, good police and fire departments, and excellent schools. Hague, however, had operated an arbitrary, corrupt machine that controlled Jersey City politics. His machine had passed its prime by June 1947, when his nephew, Frank Hague Eggers, succeeded him as mayor.[23]

Several factors influenced Hague's retirement as mayor and the decline of his political machine. Hague either may have tired of the political arena or lost the will to rule, as reflected by his more frequent absences from Jersey City. He increasingly stayed at his Key Biscayne, Florida, home or his Park Avenue penthouse, avoiding pending lawsuits against him regarding salary kickbacks and averting prosecution despite the many charges of corruption and impropriety. The altered demography of

Jersey City also had diminished Hague's political influence. Jersey City's population peaked at 316,715 in the 1930 census and declined by over 15,000 to 301,012 in the 1940 census. The decrease in property owners and voters lowered the city's revenue base. Older ethnic groups, including the Irish-Americans, left the inner city for the suburbs, being replaced by Polish-Americans, Italian-Americans, and African-Americans. Hague had failed to give the new constituent groups representation in his administration. New government-sponsored social services replaced Hague's patronage system and ward leaders in providing economic assistance for Jersey City residents.[24]

Hague fought attempts to revise the New Jersey constitution, resisting a state income tax, changes in the tenure and pensions of public employees, and taxation of church property. Republican Alfred Driscoll, who replaced Walter Edge as Governor in 1947, led the movement to rewrite the New Jersey constitution. Hague's personal control of Jersey City and state politics crumbled, as the Republicans swept local elections in May 1949. John Kenney, one of Hague's former subordinates, resoundingly unseated Eggers as Jersey City mayor, securing 57 percent of the popular vote.[25] The impact of Hague's departure on Norton's political future in Congress remained unclear.

President Truman, meanwhile, welcomed Norton's inspirational messages during his often stormy first term and especially his 1948 presidential campaign. He liked her "gratifying assurances" adding, "I cannot tell you how much I appreciate your splendid cooperation." In March 1948, Truman reported finding "the strength which you are praying that God will give me in the fight in which we are engaged. These are indeed difficult times and one appreciates a pledge of loyal support such as you give."[26]

Norton served for the seventh time as a delegate at large at the Democratic National Convention in July 1948 at Philadelphia, Pennsylvania. The convention was held in extremely hot weather. "I went reluctantly," Norton confessed, "dreading the next few days." She zealously backed President Truman against stern challenges from Governor Strom Thurmond of South Carolina and former Vice President Henry Wallace. Thurmond became the States Rights candidate for president in 1948, resisting Truman's civil rights policies and appealing to some Southern conservatives. Wallace became the Progressive Party candidate for president in 1948 and was backed by some Northern liberals, who opposed Truman's containment policies toward the Soviet Union. Other Northern Democrats considered Truman's prospects hopeless and privately courted General Dwight D. Eisenhower for president.

The Democratic National Convention drained Norton physically, but she remained solidly in Truman's camp. Although admiring Eisenhower's military record, Norton did not consider him a good Democratic presidential candidate. "It was a difficult situation and terribly depressing as the wrangling went on," she detected, "with the newspaper writers and the radio commentators talking about a party committing suicide." From the outset, she declared, "I was for Truman. I couldn't see it any other way. Even if I had, I would have maintained my stand, for I had personally pledged my loyalty to him. I profoundly believe he deserved it."

Norton in 1948 also became the first woman to chair the Credentials Committee at a political party convention. The Democratic National Committee designated Norton because of her vast congressional experience, common sense, and popular party standing. As Credentials Committee Chair, she favored seating those delegates defending labor gains and supporting containment. After confronting several credentials battles, however, she confessed, "I would gladly have passed the honor along to someone else!"[27]

Norton had to decide which of two competing delegations to seat from Mississippi. The Mississippi contingent clashed over whether the party platform should include a civil rights plank. The regularly elected delegation opposed including a civil rights plank, while the contesting contingent supported it. Although sympathizing with the contesting delegation, she did not let her personal views influence the Credentials Committee decision. "If I did," Norton knew, "it would be a long, long time before any woman would again have the opportunity to be chairman of a committee." The convention waited several hours for the Credentials Committee report so that the Mississippi contingent could be seated and the delegates could transact business. The Credentials Committee remained deadlocked until a late arriving member cast the tie-breaking vote for the regularly elected Mississippi delegation. George Vaughan, a Missouri delegate who favored seating the contesting contingent, vowed to submit a minority report and insist upon a roll call vote. Norton, though, knew that a roll call of the 1,234 convention delegates would take considerable time and reached an understanding with Vaughan. Norton agreed that, after submitting her majority report, she would yield most of her twenty minutes for Vaughn to give his minority report if he did not demand a roll call.[28]

Norton delivered the majority Credentials Committee report to the convention delegates in just five minutes, letting Vaughan use the remaining fifteen minutes to lobby for a civil rights plank. Vaughan, an eloquent speaker, stirred the convention delegates, especially those from New York, New Jersey, Illinois, and California. "The Mississippi Democrats may be absolutely certain that their delegates will positively withdraw from the convention," he warned, "unless the party embodies in its platform a positive plank that it will fight to uphold civil rights!" Norton empathized with Vaughan, noting, "He was fighting for something we all believed in, something for which I had fought all the years I was in Congress—civil rights."[29]

Senator Alben Barkley of Kentucky, the temporary convention chairman, encountered difficulty in keeping order among the contentious delegates. Senator Carl Hatch of New Mexico argued that the majority of the Credentials Committee favored seating the regularly elected Mississippi delegation. Norton moved that the majority Credentials Committee report be accepted. The motion carried on a voice vote. "Had he (Vaughan) insisted on a roll call," Norton believed "he would have won. The outcome that night brought no personal satisfaction to me, for it meant victory for the element that had opposed almost everything I had stood for in the House—NLRB, the Wage and Hour Law, FEPC, abolition of the poll tax." The delegates adopted the party platform, which eventually included a civil rights plank, elected House Majority Leader Sam Rayburn of Texas convention chairman and heard Rayburn deliver the keynote address.

Later that evening, Norton and Representative Helen Gahagan Douglas of California made a stirring appeal to women to participate in the 1948 presidential campaign and vote in the November election. Norton's speech unfortunately did not begin until after midnight. "I would gladly have withdrawn," she recollected, "but the fact that Helen Gahagan Douglas and I had been put on the program at an evening session meant a good deal to the women." Norton already had been seated on the hot platform stage for over five hours and did not get to bed until around 2:30 a.m.[30]

"The following night, however, more than made up for the heat, fatigue, and frustration of that day," Norton reminisced. Delegates nominated Truman as their presidential candidate and Barkley as their vice presidential selection. When Eisenhower removed his name from consideration, the Northeastern, Midwestern, and Western delegates rallied behind Truman. The Southern delegates, who had resisted the inclusion of a civil rights plank in the party platform, backed Senator Richard Russell of Georgia for president and walked out of the convention when Truman won the nomination. Norton saw Truman shortly afterward just inside the convention hall entrance. "The President, dressed in an immaculate white linen suit," she remembered, "was calm and relaxed, the last man in the world you would have guessed might be the subject of so much controversy." A few minutes later, Truman delivered a stirring acceptance speech. He cited the monumental gains that farmers, laborers, and the poor had made since 1933 and chastised the Republican-dominated Eightieth Congress for not passing his housing, education, medical care, and civil rights legislation.[31]

Norton campaigned strenuously for Truman in New Jersey, rallying women behind the Democratic Party. "We all worked hard in that campaign," she recollected. "Frank Hague threw his whole heart into it and put on a show for President Truman in New Jersey surpassing anything he had done previously for Smith or Roosevelt." New Jersey voters, though, rejected the Norton and Hague pleas. Governor Thomas Dewey of New York, the Republican presidential candidate, bested Truman in the November 1948 election by nearly 100,000 votes out of almost 1.8 million votes cast in the Garden State.[32]

Truman, however, pulled one of the biggest upsets in American political history, defeating Dewey nationally by over two million popular votes and by 303 to 189 in the Electoral College to retain the presidency. Norton explained, "It was really Harry Truman himself who won that fight—by just being Harry Truman, talking straight from-the-shoulder to Mr. and Mrs. America at the whistle stops." Truman had crisscrossed the United States by train, delivering numerous passionate impromptu talks denouncing the Eightieth Congress. Following the election, Truman wrote Norton, "I do, of course, feel very deeply the responsibilities entrusted to me, but with the cooperation of all I hope to bring to a successful conclusion the momentous issues facing us."[33]

The Democrats regained control of the U.S. Congress, adding 9 Senate seats for a 54 to 42 advantage and 75 House seats for a 263 to 171 advantage. Norton won reelection for a thirteenth consecutive term with over 68 percent of the vote, outpolling Republican challenger Leon Banach, 84,487 to 39,661. She campaigned actively this time, vowing to repeal the Taft-Hartley Act, and bettered her 1946 performance by 4 percent. Hague's diminished political influence in Jersey City did not appear to hurt her. Democrats gained three seats in the New Jersey delegation, with Charles Howell, Peter Rodino Jr., and Hugh Addonizio defeating nonincumbent Republicans. To Norton's delight, Rodino replaced Hartley, who had not sought reelection. Democrats regained the House leadership, with Sam Rayburn of Texas succeeding Republican Joseph Martin of Massachusetts as speaker.

Norton became chairman of the House Administration Committee in January 1949, making her the only woman ever to head four congressional committees. She already was the dean of women members and the oldest woman in the U.S. Congress. Norton enjoyed this position as much as her three previous chairmanships, but found it much less stressful and arduous. "Serving as chairman of the House Administration Committee," she acknowledged, "was one of the happiest experiences I had during all my years in Congress." As committee chair, Norton secured the House adoption of more than seventy resolutions and bills. She enlisted niece Jeanne McDonagh, younger sister of Marion and Lucille, to work as secretary and Administration Committee clerk. McDonagh served two years in that capacity, resigning in November 1950 to join a public relations firm in New York City. According to Norton, "She was a very great help to me and is really a remarkably efficient young lady."[34]

Shortly after Norton assumed control of the Administration Committee, Congress restricted the power of the House Rules Committee. Norton often had battled with the Rules Committee over labor legislation when head of the Labor Committee. The House adopted a Democratic Party caucus resolution preventing the Rules Committee from wielding its power arbitrarily to withhold legislation from the House floor for more than twenty-one days. House committee heads could introduce a resolution asking for House debate on any measure already favorably reported by a standing committee and not acted upon in twenty-one days by the Rules Committee. The twenty-one-day rule prevented a few Rules Committee members from killing legislation by blocking measures from reaching the House floor for debate. The House action, Norton affirmed, "gave me more satisfaction than anything that had happened in the House in years." "The Rules Committee," she declared, "was at last shorn of the power it had exercised in so high-handed a manner." The twenty-one-day rule, though, lasted only for the duration of the Eighty-first Congress and was rescinded in January 1951.[35]

Norton's most spirited confrontation as Administration Committee head came in 1949 when she introduced a controversial civil rights measure forbidding states from requiring citizens to pay a poll tax before voting primaries and elections for national offices. Since the 1890s, Southern states had compelled voters to pay a poll tax to vote in primary or general elections affecting Congress and other federal offices. Poll taxes had disenfranchised numerous African-American voters in southern states. Norton's bill attempted to expand voting rights to all persons regardless of race by eliminating the poll tax. Anti–poll tax legislation had stalled in Congress for decades, but the 1948 Democratic Party National Convention had revived the issue by including civil rights in its platform.

The Administration Committee approved Norton's civil rights measure, but the conservative-dominated House Rules Committee sought to block House floor debate. In order to force her bill out of the Rules Committee, Norton employed the new twenty-one-day rule. "We patiently waited for the time to run out," she recalled, "and then invoked the 21-Day Rule—the first time it was used."[36] The House in July 1949 brought Norton's anti–poll tax measure out of the Rules Committee to the floor for consideration.

Amidst a torrid late July heat wave, the House debated Norton's anti–poll tax bill for two days. Norton directed the floor battle for her legislation, but conservative Southern Democrats delayed House floor action by forcing eight quorum calls. Norton, undeterred in her quest for a House vote on her anti–poll tax measure, vowed, "If necessary, members will be kept in session all night to complete debate on this bill!" Representatives on July 26 overwhelmingly approved her anti–poll tax legislation, 273 to 116. "It was the last general bill I sponsored,"[37] Norton recollected. Conservative Southern senators, however, filibustered to block passage of Norton's measure, delaying congressional approval for another fifteen years. Congress did not enact anti–poll tax legislation until the Civil Rights Act of 1964.[38] Norton's Administration Committee also secured funding for expanding the Legislative Reference Service of the Library of Congress, the principal research branch for Senate and House members.

To plan events for the 150th anniversary of the federal government in Washington, D.C., President Truman in 1949 appointed Norton to the National Capitol Sesquicentennial Commission. The nation's capitol had moved from New York City to Washington, D.C., in 1800. Norton in late 1949 introduced a bill authorizing $3 million for the Washington, D.C., sesquicentennial celebration and led the floor debate for her measure. Besides emphasizing that her bill would commemorate the 150th anniversary of the federal government in Washington, she noted that previous congressional appropriations had helped fund fairs in New York City, Chicago, and many other cities. Norton grumbled, "No matter what happens in the District, it seems to be nobody's business, because everybody seems to think we're doing something for the District, whereas we should be doing it as members of Congress whose duty it is to legislate for the District of Columbia!" She hoped the measure would "not be used as a whipping boy by people who are talking about what they are going to save the taxpayers." Norton realized, though, "Once more I was on my feet battling the indifference and prejudice of the members toward their national capital."

Conservative representatives fought using taxpayer money as gifts to the District of Columbia and insisted that Washington, D.C., should support itself. Norton countered, "Let us not say we are doing this for the District of Columbia. We are doing it because we want the people not only in the United States but all over the world to know that we appreciate the fact that this Government has been meeting here in the Capital of the United States for 150 years." Norton's passionate speech stirred Democrat McCormack of Massachusetts to term it "the most effective . . . ever made on the floor of the House." Congress initially rejected the $3 million appropriation, but later approved it.[39]

The Eighty-first Congress, spurred by the Democratic Party resurgence, enacted the most progressive legislation since the Second New Deal. Norton ardently backed Truman's Fair Deal measures, including an amendment to the Fair Labor Standards Act raising the minimum wage from 40 cents to 75 cents an hour and the National Housing Act providing funding for slum clearance and the construction of 800,000 housing units for low-income families. These bills particularly benefited her Jersey City and Bayonne constituents. Congress also adopted legislation raising social security benefits for retirees and broadening coverage to include ten million additional persons, extending rent controls, admitting 400,000 refugees to the United States, and increasing the salaries and benefits of postal workers and other federal employees. To Norton's chagrin, however, that Republicans and conservative Democrats thwarted measures for national health insurance, federal aid to education, civil rights, and repeal of the Taft-Hartley Act.[40]

New Jersey and constituent issues still commanded Norton's attention. Norton recommended the appointment of over 100 postmasters for New Jersey and handled hundreds of veterans and immigration cases from her district and throughout the Garden State. When Secretary of Defense Louis Johnson proposed the reduction of defense personnel, she fought to retain an adequate contingent in the military and naval establishments in her district and across New Jersey.

Norton, filled with human compassion, relished steering through the House a measure permitting Burmese nurses Ruby Thaw and Ella Sein to stay permanently in the United States. Thaw and Sein had volunteered as nurses with General Joseph Stilwell during his retreat from Burma in March 1942 and had worked at first aid depots when the American soldiers returned. Dr. Gordon Seagrave, a medical missionary, arranged for Thaw and Sein in 1947 to pursue postgraduate study in obstetrical nursing at Margaret Hague Maternity Hospital in Jersey City. Immigration laws required Thaw and Sein to return to Burma unless Congress let them stay. "Had they returned to their native land," Norton feared, "they would very likely have been shot." She stressed, "All who knew the girls and were familiar with the heroic service they had given agreed wholeheartedly that they should be allowed to remain permanently in this country." The House, moved by Norton's humanitarian story, permitted the nurses to remain in the United States. "This was the last 'private bill' I introduced," Norton related. "None gave me more satisfaction."[41]

Norton's energy, intelligence, integrity, and candor continued to impress and inspire her colleagues. Democrat Reva Beck Bosone of Utah, who joined the U.S. House of Representatives in January 1949 and often lunched with the New Jersey Democrat, wrote, "Mrs. Norton is 74 years of age, but one would never know it." She added, "Mrs. Norton has the respect of everyone on Capitol Hill. She is a colorful personality, who is loved because she is fair and fearless." Bosone observed, "If anyone ever had doubts about whether or not a woman was so politically constituted to withstand the rigors of this strenuous life here in Washington, they would be dispelled. Mrs. Norton has never been 'wishy-washy'; she has taken very definite stands on all important legislation." The response of male colleagues toward Norton likewise impressed Bosone. "She is beloved by all of the men because of her stalwart character."[42]

During the twilight of her congressional career, Norton received several awards for distinguished public service. The Women's National Press Club of Washington, D.C., in 1946 gave her the Woman of Achievement Award as that year's outstanding woman in government and one of the nation's ten most outstanding women. In May 1947, Theta Phi Alpha, the National Catholic University Women sorority, presented Norton the Siena medal for being the Roman Catholic woman of the year in community and national service. Archbishop Richard Cushing gave Norton the medal at a pontifical mass at St. Catherine's Church in Norwood, Massachusetts, on the six hundredth anniversary of the birth of St. Catherine of Siena, a fourteenth century Dominican nun.[43] Norton knew, "It was far more than I deserve." "Some honors have come to me during my long life, but none has given me the joy I experienced on that morning." The sorority made her a lifetime member. She concluded, "It does give one some satisfaction not to have to wait until one dies to hear nice things about themselves."[44] The International Relations Club of the College of St. Elizabeth in 1949 also recognized her for performing outstanding government service. These awards came as Norton entered the final phase of her illustrious congressional career.

NOTES

1. Mary T. Norton, "Madam Congressman: The Memoirs of Mary T. Norton of New Jersey," (Hereafter cited as "Memoirs"), Mary T. Norton MSS, New Jersey Collection, Archibald Stevens Alexander Library, Rutgers, The State University of New Jersey, p. 229.

2. Norton, "Memoirs," pp. 230–31.

3. Mary T. Norton, "The War is Not Over," Report, International Labor Organization Conference, Paris, France, October 1945, Norton MSS, Box 5, Speeches, 1941–1952; Norton, "Memoirs," pp. 227, 234.

4. Norton, "Memoirs," pp. 235–36; Marion McDonagh Burke, Interview with Author, August 7, 1981; Mary T. Norton Press Release, January 1947, Norton MSS, Box 4, Personal Biographical Material.

5. Norton, "Memoirs," pp. 236–37.

6. Susan M. Hartmann, *Truman and the 80th Congress* (Columbia, MO: University of Missouri Press, 1971), pp. 63–64, 164.

7. Mary T. Norton to Harry S. Truman, May 22, 1946, Norton MSS, Box 2, Corr., Truman, 1946–1949; Harry S. Truman to Mary T. Norton, May 28, 1946, Norton MSS, Box 2, Corr., Truman, 1946–1949; David McCullough, *Truman* (New York: Simon & Schuster, 1992), p. 468; Daniel Paul Gitterman, *Boosting Paychecks: the Politics of Supporting America's Working Poor* (Washington, D.C.: Brookings Institution, 2009), pp. 48, 50; Mary T. Norton Record on Labor, circa 1949, Norton MSS, Box 4, Personal Biographical Material; Harry S. Truman, "Special Message to the Congress Presenting a 21-Point Program for the Reconversion Period," September 6, 1945, American Presidency Project, http://www.presidency.ucsb.edu.

8. Norton, "Memoirs," p. 237; Norton to Kendrick, July 29, 1946; "Statistics of the Congressional Election of November 5, 1946," (Washington, D.C.: U.S. Government Printing Office, 1947), p. 22.

9. Norton, "Memoirs," p. 238.

10. Angeline Bogucki, "Summary of the Legislative Career of Representative Mary T. Norton," Legislative Reference Service, Library of Congress, Washington, D.C., November 3, 1950, p. 14; Hope Chamberlin, *A Minority of Members: Women in the U.S. Congress* (New York: Praeger Publishers, 1973), p. 58; Mary T. Norton, Press Release, Washington, D.C., January 1947, Norton MSS, Box 4, Personal Biographical Material; Norton Labor Record; Margot Gayle, "Battling Mary Retires," *Independent Woman* 29 (July 1950), p. 198; Norton, "Memoirs," p. 238; *Washington Post*, August 3, 1959, p. B2.

11. *Washington Post*, Aug. 3, 1959, p. 2B; Norton, Press Release, Jan. 1947; Bogucki, "Summary," p. 14; U.S. Congress, House of Representatives, Hearings, Subcommittee no. 4, Committee on Education and Labor, Minimum Wage Standards, 80th Cong., 1st

Sess., pp. 39–51; Mary T. Norton, Radio Interview, WOL, Washington, D.C., January 22, 1947, Norton MSS, Box 5, Speeches, Labor, 1937–1949; Gayle, "Battling Mary Retires," p. 198.

12. *New York Times*, August 3, 1959; Mary T. Norton, Speech, New Jersey CIO Convention, December 6, 1947, Norton MSS, Box 5, Speeches, Labor, 1937–1949; Hartmann, *Truman and the 80th Congress*, p. 83; Harry A. Millis and Emily Clark Brown, *From the Wagner Act to Taft-Hartley: A Study of National Labor Policy and Labor Relations* (Chicago, IL: University of Chicago Press, 1950), pp. 383–94; Richard S. Kirkendall, ed., *The Harry S. Truman Encyclopedia* (Boston, MA: G. K. Hall & Company, 1989), p. 354. For history of the Taft-Hartley Act, see R. Alton Lee, *Truman and Taft-Hartley: A Question of Mandate* (Lexington, KY: University of Kentucky Press, 1966).

13. Hartmann, *Truman and the 80th Congress*, p. 82; Norton Labor Record.

14. *New York Times*, April 18, 1947, pp. 1, 6; *New York Times*, Aug. 3, 1959.

15. Millis, *Wagner Act to Taft-Hartley*, pp. 383–84; Gilbert Y. Steiner, *The Congressional Conference Committee: Seventieth to Eightieth Congresses* (Urbana, IL: University of Illinois Press, 1951), pp. 167–68; Hartmann, *Truman and the 80th Congress*, pp. 84–86.

16. Norton, "Memoirs," p. 239.

17. Norton, Speech, New Jersey CIO Convention, Dec. 6, 1947; *New York Times*, Aug. 3, 1959; *Washington Times-Herald*, June 8, 1947.

18. Marcy Kaptur, *Women of Congress: A Twentieth Century Odyssey* (Washington, D.C.: Congressional Quarterly, 1996), pp. 48–49.

19. Norton, Speech, New Jersey CIO Convention, Dec. 6, 1947; Mary T. Norton to Teresa, March 13, 1948, Norton MSS, Box 1, Gen. Corr., 1948.

20. Bogucki, "Summary," Nov. 3, 1950, p. 15; *Congressional Record*, 81st Cong., 1st Sess., p. 5267; Norton, "Memoirs," p. 240.

21. Katherine Kempfer and Dorothea K. Blender, "Our Congresswomen in Action," *Women's Lawyers Journal* 33 (Summer 1947), p. 204; Mary T. Norton to Charlotte Kendrick, July 29, 1946, Norton MSS, Box 1, Gen. Corr., 1946.

22. Norton, Press Release, Jan. 1947; Norton, "Memoirs," pp. 249–51.

23. Carmela Karnoutsos, "Frank Hague, 1876–1956," *Jersey City Past and Present Home Page*, New Jersey State Historical Commission, http://www.njcu.edu; Thomas Fleming, "I Am the Law," *American Heritage* XX (June 1969), pp. 45–46, 48.

24. Karnoutsos, "Frank Hague"; Fleming, "I Am the Law," p. 48.

25. Norton, "Memoirs," pp. 253–54; *New York Times*, April 25, 1952; *Washington Star*, January 2, 1956, p. 22.

26. Harry S. Truman to Mary T. Norton, January 5, 1946, Norton MSS, Box 2, Corr., Truman, 1946–1949; Harry S. Truman to Mary T. Norton, March 22, 1948, Norton MSS, Box 2, Corr., Truman, 1946–1949; Burke, Interview with Author, Aug. 7, 1981.

27. Norton, "Memoirs," pp. 242–43; Mary Tobin, Press Release, Woman's Division, Democratic National Committee, May 24, 1948, Norton MSS, Box 3, Political, Miscellaneous.

28. Norton, "Memoirs," p. 244.

29. Norton, "Memoirs," pp. 244–45.

30. Norton, "Memoirs," pp. 245–46.

31. Norton, "Memoirs," pp. 246–47. For an account of the 1948 Democratic Party convention, see McCullough, *Truman*, pp. 632–43.

32. Norton, "Memoirs," p. 247.

33. Hartmann, *Truman and the 80th Congress*, p. 208; Norton Labor Record; Truman to Mary T. Norton, November 18, 1948, Norton MSS, Box 2, Corr., Truman, 1946–1949. For the election, see McCullough, *Truman*, pp. 709–19 and Irwin Ross, *The Loneliest Campaign: The Truman Victory of 1948* (New York: New American Library, 1968).

34. "Statistics of the Presidential and Congressional Election of November 2, 1948," (Washington, D.C.: U.S. Government Printing Office, 1949), p. 26; Emily A. Geer, "A Study of the Activities of Women in Congress With Special Reference to the Congressional Careers of Margaret Chase Smith, Mary T. Norton, and Edith Nourse Rogers," (Masters thesis: Bowling Green State University, 1952), p. 135; Kaptur, *Women of Con-*

gress, p. 49; Norton, "Memoirs," p. 249; "Record of Honorable Mary T. Norton (D. N. J.) in the Eighty-first Congress, 1st Session," Norton MSS, Box 3, Congressional Voting Record, Statistics; Mary T. Norton to Rev. Mother O'Byrne, December 5, 1950, Norton MSS, Box 2, Gen. Corr., June-December, 1950.

35. Norton, "Memoirs," pp. 248–49.

36. Norton, "Memoirs," pp. 251–52; Norton Record, Eighty-first Congress; Kaptur, *Women of Congress*, pp. 48–49.

37. Gayle, "Battling Mary Retires," p. 198; Norton, "Memoirs," p. 252.

38. Kaptur, *Women of Congress*, p. 49; Rudolf Englebarts, *Women in the United States Congress, 1917–1972: Their Accomplishments: with Bibliographies* (Littleton, CO: Libraries Unlimited, 1974), pp. 30–32.

39. Norton, "Memoirs," p. 253; *Congressional Record*, Vol. 95, Pt. 11, p. 14255; Norton Record, Eighty-first Congress; Bogucki, "Summary," p. 10.

40. For a summary of Fair Deal legislation, see Alonzo Hamby, *Beyond the New Deal: Harry S. Truman and American Liberalism* (New York: Columbia University Press, 1973).

41. Norton, "Memoirs," pp. 256–57; Norton Record, Eighty-first Congress.

42. Reva Beck Bosone to the Readers of the *American Fork-Citizen*, "Life with Congress," April 9, 1949, Norton MSS, Box 1, Gen. Corr., 1949. For comments by Norton's male colleagues, see Chapter 9.

43. Mary T. Norton to Elizabeth A. Conkey, February 11, 1946, Norton MSS, Box 1, Gen. Corr., 1946; Norton, "Memoirs," pp. 241–42.

44. Katherine Keliher Moran to John McCormack, May 1, 1947, Norton MSS, Box 1, Gen. Corr., January-May, 1947; Mary T. Norton to Archbishop Cushing, May 1947, Norton MSS, Box 1, Gen. Corr., Jan.-May, 1947; Mary T. Norton to Mrs. John McCormack, May 6, 1947, Norton MSS, Box 1, Gen. Corr., Jan.-May 1947; Mary T. Norton to Elizabeth, May 21, 1947, Norton MSS, Box 1, Gen. Corr., Jan.-May 1947.

NINE

The Finale and Legacies

The New Jersey political scene had changed significantly by 1949 when Norton began serving her thirteenth term in the U.S. House of Representatives. The collapse of Mayor Frank Hague's political control of Jersey City, the adoption of a new state constitution, and the shift of political power from the Democratic-leaning cities to the Republican-inclined suburbs sharply diminished the influence of the New Jersey Democratic Party. New Jersey's elections increasingly became more competitive. Urban parties no longer held safe seats, for which victories were ensured. Norton needed to file by March 9, 1950, if she planned to seek reelection for another congressional term. She already was the dean of the New Jersey congressional delegation and had served in the U.S. House of Representatives longer than any other woman.[1]

As the twenty-fifth anniversary of her joining the House approached in 1950, Norton began contemplating retirement. "I set as my goal twenty-five years in Congress," she revealed, "and always in the back of my mind I had the idea that when I had achieved that goal I would retire." The news of Norton's possible retirement alarmed her Thirteenth Congressional District constituents. "The pressure on me to continue was heavy," she recalled. "Mail began to pour in from my district." The constituent response, coupled with Norton's vast House experience and her desire to inspire other women to serve in Congress, prompted her to delay retirement. According to Norton, "Some of my friends in the House talked to me long and earnestly, pointing out that my years of experience could be of great value both to my party and to my country in this difficult period. I realized, too, that there were too few women in the House."[2]

Democrat Reva Beck Bosone of Utah on March 3 gave Norton several reasons why she should remain in Congress and persuaded her to reconsider. "She was so convincing," Norton admitted, "that as I left the floor that afternoon I whispered to her, 'You win!'" Norton decided to seek a fourteenth consecutive House term. She planned to announce her decision on March 7, her seventy-fifth birthday, and to travel to Jersey City the next day to meet the March 9 filing deadline. "I went to bed that Friday night relieved that at last I had made my decision," she recollected. "Once more I would be a candidate for Congress."[3]

Norton, however, woke up the next morning with a migraine headache and postponed the dinner she had scheduled with her sisters, Anne and Loretta, and Jeanne McDonagh to celebrate her twenty-fifth anniversary in Congress. "By 3 o'clock I realized that I was really ill," Norton recalled. "Dr. (George) Calver had come out from the Capitol and wanted to send me to the Naval Hospital at Bethesda at once." Norton initially resisted Dr. Calver's wishes, but promised to go if her fever rose. "By 7 o'clock it had reached 104," she remembered, "an ambulance was called, and I was on my way to the hospital. Dr. Calver knew how sick I was and had made all the arrangements." Norton not only had contracted pneumonia and influenza, but also suffered considerable pain from the congestion in her lungs.[4]

The hospitalization dashed Norton's reelection plans. Health problems, she realized, would prevent her from campaigning for another congressional term. After a visit from Dr. Calver, Norton on March 7 scribbled on the back of an envelope: "Please advise my friends that I will not be a candidate in November." When Jeanne McDonagh brought Norton gifts and numerous birthday messages the next morning. Norton handed her the retirement note. After reading the note, Jeanne stared at Norton. "I prayed for a sign," Norton told McDonagh, "and I certainly got it!" A March 8 press release officially stated that Norton would not be a candidate for reelection to the Eighty-second Congress in November 1950 because of ill health. "This critical illness had come so suddenly that it seemed to me it must be an answer to my weeks of indecision and probably to prayer," Norton concluded. "I accepted it."[5]

India Edwards, vice chairman of the Democratic National Committee and director of its Women's Division, had planned a surprise birthday party for Norton on March 7. One hundred people, including colleagues, other politicians, friends, and family, had been invited to a luncheon in the Speaker's dining room at the Capitol Building. Norton's hospitalization for pneumonia forced postponement of that celebration until April 26. The invitees instead sent her a moving testimonial letter commending her successful career, noting her "sense of humor, charity, true Christianity, and loyalty to your friends that knows no price too high to pay." The House Administration Committee likewise postponed a surprise birthday party for Norton.[6]

During her hospitalization, Norton reflected on her health problems. "Some mean Republican must have put the 'double cross' on me," she wrote President Truman, "else surely I could not have spent such an important birthday in the hospital." But, Norton added, "I have fooled him for I am going to be as well as ever soon." She concluded, "My unfortunate attack has made me realize how very fortunate I am in the warm friendships I have made through my long years in Congress, expressed so beautifully in the hundreds of letters and telegrams I received at a time when I needed encouragement to get well."[7]

Norton's hospitalization gave her an appreciation of the overwhelming concern shown by colleagues and more time to reflect upon her significant career. "I cannot tell you," she wrote Republican Senator Margaret Chase Smith of Maine, "how much the messages and letters from my friends have meant to me during these tedious days." "It certainly was unfortunate to have been stricken before my birthday," Norton acknowledged, "when so much time and thought had been given to making it one for me to remember." She exclaimed, "My twenty-six years in the Congress have been years of rich reward. They will mean much to me in the days ahead and always I shall feel that I have been greatly privileged to have served my country and my district at a time when history was in the making."[8]

Southern Democrats, often among Norton's most vocal critics, even set aside their political and ideological differences. House Appropriations Committee Chairman Clarence Cannon of Missouri observed that they had served together during "the greatest period in the annals of America and the history of the world" and commended Norton for having "a very large part in that history and a still larger part in that record of accomplishments."[9] House Ways and Means Committee Chairman Robert Doughton of North Carolina stressed, "No one has performed his or her duties more faithfully, efficiently or conscientiously." "You have such an understanding heart, you are such a dignified, fine looking woman, a woman who has succeeded in every possible way that it is for any woman," Frank Boykin of Alabama wrote. "There is no one who has more judgment, more energy and ability and a bigger and a better heart."[10] Wright Patman of Texas declared, "I know of no one who is held in higher esteem," while J. Hardin Peterson of Florida wrote, "I can well believe the long, fine service you have rendered your state and your nation and the wonderful record you have made in the House, both in accomplishments and in making friends among the members." Oft-time adversary Edward Cox of Georgia even termed Norton "one of the very ablest members of Congress with whom I have been privileged to serve."[11]

Northern Democrats echoed similar sentiments. Francis Walter of Pennsylvania proclaimed, "If I could live as useful a life as you have all the prayers of a devoted mother would have been answered. You have been an inspiration to many members of Congress." Philip Philbin of Massachusetts lauded her "magnificent service" to her district, state, and

nation and wrote, "Your service has been outstanding, your fidelity un-
excelled and your devotion to American ideals an example to all." He
implored her to continue "to lighten our burdens by the grace of your
presence, your friendliness, your kindness, your generosity, and your
devotion to good causes."[12] House Rules Committee Chairman Abe Sabath of Illinois affirmed that Norton had "served the people and the
country honestly, faithfully and courageously at all times," while John
Dingell of Michigan wrote her, "You have proved to the world that this is
not alone a man's world. Although the rules of the game have been
established by men, you have played the game without handicap and
you have more than held you own. You have been an inspiration and
guide to the women of this Nation."[13] Republican Charles Eaton of New
Jersey likewise commended her "remarkable record in Congress." Norton, visibly moved, pondered, "It's wonderful to be able to read your
obituary before you die."[14]

Norton's hospitalization for pneumonia lasted about one month. Dr.
Parker, Norton's hospital physician, told her, "Do you know you're the
miracle of the hospital?" Norton suddenly realized that she had experienced "a narrow escape." She philosophized, "Why it happened in the
way it did, so swiftly and suddenly at such a crucial time, I accepted as
one of those mysteries that are difficult to understand." "The weeks in
the hospital," Norton reflected, "gave me a deeper understanding and
appreciation of the friends I had made during my years at the Capitol."[15]

Norton finally returned to the House on April 26, when colleagues
held her long belated birthday party. "I suspected something was afoot
that morning," she recollected, "for Jeanne kept hovering around while I
was dressing, insisting that I wear a new dress I had bought just before
my illness. I did not agree and dressed as I would for any ordinary day in
the House." Jeanne, however, never leaked a word about the surprise
party.[16]

The House already was in session when Norton arrived at the Capitol
building. Democrats Bosone of Utah and Edna Kelly of New York joined
her as she entered the House Chamber. Republican Frances Payne Bolton
of Ohio delivered a testimonial to Norton. "We women of the House
regret very keenly that we shall not have her with us in the future sessions of Congress," she stated. "We wish her every possible and conceiv-
able joy and satisfaction out of the many things she has done for humanity, for her people, for other women, and for so many children."[17] Bolton
asked Republicans Cecil Harden of Indiana, Edith Nourse Rogers of Massachusetts, and Katharine St. George of New York to join Democrats
Bosone, Kelly, Helen Gahagan Douglas of California, and Chase Woodhouse of Connecticut around Norton. The 435 House members, only 15 of
whom had served longer than Norton, applauded her heartily.[18]

Congressional women colleagues presented Norton with a unique
gold link bracelet, each of the eight links engraved with the autograph of

a different woman House member from her final term. A round gold disk, signed by Senator Smith of Maine, hung from the bracelet. Smith had served in the U.S. House from 1940 to 1949 and in 1948 had become the first woman elected to the U.S. Senate in her own right.[19] Dingell of Michigan noted, "Mary asked no quarter, concession, or handicap because of her sex." "She could do anything any man in the House could do," he said, "and frequently do it better."[20]

The genuine outpouring of friendship by colleagues stirred Norton's emotions. "I have been quite overwhelmed since my return to Congress," Norton wrote Bolton, "not only on account of the lovely bracelet but particularly by the beautiful tribute on the Floor of the House to welcome me back to our group." She claimed, "Nobody could have paid a more eloquent and sincere tribute to anyone." Norton acknowledged, "It has been an everlasting privilege to have served in the House during so many eventful eras in our history." "I am leaving the Congress with very mixed feelings," she admitted. Norton added, "I shall miss you all very much and it will be difficult to make up for what I am losing." But she realized, "I could not go on very much longer and do the kind of work that I have always liked to do."[21]

Norton addressed her House colleagues for the final time on June 26, the day after the outbreak of the Korean War. North Korean armies had crossed the thirty-eighth parallel and invaded South Korea. Norton had introduced a bill to increase the salaries of U.S. senators and U.S. Representatives. Members of the Eighty-first Congress received a $12,500 annual salary and $2,500 for expenses. Norton had long favored raising congressional salaries and realized that the time was right to propose such legislation. "I could do it," she explained, "because I was leaving and could not benefit by the raise."

Congressional pay had fallen behind the increased cost of living. Senators and representatives had to maintain homes in both their home state and in Washington, D.C., because the U.S. Congress met most of the year. They could no longer pursue side occupations because of their full-time legislative responsibilities. House members faced reelection every two years and needed to campaign frequently, spending up to $2,500 annually and contributing to their political party. Norton argued, "Members must meet all demands on a salary completely inadequate." Federal government salaries were not competitive with those of business corporations. Norton cited the salaries of board chairmen and presidents of 34 large corporations, 27 of whom earned from $100,000 to $500,000 a year. "The United States Government is the greatest corporation in the world and the Congress is the board of directors," Norton emphasized. "It should have the best brains to conduct its business." She pleaded with colleagues, "I sincerely hope that it will become law before I say adieu."[22]

Norton wanted Democratic Party leaders to send the salary measure to her House Administration Committee, but it was referred instead to the House Post Office and Civil Service Committee, chaired by Democrat Tom Murray of Tennessee. Murray, a wealthy bachelor and fiscal conservative, opposed raising congressional salaries and pigeonholed Norton's legislation. Murray's response sorely dismayed Norton. "I could have helped get it before the Congress," she insisted.

As Norton's retirement neared, colleagues deluged her office with congratulatory messages. Republican Senator Robert Hendrickson of New Jersey wrote, "I admired you for the splendid manner in which you handled your high office and your devotion to duty has ever been an inspiration. The women of New Jersey have every right to be proud of your long and faithful record of service." Republican Senator H. Alexander Smith of New Jersey echoed similar sentiments about Norton. "I have tried as far as I can to look above and beyond partisanship since I have been in the Senate and to think in terms of those characters who have made a real contribution during their terms here. You are certainly in this class and you deserve the warm commendation and hearty thanks not only from people of New Jersey, but from the people of the United States as well."[23] Cannon of Missouri reflected, "No retirement from the House grieves me more than yours." He added, "Your retirement leaves a blank here in the House in your many friendships in both houses that cannot be filled." Veteran Rules Committee chairman Sabath penned Norton, "Your gracious presence will be missed in the daily routine on the floor, but I shall look forward with pleasure to greeting you often upon your visits to the halls in which you have so indelibly left the fruits of your labors." Republican Karl LeCompte of Iowa, a House Administration Committee colleague, wrote her: "You have the most distinguished service and the most distinguished career of any women I have ever known." Democrat Thomas Stanley of Virginia, remarked, "It has certainly been a pleasure to serve under you as Chairman of the Committee on House Administration."[24]

Industrial labor union leaders likewise lauded Norton's legislative achievements. Philip Murray, president of the Congress of Industrial Organizations, wrote, "We in the labor movement are mindful of your many contributions to the cause of the men and women who work for a living. You have sponsored noteworthy legislation designed to protect and advance the interests of American workers."[25] Besides chairing the House Labor Committee, Norton had led the legislative battles for the Fair Labor Standards Act and a permanent Fair Employment Practices Committee.

On her final day in Congress, Norton praised President Truman for his domestic and foreign policies and inspirational courage and reflected on her own congressional career. "No President," she wrote, "has ever had to solve greater problems than have come to you. And, nobody, could have done a better job." "I have loved my work in Congress," Norton reminisced, "and am very proud of the fact that I am a Democrat and have always followed the leadership of my Party. I am retiring with the happy feeling that I hold the respect and affection of the Members with whom I have been associated for more than a quarter of a century." Although leaving Congress, she volunteered to help President Truman in some other capacity. The president replied, "I was sorry to see you leave the Congress because I think you always made a great contribution to the welfare of the country."[26]

Norton walked into the House chambers for the last time as a representative on January 1, 1951. Congresswomen Woodhouse, Bosone, Kelly, and Douglas shared with her memories from their respective legislative careers. Woodhouse and Douglas also were there for the last time as House members, too. Woodhouse had lost her House reelection bid to Republican Horace Seely-Brown Jr. of Connecticut, while Douglas had been defeated in a U.S. Senate race by Republican Richard Nixon of California. Bosone of Utah, who had entered Congress in 1949, served one more House term. That afternoon, Norton visited the House Administration Committee rooms under the Capitol Dome for the final time as a member.

Norton packed cases and boxes in her congressional office the next afternoon. She heard the bells in the corridor ring three times, notifying representatives of an imminent roll call vote. "The idea passed through my mind that I ought to go over," Norton acknowledged. "It would be my last roll call. But I didn't go." She explained, "I have always dreaded the possibility of showing emotion in public. I didn't know how my emotions might react to that strain."[27] Only the rich memories of her notable congressional career remained.

Norton left Congress with mixed emotions on January 2, having made so many close friends. "I was glad to lay down the burden," she confessed. "But I was sorry to leave the men and women with whom I had served and who had meant so much to me during those twenty-six years." The humanitarian Norton truly had enjoyed helping other people while treating district, state, national, and world problems. She always regarded her congressional responsibilities in a very personal way, knowing, "Some one was depending on you to do something which meant so much to that person."[28]

Norton's retirement marked the end of the Hague era in Jersey City and Hudson County, too. Norton had been the last major figure linked to Mayor Hague who still held political office. The Hague administration had controlled Jersey City and Hudson County politics from 1917 to 1949. Norton's Thirteenth District Congressional seat, however, remained in Democratic Party control. Democrat Alfred Sieminski, who replaced Norton, defeated Republican Edward Binkowski in the November 1950 election. He received only 52 percent of the popular vote, 16 percent less than Norton had tallied in her final congressional race. Sieminski, a laundry executive, was elected while on active duty as an army major in Korea.

He had volunteered for combat duty during the Korean War after winning the Democratic party primary, leaving his wife to campaign for him. Sieminski served four House terms, surviving by just 57 votes against Republican Norman Roth in 1956.

The Washington media, which had nicknamed Norton "Battling Mary" and "Aunt Mary," viewed her as a strong, able leader with a kind, caring heart. When Norton retired, *Washington Star* columnist Mary McGrory wrote, "They'll Miss the Back of Mary's Hand." McGrory described how Norton had impacted the U.S. House of Representatives as a "caustic humanitarian." She added, "The ability of the gentlewoman from New Jersey to take care of herself in the hurly-burly of the House has become a legend," yet "her quickness to give the back of her hand to fractious lawmakers seems to have inspired no deep resentment on their part." She concluded, "For strength and warmth, the House is not likely to see her like soon again." [29]

Public service soon beckoned Norton. The Washington press corps expected her to join the District of Columbia Commission, but she declined that post and really wanted to replace Arthur Quinn as Comptroller of the Customs of the Port of New York. In February 1951, however, Secretary of Labor Maurice Tobin appointed her as a Labor Department consultant on manpower and as chairman of the newly formed Woman's Advisory Committee of the Defense Manpower Administration. Norton wanted to make sure that her consultant appointment did not interfere with the defense manpower position or with President Truman's consideration of her for the Customs position. Truman assured her that the two positions were unrelated and convinced her to accept the consultant job. "I shall be glad," Norton wrote Tobin, "to give all the time necessary to this assignment." "I am most anxious," she affirmed, "to give my time and whatever ability I have, wherever it will help most at this very critical time." The consultant position helped Norton financially because, according to niece Marion McDonagh Burke, "she was nearly broke after leaving Congress." [30]

The Woman's Advisory Committee of the Defense Manpower Administration, consisting of twenty-one leaders from civic organizations, management, trade unions, state agency administrative groups, and the public, recommended policies and programs governing women in industry and identified business trends regarding employment of women. The committee, according to Norton, reflected "the strength which the women of America add to our body politic and economics in this time of national emergency." It also recognized the skills and abilities of women "to produce the arms needed to ward off the threat of totalitarian aggression and the goods essential to the maintenance of a sound civilian economy." [31]

Norton continued striving to do what she could to help women workers. In December 1951, she proposed mobilizing 36 million women over age sixteen in industrial employment. Although recommending that priority be given to hiring childless women, Norton insisted that day care centers and adequate school facilities be established to help those with children. Above all, she wanted state laws enforced to protect women workers and to help prevent gender discrimination in employment. Management, labor, and local communities, she concluded, should draw extensively upon women workers.[32]

Gender discrimination issues still troubled Norton. The Korean War, unlike World War II, did not enhance employment opportunities for women. Norton favored the creation of a federal commission to investigate gender inequity, but encountered formidable resistance from conservative senators and representatives. Although 19 million women were employed in 1950, thirty-six states did not have equal pay laws. Norton deemed equal pay legislation essential "as a matter of simple justice and to prevent the use of women as wage cutters." Women, she argued, faced "an uphill fight" requiring "all the courage and all of the resourcefulness we have." Norton insisted that the challenge be met "if the vote we acquired in 1920 really means anything to the women of our Country, and particularly to the women who find it necessary to compete with men in the labor market." She persuaded Democratic Representative John F. Kennedy of Massachusetts to introduce equal pay legislation, but his measure failed because the American Federation of Labor opposed it and the Korean War produced no labor shortage.[33]

Norton still encouraged more women to enter politics. In the 1952 elections, only fifteen Democratic women and nine Republican women sought House seats. She explained, "Women themselves are to blame. If the urge was greater, they would find a way to increase the number of women candidates." Women possessed the numerical strength to determine the outcome of elections, but confronted formidable financial problems, resistance from conservative men controlling party machinery, and weak organization. Norton lamented, "Campaign expenses come high and many women with ability find it impossible to meet the expense. Also, women have learned that unless the men who control the political machinery are willing to co-operate, it is almost impossible to be elected. And women do not organize as they could to help elect women! They could, because of their numerical strength, control elections, but it is my opinion they never will." Norton insisted that women had more opportunities to enter politics than ever before and believed that women should work within the existing party machinery, regardless of opposition from some male leaders. She already had shown that women were as capable as men when they worked inside the political system. Women, however, still lacked experience in organizing within the political party apparatus. Norton, therefore, did not expect the number of women seeking congressional positions to increase significantly during the 1950s. "It takes a lot of courage, common sense, faith in oneself and what I call 'stick-to-itiveness,'" she stressed, "plus a great deal of hard work and, of course, ability."[34]

Norton's political career ended when Republican Dwight D. Eisenhower assumed the presidency in January 1953. Norton resigned as manpower consultant to the Secretary of Labor and as chairman of the Woman's Advisory Committee of the Defense Manpower Administration. Secretary of Labor Martin Durkin, Tobin's successor, persuaded Norton to remain a consultant for another nine months. After moving into a New York City apartment, Norton relocated to Greenwich, Connecticut, in 1956 to live with her sister, Mrs. Joseph McDonagh.

During the 1950s, Norton dined occasionally with Eleanor Roosevelt and Lorena Hickok at the Roosevelt estate in Hyde Park, New York. Hickok, an intimate friend of Roosevelt, had reported for the Associated Press from 1928 to 1933, served as chief investigator for the Federal Emergency Relief Administration from 1933 to 1940, and worked as executive secretary of the Women's Division of the Democratic National Committee from 1940 to 1945. Norton and Hickok, who suffered from diabetes and partial blindness and resided in a cottage at the Roosevelt estate, shared the same birthdays, the latter being eighteen years younger. After celebrating their birthdays in March 1954, Roosevelt wrote, "Congresswoman Norton is perfectly remarkable. She insists that she is 79 years old, but nobody would ever know it by watching her! She sat with us Saturday night and listened to Adlai Stevenson's speech and was as keen—and interesting in her comments—as anyone in the room." Roosevelt added, "Old age which comes as gracefully as it has come to her is certainly nothing to be feared for she is more interesting and a more entertaining companion today than she was 40 years ago. She is lovable and kind and I am sure every member of her family adores her and she certainly has many, many friends. I feel it both an honor and a pleasure to be one of her friends."

Norton wrote an autobiography with Hickok's assistance. Frances Parkinson Keyes, a novelist and wife of three-term Republican Senator Henry Wilder Keyes of New Hampshire, had encouraged Norton in 1931 to begin penning handwritten notes for a possible autobiography. Norton, however, resisted the idea until her retirement from political life. "Searching the past," she feared, "often revives memories of events best forgotten." In 1951, however, Hickok persuaded Norton to write her memoirs to inspire other women to play more prominent roles in the daily work of government and the Democratic Party. She also convinced Norton that writing a story about her life could earn book royalties and guarantee her a permanent place in history. "You're always talking about how young women should get in involved in politics," Hickok admonished Norton. "Well, here's your chance to tell them now."

Norton, who had very few close political friends or confidants, initially seemed very reluctant to discuss her personal life. "It has always been difficult for me to talk about myself," she confessed, "but how can you write an autobiography without using the letter 'I'?" Hickok's relentless persistence troubled Norton, who did not want to expose private matters to public scrutiny and disliked criticizing others even when warranted. "'Hick prodded me so in the next few weeks," Norton recalled, "that it put quite a strain on our friendship."[35]

Norton acceded to Hickok's wishes and authored her memoirs mainly "to encourage older people—especially women." Hickok, who moved in with Norton, spent 1951 drafting the autobiography and finished it in January 1952. Norton's account reminisces about her extensive congressional service; details her leadership roles on the House District of Columbia, Labor and Administration Committees; relives the major legislative battles of the Franklin D. Roosevelt and Truman eras; provides deft portraits of political colleagues; and outlines the political texture of three decades. Although less candid about her personal life, Norton's memoirs describe her early family life, marriage, welfare activities, and entrance into politics. Her stories portray the struggles of a brave, courageous woman pioneer in New Jersey and national politics before history books and academic curricula recognized the dynamic role and impact of women in American life. Norton struggled with finding a short, snappy title for her memoirs. "Summing up your life—what you've tried to do; what you stand for—in one to five short words isn't easy, especially when your life has been as long as mine," she explained. "And a lot has happened." Some advisers suggested "Madame Congresswoman" for the title, but she preferred "Madame Congressman" instead. "I never legislated as a woman," she objected.

Norton could not find a publisher for her memoirs, causing perhaps the greatest disappointment in her life. She wanted her autobiography published by a commercial press as a trade book with a large print run. Nine publishers and three magazines wanted to see her manuscript, but her memoirs did not pique their interest, being written in an era before the nation paid much attention to women's participation in politics and public leadership. Norton's manuscript is of importance as a historical document for those studying the history of American women, politics, labor, cities, and New Jersey. Several problems, however, limited the effectiveness of her autobiography. Norton's memoirs were written in a relatively short time. Norton describes her numerous activities, but often does not show how they illuminate the broader stage of the place, time, and culture in which she played a valuable part as a prominent political figure. Norton's memoirs also should have included more about her family, precongressional and congressional careers, and personal and professional relationships, and especially should have shed more light on the social, cultural, and political history of her period.

On August 1, 1959, Norton suffered a heart attack at the home of her sister, Mrs. Joseph McDonagh, in Greenwich, Connecticut. She died the following day at age eighty-four at Greenwich Hospital and is buried in Holy Name Cemetery in Jersey City.[36]

Norton, a shrewd, conscientious politician who never lost an election, had represented the Twelfth and Thirteenth Congressional Districts in New Jersey for thirteen terms from 1925 through 1951. She set the record for length of service by a woman representative, a mark soon surpassed by Rogers of Massachusetts. She had served under Presidents Calvin Coolidge, Herbert Hoover, Franklin D. Roosevelt, and Truman and under seven House Speakers, including Nicholas Longworth, John Nance Garner, Henry Rainey, Joseph Byrnes, William Bankhead, Joseph Martin Jr., and Sam Rayburn. During Norton's tenure, thirty-five women had followed her path into the U.S. Congress.[37]

Significant historical developments had occurred during Norton's tenure. Norton likened her story to "the reader of a historical novel, who, having finished one chapter and enjoying every paragraph of it, turns the page to find a whole new chapter opening up." Her legislative service had spanned the post—World War I era, the Great Depression, World War II, and the Cold War, along with major technological advances in urban America. Norton had entered the U.S. Congress during the economically prosperous, increasingly isolationist 1920s. The nation soon had experienced its greatest economic depression, ending Republican Party control of the executive and legislative branches. President Roosevelt had helped the United States rebound from the economic depression with his New Deal relief, recovery, reform and social justice programs and had guided the democratic nation through World War II against totalitarian challenges from Nazi Germany, Fascist Italy, and the Japanese Empire. President Truman had expanded the New Deal with his Fair Deal policies and had contained the spread of Communism abroad with the Truman Doctrine, Marshall Plan, and the North Atlantic Treaty Organization. Norton had left Congress during the Korean War and had hoped that the United Nations would hasten the path toward an everlasting international peace. "Some day," she dreamed, "perhaps the world will realize that wars never settle anything, and there will finally be established a court or forum where differences between nations can be settled in a civilized fashion."[38]

Historians tracing the role of American women too often either have ignored or underplayed Norton's significant impact on the national political scene. Norton rose to prominence after the suffragettes had secured the vote for women in national elections and had left the political arena over a decade before the modern feminist movement surfaced. She combined traditionalism and reform, representing an eastern, urban, predominately Roman Catholic, working-class district covering Bayonne and part of Jersey City, and made legislative history. Besides being the first Democratic Party congresswoman, the pioneering legislator was the first woman elected from an eastern state and to head a standing congressional committee. Norton chaired the House District of Columbia Committee, becoming the nation Capitol's initial and only "Lady Mayor." She was the first woman to direct a major congressional committee, namely the House Labor Committee. The devout Democrat became the only woman to chair four committees and held various leadership positions in Congress, within the state party organization, and at national political conventions.

Norton adeptly utilized her lobbying, oratorical, and formative abilities. The effective lobbyist was "known to change many a vote on the Democratic side of the House, for a bill in which she was interested, by her persuasiveness and ability." Margot Gayle pictured the clear-thinking, lucid Norton as "a legislator with whom one did not carelessly tangle in debate." Norton also was in frequent demand as a speaker, often delivered radio addresses, and was widely recognized for her organizational skills.

The first generation congresswoman established numerous political precedents for women. She was an outsider to her Capitol Hill colleagues because of her gender and to the Washington elite because of her working-class background but gradually climbed the political party and congressional seniority systems and demonstrated that women could master parliamentary skills and provide deft leadership. Despite being neither a feminist crusader nor having any major legislation named after her, she piloted several controversial labor measures to enactment.

Norton, who proved that women could win elections, retain constituent support, and exert leadership, did not reflect the typical socioeconomic backgrounds of the congresswomen from the 1917 to 1934 era. Most were affiliated with Protestant denominations and came from wealthy families, who sent them to private secondary schools and colleges or universities. Norton, though, grew up in an Irish Roman Catholic family and attended school only through the eighth grade. She was elected to Congress at age fifty, sooner than the typical female representative. Norton was one of only three Congresswomen from that era with previous electoral experience, having served as a New Jersey freeholder, and had not replaced a deceased husband. Nevertheless, she shared a few characteristics with the 1917 to 1934 congresswomen, being Caucasian and having been involved in civic organizations and social welfare endeavors.

Norton lived a simple, unpretentious, family-oriented life and did not crave media publicity. She often shunned Washington elite society partly because of her limited eighth grade education, gender, and Roman Catholic religious affiliation. Norton helped care for her younger siblings, was a dedicated housewife, and remained very close to her nieces Marion McDonagh Burke, Lucille McDonagh Considine, and Jeanne McDonagh. Marion worked as assistant clerk of the House District of Columbia Committee and clerk for the House Labor Committee, while Lucille clerked for the Labor Committee and Jeanne clerked for the House Administration Committee.

The New Jersey Democrat fought for economic and social reforms to improve working and living conditions for downtrodden Americans. She valiantly espoused the advancement of social welfare, stabilization of labor-management relations, and improvement of public institutions. At the district, state, and national levels, Norton championed those economic and social programs she considered in the best public interest. Eleanor Roosevelt boasted that Norton "fought for the underdog," while New Jersey Representative Peter Rodino deemed her a "champion of human rights and ardent advocate of the cause of welfare."[39]

Norton rallied behind organized and especially unorganized industrial workers, winning the respect and admiration of both labor leaders and the rank and file. In the Labor Committee, she battled for major New Deal measures benefiting workers and raising the national standard of living. A labor magazine observed, "From the very first day of her service, she has been on the side of the workers." One labor union deemed Norton "one of labor's most stalwart friends."[40]

Above all, Norton implored women to participate in politics, vote in elections, and seek public office. "All my life," she declared, "I've been completely out of patience with the idea that it isn't ladylike for women to go into politics!" Norton asserted, "Women in the United States have never used their power." She counseled women to work diligently daily in politics and to remain both tactful and steadfast. "They can't stay at home and let John do it," Norton advised. One contemporary observer lauded her as "the first woman to prove that she had what it took to play the game of politics." Norton wanted congresswomen to be treated the same way as their male colleagues.[41]

In 1990, the Women's Project of New Jersey designated Norton as a significant political role model for women. Norton's speeches, writings, and legislative achievements demonstrated that she adeptly understood the challenges facing working-class women. These gender problems included maternity leave, childcare, job training programs, displaced homemakers, and equal pay for equal work. In 1996, Hudson County Community College recognized Norton's work on behalf of women by naming a conference room after her.

Norton's life inspired other women of limited educational background and meager financial resources to participate in civic affairs and pursue political careers. "Norton often bemoaned the small number of women who were willing to run for public office. She constantly encouraged them to join her." In 1957, Republican Florence Dwyer of New Jersey described Norton's impact on her life. "Many years ago when I became interested in politics," Dwyer wrote Norton, "I looked up to you as the outstanding woman in the entire country. Your record as chairman of the Labor Committee in the House was well known and you can always be proud of the remarkable performance you made in the Congress of the United States." Dwyer concluded, "You were a symbol of the aspirations of all political minded women."[42] Norton likewise would have been proud of Dwyer, who became New Jersey's second woman House member in 1958 and served seven terms from 1959 to 1973.

The only cloud hanging over Norton's legacy concerned her connection with Mayor Hague and his Jersey City political machine. Norton supported "Hague's desires to promote the interests of the district's mostly working-class and Roman Catholic constituency." Besides learning politics from Hague, she benefited from his knowledge and influence and steadfastly supported his nominees for political office.[43] Norton initially needed Hague's support to win reelection. The *Washington Post* wrote, "She demonstrated a sense of organizational loyalty which sprang from her political beginnings. She frequently was criticized by her opponents as the 'right-hand woman' in the Hague machine." Hague, whom Norton called "a very good friend," endorsed her in all thirteen congressional election races in the predominantly Roman Catholic, Democratic Party district. Norton termed Hague a "hardworking," "clean-living," and "remarkable executive" who built Jersey City into "an outstanding metropolitan city." Hague's achievements in law enforcement, fire safety, welfare, and medical care impressed her. Hague usually received Norton's support in Congress and used her "to give respectability to his machine politics." Throughout her legislative career, "Norton was loyal to Hague, whom she called her 'political foster father,'" Burke, Norton's niece, admitted Hague "cramped Mary's style."[44]

Hague's Jersey City machine, however, did not dictate Norton's congressional actions. "Norton denied interference from Hague and the supposition that she was in daily contact with him." Although befriending Hague, she claimed that the mayor seldom tried to influence her legislative votes. During her initial term, Norton asked Hague's advice on one particular bill. The mayor counseled her to be guided by her "sense of values" and serve her constituents faithfully. "God," Hague replied, "gave you as much sense as he gave me." For the next decade, Norton insisted that she "never had a request or any advice regarding my congressional work."[45] She followed the dictates of her conscience whenever disagreeing with the Jersey City mayor on labor and other legislative issues. "In many instances, Norton's legislative agenda for her constituents transcended those of Hague and her legislative successes benefited Hague's constituents as well." During House consideration of the Wage and Hour Bill of 1937, Norton showed her independence by denying Hague's request to intervene on behalf of the American Federation of Labor. She claimed the mayor "understood my position and respected me for refusing to be stampeded."[46]

Norton insisted that Hague never compelled her to vote against her convictions. "I have never had any interference from Mayor Hague with the way I voted," she claimed. "People think I'm in constant communication with him, but that's not true." Hague, Norton insisted, "never asked any of us to do anything our consciences would not approve." The thirteen-term representative "made New Jersey so proud of her that probably even Hague would not have been able to depose her." Although "bossism ruled the day," Christine Wiltanger observed, "Norton more than held her own." Carmela Karnoutsos wrote, "Congresswoman Mary T. Norton was Jersey City's most prominent political figure during the era of Frank Hague, with the possible exception of the mayor himself."[47]

The Hague machine had opened the doors for Norton politically, but she had made an enormous impact of her own on the U.S. Congress and other women. Norton maintained, "I was representing not only my own district, but all women at a time when we were pioneers in politics." The multidimensional, complex, ambitious, determined, and gritty New Jersey Democrat with limited formal education accomplished much on Capitol Hill. "Her political philosophy, personal morality, and feminism made her a powerful leader during the period just after women were granted the right to vote." Norton improved the lives of Washingtonians as chair of the House District of Columbia Committee, championing home rule for the nation's capitol. She bettered the conditions for military personnel as a Veterans Affairs Committee member, obtaining funds for the construction of the first veterans' hospital in New Jersey.

On a much broader scale, Norton uplifted the status of working-class Americans, including her Jersey City and Bayonne constituents, as chair of the House Labor Committee. She helped sponsor the Wagner National Labor Relations Act of 1935, which outlawed unfair labor practices against unions and guaranteed organized labor the right to bargain collectively. Norton steered through the Labor Committee and secured House adoption of the landmark Fair Labor Standards Act of 1938, which set a minimum wage of 25 cents an hour, established a forty-hour work week for workers of firms engaged in interstate commerce, and outlawed child labor. "Her finest hour may have been passage of the controversial Fair Labor Standards Act of 1938," widely considered as the final piece of major New Deal legislation. During World War II, Norton helped create a temporary Fair Employment Practices Committee to prevent racial and gender discrimination in hiring. She also helped secure pensions for federal elective and executive offices and expand the retirement system for federal employees. Norton had "played an integral role in successfully enacting this critical legislation that would shape our nation for years to come." The National Women's History Museum concluded, "Norton merits more recognition than she gets from today's working women: because of her leadership in Congress (and Frances Perkins in the executive branch) today's workers are assured decent pay, health and safety protections, retirement benefits, and economic opportunity."[48]

Norton's official portrait hangs in the offices of the House Democratic Party leader as a vivid reminder of the trailblazing woman who helped shape legislative history. During Women's History Month in March 2004, House Democratic Leader Nancy Pelosi of California unveiled Norton's picture at a reception. Democratic Representative Marcy Kaptur of Ohio had rescued the portrait from a closet in the House Annex Building. At the reception, Pelosi remarked, "It is an appropriate time to celebrate the lives of women such as Mary Norton" and "to recommit ourselves to finding and inspiring the next generation of women leaders. It is with pride and hope that we hang this portrait of Mary Norton today to celebrate the good work in Congress that she described as a 'soul-satisfying experience.'" Pelosi lauded Norton as "a great role model for women."[49]

Norton's legacy remains alive. On the seventieth anniversary of the Fair Labor Standards Act, Democrat Rosa DeLauro of Connecticut in 2008 introduced a resolution recognizing Norton's crucial role in the passage of that milestone measure. "Congresswoman Norton was a tireless champion of the American worker and her dedication and resolve are an inspiration to all of us—women, men and elected officials—who follow in her footsteps," she remarked. DeLauro stressed that passage of the "landmark" measure "never would have happened without Norton's leadership, creating the minimum wage and establishing the basic worker protections we take for granted today. Her work laid the foundation that we continue to build upon to this day. And she did it all with a skillful blend of strength and compassion."[50] "Battling Mary" indeed was a congressional trailblazer.

NOTES

1. Barbara J. Tomlinson, "Making Their Way: A Study of New Jersey Congresswomen, 1924–1994," (Ph.D. dissertation: Rutgers, The State University of New Jersey, 1996), pp. 41, 44.
2. Mary T. Norton, "Madam Congressman: The Memoirs of Mary T. Norton of New Jersey," (Hereafter cited as "Memoirs"), Mary T. Norton MSS, New Jersey Collection, Archibald Stevens Alexander Library, Rutgers, The State University of New Jersey, pp. 257–58.
3. Norton, "Memoirs," p. 258.
4. Norton, "Memoirs," p. 259.
5. Norton, "Memoirs," pp. 259–60.
6. Norton, "Memoirs," pp. 260–61; Margot Gayle, "Battling Mary Retires," *Independent Woman* 29 (July 1950), p. 199.
7. Mary T. Norton to Harry S. Truman, April 6, 1950, Norton MSS, Box 2, Correspondence, Truman, 1950–1952.
8. Mary T. Norton to Margaret Chase Smith, April 6, 1950, Norton MSS, Box 2, Gen. Corr., April 1950; Mary T. Norton to J. Howard McGrath, April 6, 1950, Norton MSS, Box 2, Gen. Corr., Apr. 1950.
9. Clarence Cannon to Mary T. Norton, March 4, 1950, Box 1, Gen. Corr., March 1–6, 1950.

10. Robert L. Doughton to Mary T. Norton, March 4, 1950, Norton MSS, Box 1, Gen. Corr., Mar. 1–6, 1950; Frank W. Boykin to Mary T. Norton, March 4, 1950, Norton MSS, Box 1, Gen. Corr., Mar. 1–6, 1950.

11. Wright Patman to Mary T. Norton, March 7, 1950, Norton MSS, Box 1, Gen. Corr., March 9–31, 1950; J. Hardin Peterson to Mary Norton, March 4, 1950, Norton MSS, Box 1, Gen. Corr., Mar. 1–6, 1950; Edward Cox to Mary T. Norton, April 19, 1950, Norton MSS, Box 2, Gen. Corr., Apr. 1950.

12. Francis Walter to Mary T. Norton, March 6, 1950, Norton MSS, Box 2, Gen. Corr., Apr. 1950; Philip J. Philbin to Mary T. Norton, March 7, 1950, Norton MSS, Box 1, Gen. Corr., March 7–8, 1950.

13. A. J. Sabath to Mary T. Norton, March 6, 1950, Norton MSS, Box 1, Gen. Corr., Mar. 1–6, 1950; John D. Dingell to Mary T. Norton, March 7, 1950, Norton MSS, Box 1, Gen. Corr., Mar. 9–31, 1950.

14. Charles A. Eaton to Mary T. Norton, March 13, 1950, Norton MSS, Box 1, Gen. Corr., Mar. 9–31, 1950; Norton, "Memoirs," p. 261.

15. Norton, "Memoirs," p. 260.

16. Norton, "Memoirs," p. 263.

17. Gayle, "Battling Mary Retires," pp. 199–200; *Congressional Record*, Vol. 96, Part 5, p. 5797.

18. Emily A. Geer, "A Study of the Activities of Women in Congress With Special Reference to the Congressional Careers of Margaret Chase Smith, Mary T. Norton, and Edith Nourse Rogers," (Masters thesis: Bowling Green State University, 1952), p. 139.

19. Marcy Kaptur, *Women of Congress: A Twentieth Century Odyssey* (Washington, D.C.: Congressional Quarterly, 1996), p. 50; Norton, "Memoirs," p. 264. Norton, who admired Republican Smith, wrote, "You are doing a grand job in the Senate and I am proud of you. I know that you will have a long and very successful career and I shall continue to cheer for your from the sidelines." Norton to Smith, Apr. 6, 1950.

20. Gayle, "Battling Mary," pp. 199–200.

21. Norton wrote the Republican Bolton, "You have done a wonderful job in the Congress and I hope sincerely that you will be there for many years to come and that some day you, too, will celebrate your twenty-fifth anniversary in the Congress of the United States." Mary T. Norton to Frances Bolton, May 2, 1950, Norton MSS, Box 2, Gen. Corr., May 1950.

22. Norton, "Memoirs," pp. 265–67.

23. Robert C. Hendrickson to Mary T. Norton, December 8, 1950, Norton MSS, Box 2, Gen. Corr., June-December 1950; H. Alexander Smith to Mary T. Norton, December 11, 1950, Norton MSS, Box 2, Gen. Corr., June-Dec., 1950.

24. Clarence Cannon to Mary T. Norton, December 22, 1950, Norton MSS, Box 2, Gen. Corr., June-Dec. 1950; A. J. Sabath to Mary T. Norton, January 2, 1951, Norton MSS, Box 2, Gen. Corr., Jan.-June, 1951; Karl M. LeCompte to Mary T. Norton, October 10, 1950, Norton MSS, Box 2, Gen. Corr., June-Dec. 1950; Thomas B. Stanley to Mary T. Norton, December 27, 1950, Norton MSS, Box 2, Gen. Corr., June-Dec, 1950.

25. Philip Murray to Mary T. Norton, October 10, 1950, Norton MSS, Box 2, Gen. Corr., June-Dec. 1950.

26. Mary T. Norton to Harry S. Truman, January 2, 1951, Norton MSS, Box 2, Corr., January-June 1951; Harry S. Truman to Mary T. Norton, January 4, 1951, Norton MSS, Box 2, Corr., Truman, 1950-1952.

27. Norton, "Memoirs," p. 271.

28. RBC, Associated Press Release, January 1951; Mary T. Norton to *Newark Star-Ledger*, January 1951, Norton MSS, Box 2, Gen. Corr., January-June 1951.

29. *New York Times*, December 16, 1990; Our Campaigns, "NJ - District 13 - History," http://www.ourcampaigns.com; "Alfred Sieminski," http://www.politickernj.com; Mary McGrory, "They'll Miss the Back of Mary's Hand," *Washington Star*, March 1951 in Nancy Pelosi, Press Release, "Pelosi Remarks on Portrait Unveiling of Former Congresswoman Mary T. Norton," March 18, 2004, http://pelosi.house.gov.

30. *Washington Post*, August 3, 1959, p. B2; Mary T. Norton to Harry S. Truman, February 3, 1951, Norton MSS, Box 2, Corr., Truman, 1950–1952; Harry S. Truman to Mary T. Norton, February 7, 1951, Norton MSS, Box 2, Corr., Truman, 1950–1952; Marion McDonagh Burke, Interview with Author, August 7, 1981.

31. Mary T. Norton, Speech, National Conference on Labor Legislation, Washington, D.C., December 4, 1951, Norton MSS, Box 5, Speeches, The American Woman, 1932–1951.

32. Norton, Speech, National Conference, Dec. 4, 1951.

33. Barbara J. Tomlinson, "Making Their Way," p. 42; Mary T. Norton, Panel Discussion, 1952, Norton MSS, Box 5, Speeches, Labor, 1937–1949; Cynthia Harrison, *On Account of Sex: The Politics of Women's Issues, 1945–1968* (Berkeley, CA: University of California Press, 1988), p. 45.

34. Mary T. Norton to Joseph F. McCaffery, June 18, 1953, Norton MSS, Box 1, Gen. Corr., 1944.

35. Mary T. Norton, "Handwritten Notes," Norton MSS, Box 1, Gen. Corr., 1931–1936; Eleanor Roosevelt, "My Day," March 10, 1954, United Feature Syndicated newspaper column.

36. Norton, "Memoirs;" Ruth Cowan, "Snappy Title Needed for Mrs. Norton's Life," *Jersey Journal*, January 14, 1952, p. 3.; Carmela Ascolese Karnoutsos, "Mary Teresa Norton, 1875–1959," in Joan N. Burstyn, ed., *Past and Promise: Lives of New Jersey Women* (Syracuse, NY: Syracuse University Press, 1997), pp. 368–70. Her obituaries are in the *New York Times*, August 3, 1959; *New York Herald Tribune*, August 3, 1959, p. 2B; *Washington Post*, Aug. 3, 1959, p. 2B; and *Chicago Tribune*, August 3, 1959.

37. Kaptur, *Women of Congress*, p. 50; *New York Times*, Aug. 3, 1959.

38. Norton to *Newark Star-Ledger*, Jan. 1951; Kaptur, *Women of Congress*, p. 49; Norton, "Memoirs," p. 269.

39. "Mary T. Norton," *Current Biography* 5 (1944), p. 502; "Mary T. Norton M. C.," Norton MSS, Box 4, Personal Biographical Material; Gayle, "Battling Mary Retires," p. 200; *New York Herald Tribune*, Aug. 3, 1959, p. 2B; *Washington Post*, Aug. 3, 1959, p. 2B; Featured House Publications, *Women in Congress, 1917–2006*, April 27, 2007, 108th Cong., 1st sess., H. Doc. 108–223, http://www.gpo.gov; Phyllis J. Read and Bernard L. Witlieb, *The Book of Women's Lists* (New York: Random House, 1992), p. 317; "Women Pioneers on Capitol Hill, 1917–1934," in http://womenincongress.house.gov.members/ profiles; Hope Chamberlin, *A Minority of Members: Women in the U.S. Congress* (New York: Praeger Publishers, 1973), p. 53; "Mary Teresa Norton," *U.S. News* 9 (May 10, 1940), p. 37.

40. Mary T. Norton to Jeanne McDonagh, 1949, Norton MSS, Box 4, Personal Biographical Material.

41. Gayle, "Battling Mary Retires," p. 200; Doris Faber, *The Life of Lorena Hickok: E. R.'s Friend* (New York: William Morrow & Company, 1980), p. 286; Annabel Paxton, *Women in Congress* (Richmond, VA: The Dietz Press, 1945), p. 35.

42. Karnoutsos, "Mary Teresa Norton," pp. 368–70; Rosa L. DeLauro, Press Release, June 25, 2008, http://www.delauro.house.gov; Barbara Griffin to editor, *The Jersey Journal*, November 5, 2010; Florence Dwyer to Mary T. Norton, January 9, 1957, Norton MSS, Box 2, Gen. Corr., 1957. For Dwyer's Congressional career, see Barbara Tomlinson, "Making Her Way: The Career of Congresswoman Frances E. Dwyer," *New Jersey History* 112 (1994), pp. 40–77.

43. Maureen Rees, "Mary Norton: A 'Grand Girl'," *Journal of Rutgers University Libraries* 47 (December 1985), p. 59; Featured House Publications, *Women in Congress, 1917–2006*; "Mary T. Norton 1875–1959," http://www.womenicongress.house.gov/ members-profiles; Burke, Interview with Author, Aug. 7, 1981.

44. Chamberlin, *Minority of Members*, p. 53; *Washington Post*, Aug. 3, 1959, p. B2; Helen Meagher, "Notes of Interview with Mary T. Norton," *Women's Voice*, March 26, 1931, Norton MSS, Box 1, Gen. Corr., 1931–1936; Mary T. Norton to Frances Parkinson Keyes, January 23, 1931, Norton MSS, Box 1, Gen. Corr., 1931–1936; Karnoutsos, "Mary Teresa Norton"; Burke, Interview with Author, Aug. 7, 1981.

45. Eleanor Andrews to Elenere Kellogg, undated, Norton MSS, Box 4, Personal Biographical Material; Norton to Keyes, Jan. 23, 1931; *Washington Post*, Aug. 3, 1959, p. B2; Karnoutsos, "Mary Teresa Norton."

46. Mary T. Norton to Franklin D. Roosevelt, May 29, 1942, Franklin D. Roosevelt MSS, President's Personal File 5418, Mary T. Norton; Faber, *Lorena Hickok*, p. 287; Karnoutsos, "Mary Teresa Norton."

47. Andrews to Kellogg, undated; Rees, "A 'Grand Girl'," p. 59; Christine Wiltanger, "Remember the Ladies," The Official Jersey City Web Site, http://www.cityofjerseycity.com; Karnoutsos, "Mary Teresa Norton."

48. RBC, Press Release, Jan. 1951, Norton MSS, Box 2, Gen. Corr. Jan.-June, 1951, Featured House Publications, *Women in Congress, 1917–2006*; National Women's History Museum, "Women Wielding Power: Pioneer Female State Legislators: New Jersey," http://www.nwhm.org.

49. Nancy Pelosi, Press Release, "Pelosi Remarks on Portrait Unveiling of Former Congresswoman Mary T. Norton," March 18, 2004, http://www.pelosi.house.gov; Robert Choen, "Jersey City's 'Fighting Mary' Reclaims Place of Honor," *Newark Star-Ledger*, March 19, 2004, in Carmela Karnoutsos, "Mary Teresa Norton, 1875–1959," http://www.njcu.edu.

50. Lisa Kutlin, "Congresswoman Mary T. Norton: Matriarch of the Living Wage," Georgetown University Library, Gender and Legal History MSS, 2004, http://www.ll.georgetown.edu; DeLaurio, Press Release, June 25, 2008.

Bibliography

MANUSCRIPT COLLECTIONS

Mary Dewson MSS, Franklin D. Roosevelt Library, Hyde Park, NY.
  Carton 1 – Wages and Hours File
Lorena Hickok MSS, Franklin D. Roosevelt Library, Hyde Park, NY.
  Box 16 – Mary Norton Correspondence, 1941–1952
Mary T. Norton MSS, New Jersey Collection, Archibald Stevens Alexander Library, Rutgers, The State University of New Jersey, New Brunswick, NJ.
  Box 1 – General Correspondence, 1926–1950
  Box 2 – General Correspondence, 1951–1959
      Correspondence, Eleanor Roosevelt, 1941–1945
      Correspondence, Franklin D. Roosevelt, 1928–1945
      Correspondence, Harry S. Truman, 1945–1952
  Box 3 – Political File – Publications, Writings, Congressional Voting Records and Statistics
  Box 4 – Personal File – Biographical Material
  Box 5 – Speeches – Defense, 1941
      General, 1927–1940
      General, 1941–1952
      Labor, 1937–1949
      Miscellaneous
      Public Welfare, 1943–1948
      The American Woman, 1932–1951
Franklin D. Roosevelt MSS, Franklin D. Roosevelt Library, Hyde Park, NY.
  Official File 2730, 3295
  President's Personal File 4193, Edwin Watson
  President's Personal File 5418, Mary T. Norton
  President's Secretary's File, Container 140, Congress
Robert Wagner MSS, Georgetown University Library, Washington, D.C.

MEMOIRS, REMINISCENCES

Burke, Mrs. Marion McDonagh, Interview with Author, Greenwich, CT, August, 1981.
Burke, Mrs. Marion McDonagh, Letter to Author, February 4, 1980.

Loucheim, Katie, ed., *The Making of the New Deal: The Insiders Speak*. Cambridge, MA: Harvard University Press, 1983.

Norton, Mary T., "Madam Congressman: The Memoirs of Mary T. Norton of New Jersey," Mary T. Norton MSS, New Jersey Collection, Archibald Stevens Alexander Library, Rutgers, The State University of New Jersey, New Brunswick, NJ.

Perkins, Frances, *The Roosevelt I Knew*. New York: Viking, 1946.

U.S. GOVERNMENT PUBLICATIONS

U.S. Congress, *Biographical Directory of the American Congress, 1774–1961*. Washington, D.C.: U.S. Government Printing Office, 1961.

U.S. Congress, *Congressional Record*, 69th–81st Congress, 1925–1951.

U.S. Congress, House of Representatives, Committee on Administration, 80th–81st Congress, *Hearings, Reports*, 1947–1951.

U.S. Congress, House of Representatives, Committee on District of Columbia, 72nd–75th Congress, *Hearings, Reports*, 1931–1937.

U.S. Congress, House of Representatives, Committee on Education and Labor, 80th–81st Congress, *Hearings, Reports*, 1947–1951.

U.S. Congress, House of Representatives, Committee on Labor, 69th–79th Congress, *Hearings, Reports*, 1925–1946.

U.S. Congress, House of Representatives, Special Committee to Investigate the National Labor Relations Board, 76th Congress, *Reports*, 1940.

U.S. Congress, House of Representatives, Statistics of the Congressional and Presidential Elections, November 1924–November 1948.

U.S. Congress, Office of the Historian, House of Representatives, *Women in Congress, 1917–1990*. Washington, D.C.: U.S. Government Printing Office, 1991.

NEWSPAPERS

Atlanta Journal
Bayonne Evening News
Bayonne Times
Chicago Herald
Chicago Tribune
Hudson Dispatch
Jersey City Free Press
Jersey Journal
Jersey City Observer
(Newark) Advocate
Newark Evening News
Newark Star Ledger
Newark Sunday Call
Newark Sunday News
New York Herald-Tribune
New York Post
New York Times
New York World-Telegram
Washington Evening Star

Washington Post
Washington Times-Herald

MAGAZINES

American Heritage
American Mercury
American Political Science Review
Collier's
Congressional Digest
Current Biography
The Delineator
Forum
Independent Women
Ladies Home Journal
Literary Digest
Law and Contemporary Problems
National Education Association Journal
National Municipal Review
New Jersey History
New Republic
Newsweek
Political Science Quarterly
Public Opinion Quarterly
Time
U.S. News
Vital Speeches
Woman's Home Companion
Woman's Voice

ARTICLES AND REPORTS BY MARY T. NORTON

"Arguments in Favor of Fair Employment Practices Bill," *Congressional Digest* 24 (June 1945), pp. 172ff.
"Democracy's Stepchild," *Woman's Home Companion* 71 (August 1944), p. 19.
"Politics is a Business," *Collier's* 89 (May 21, 1932), p. 22.
"Prohibition," *The Jeffersonian* (1932), pp. 4–5.
"Remarks on Anti-Poll Tax Measure," *Congressional Digest* 29 (February 1950), p. 60.
"Should Legal Barriers Against Birth Control Be Removed?" *Congressional Digest* 10 (April 1931), pp. 106–7.
"The War is Not Over," Report, International Labor Organization Conference, Paris, France, October 1945.
Untitled Report, Woman's World Fair, Chicago Coliseum, Chicago, IL, May 24, 1927.

SPEECHES BY MARY T. NORTON

"The Defense of America," Regional Conference of Democratic Women, Los Angeles, CA, September 13, 1941.

"The Defense of the Federal Wage and Hours Law from Attack," National Consumers League, New York City, December 8, 1939.

"Democratic Woman's Part in the World Today," National Broadcasting Company, Washington, D.C., September 27, 1943.

"The 40-Hour Week," National Broadcasting Company, Washington, D.C., April 20, 1942.

"Home Rule and Reorganization of the District of Columbia," Washington, D.C., undated.

"Selective Service," Washington, D.C., August 22, 1941.

Untitled Radio Speech, *Herald-Tribune* Forum, New York City, October 5, 1937.

Untitled Radio Speech, WOR Forum, New York City, May 15, 1938.

Untitled Speech, Baltimore Press Club, Baltimore, MD, March 1, 1927.

Untitled Speech, New Jersey CIO Convention, December 6, 1947.

"The Wage and Hour Bill," National Broadcasting Company, Washington, D.C., August 9, 1937.

"The Wage and Hour Bill," Washington, D.C., October 19, 1938.

"Wage and Hour Legislation: Object of the Law," *Vital Speeches* 4 (June 1, 1938), pp. 485–486.

"We Must Hold Our Ground," *Newsweek* Symposium on the Role Women Play in Business and Industry," New York City, 1943.

"Why Should Women Be Interested in Government?" Radio Address, Columbia Broadcasting System, Washington, D.C., May 5, 1932.

UNPUBLISHED MATERIALS

Bogucki, Angeline, "Summary of the Legislative Career of Representative Mary T. Norton," Legislative Reference Service, Library of Congress, Washington, D.C., November 3, 1950.

Democratic National Committee, Press Release, New York City, August 31, 1928.

Dodyk, Delight W., "Education and Agitation: The Woman Suffrage Movement in New Jersey," Ph.D. dissertation: Rutgers, The State University of New Jersey, 1997.

Geer, Emily A., "A Study of the Activities of Women in Congress with Special Reference to the Congressional Careers of Margaret Chase Smith, Mary T. Norton, and Edith Nourse Rogers," Masters thesis: Bowling Green State University, 1952.

Lovero, Joan, "Life of Mary Norton," Jersey City Public Library, Jersey City, NJ.

RBC, Associated Press Release, Washington, D.C., January 1951.

Tobin, Mary, Untitled Press Release, Woman's Division, Democratic National Committee, May 24, 1948.

Tomlinson, Barbara, "Making Their Way: A Study of New Jersey Congresswomen 1924–1994," Ph.D. dissertation: Rutgers, The State University of New Jersey, 1996.

BOOKS

Allswang, John M., *The New Deal and American Politics: A Study in Political Change*. New York: John Wiley & Sons, 1978.

Badger, Anthony J., *The New Deal: The Depression Years, 1933–1940*. New York: Hill and Wang, 1989.

Bernstein, Irving, *A Caring Society: The New Deal, the Worker, and the Great Depression*. Boston, MA: Houghton Mifflin, 1985.

Bernstein, Irving, *The Turbulent Years: A History of the American Worker, 1933–1941.* Boston, MA: Houghton Mifflin, 1969.

Brody, David, *Workers in Industrial America.* New York: Oxford University Press, 1980.

Burns, James MacGregor, *Congress on Trial.* New York: Harper, 1949.

Burns, James MacGregor, *Roosevelt: The Lion and the Fox.* New York: Harcourt, Brace & World, 1956.

Burstyn, Joan N., ed., *Past and Present: Lives of New Jersey Women.* Syracuse, NY: Syracuse University Press, 1997.

Campbell, Christiana M., *The Farm Bureau and the New Deal.* Urbana, IL: University of Illinois Press, 1962.

Caro, Robert A., *The Years of Lyndon Johnson: Means of Ascent.* New York: Alfred A. Knopf, 1990.

Chafe, William H., *The American Woman: Her Changing Social, Economic, and Political Roles, 1920–1970.* New York: Oxford University Press, 1972.

Chafe, William H., *The Paradox of Change: American Women in the 20th Century.* New York: Oxford University Press, 1991.

Chamberlin, Hope, *A Minority of Members: Women in the U.S. Congress.* New York: Praeger Publishers, 1973.

Chapman, Richard N., *Contours of Public Policy, 1939–1945.* New York: Garland Publishing, 1981.

Cole, Wayne, *Roosevelt and the Isolationists.* Lincoln, NE: University of Nebraska Press, 1983.

Connors, Richard, *A Cycle of Power: The Career of Jersey City Mayor Frank Hague.* Metuchen, NJ: Scarecrow Press, 1971.

Dallek, Robert, *Lone Star Rising: Lyndon Johnson and His Times, 1908–1960.* New York: Oxford University Press, 1991.

Divine, Robert A., *The Illusion of Neutrality.* Chicago, IL: University of Chicago Press, 1962.

Engelbarts, Rudolf, *Women in the United States Congress, 1917–1972: Their Accomplishments with Bibliographies.* Littleton, CO: Libraries Unlimited, 1974.

Faber, Doris, *The Life of Lorena Hickok: E. R.'s Friend.* New York: William Morrow & Company, 1980.

Fauntroy, Michael K., *Home Rule or House Rule; Congress and the Erosion of Local Governance in the District of Columbia.* Lanham, MD: University Press of America, 2003.

Foner, Phillip, *Women and the American Labor Movement from World War I to the Present.* New York: The Free Press, 1980.

Freidel, Frank, *F.D.R. and the South.* Baton Rouge, LA: Louisiana State University Press, 1994.

Gertzog, Irwin, *Congressional Women: Their Recruitment, Treatment and Behavior.* New York: Praeger Publishers, 1984.

Gitterman, Daniel Paul, *Boosting Paychecks: The Politics of Supporting America's Working Poor.* Washington, D.C.: Brookings Institution, 2009.

Goldman, Eric, *Rendezvous with Destiny.* New York: Alfred A. Knopf, 1952.

Goodwin, Doris Kearns, *No Ordinary Time: Franklin and Eleanor Roosevelt: The Home Front in World War II.* New York: Simon and Schuster, 1994.

Gordon, Felice, *After Winning: The Legacy of the New Jersey Suffragists, 1920–1947.* New Brunswick, NJ: Rutgers University Press, 1986.

Graham, Otis L., Jr. and Meghan Robinson Wander, eds., *Franklin D. Roosevelt: His Life and Times: An Encyclopedic View.* Boston, MA: G. K. Hall & Company, 1985.

Hamby, Alonzo, *Beyond the New Deal: Harry S. Truman and American Liberalism.* New York: Columbia University Press, 1973.

Hamilton, Virginia Vander Veer, *Hugo Black: The Alabama Years.* Baton Rouge, LA: Louisiana State University Press, 1972.

Harrison, Cynthia, *On Account of Sex: The Politics of Women's Issues, 1945–1968.* Berkeley, CA: University of California Press, 1988.

Hartmann, Susan M., *Truman and the 80th Congress*. Columbia, MO: University of Missouri Press, 1971.

Huthmacher, J. Joseph, *Senator Robert F. Wagner and the Rise of Urban Liberalism*. New York: Atheneum, 1968.

Kaptur, Marcy, *Woman of Congress: A Twentieth Century Odyssey*. Washington, D.C.: Congressional Quarterly, 1996.

Karnoutsos, Carmela Ascolese, *New Jersey Women: A History of Their Status, Roles, and Images*. Trenton, NJ: New Jersey Historical Commission, 1997.

Kennedy, David M., *Freedom from Fear: The American People in Depression and War, 1929–1945*. New York: Oxford University Press, 1999.

Kessler-Harris, Alice, *Out to Work: A History of Wage-Earning Women in the United States*. New York: Oxford University Press, 1982.

Kirkendall, Richard S., ed., *The Harry S. Truman Encyclopedia*. Boston, MA: G. K. Hall & Company, 1989.

Kyvig, David E., *Repealing National Prohibition*. Chicago, IL: University of Chicago Press, 1979.

Lash, Joseph, *Dealers and Dreamers: A New Look at the New Deal*. New York: Doubleday & Company, 1988.

Leach, Bob, *The Frank Hague Picture Book*. Jersey City, NJ: Jersey City Historical Project, 1998.

Lee, R. Alton, *Truman and Taft-Hartley: A Question of Mandate*. Lexington, KY: University of Kentucky Press, 1966.

Leuchtenburg, William, *Franklin D. Roosevelt and the New Deal 1932–1940*. New York: Harper & Row, 1963.

Levine, Edward M., *The Irish and Irish Politicians*. Notre Dame, IN: University of Notre Dame Press, 1966.

Martin, Ralph G., *The Bosses*. New York: G. P. Putnam's Sons, 1964.

McCullough, David, *Truman*. New York: Simon & Schuster, 1992.

McJimsey, George, *The Presidency of Franklin Delano Roosevelt*. Lawrence, KS: University Press of Kansas, 2000.

McKean, Dayton, *The Boss: The Hague Machine in Action*. Boston, MA: Houghton-Mifflin, 1940.

Millis, Harry A. and Emily Clark Brown, *From the Wagner Act to Taft-Hartley: A Study of National Labor Policy and Labor Relations*. Chicago, IL: University of Chicago Press, 1950.

Muir, Malcolm, Jr., ed., *The Human Tradition in the World War II Era*. Wilmington, DE: Scholarly Resources Books, 2001.

Parrish, Michael. *Anxious Decades: The United States, 1920–1941*. New York: W. W. Norton, 1994.

Patterson, James T., *Congressional Conservatism and the New Deal*. Lexington, KY: University of Kentucky Press, 1967.

Paxton, Annabel, *Women in Congress*. Richmond, VA: The Dietz Press, 1945.

Polenberg, Richard, *War and Society: The United States, 1941–1945*. Philadelphia, PA: J. B. Lippincott, 1972.

Porter, David L., *Congress and the Waning of the New Deal*. Port Washington, NY: Kennikat Press, 1980.

Porter, David L., *The Seventy-sixth Congress and the World War II*. Columbia, MO: University of Missouri Press, 1979.

Read, Phyllis and Bernard L. Witlieb, *The Book of Women's Firsts*. New York: Random House, 1992.

Roediger, David R. and Philip S. Foner, *Our Own Time: A History of American Labor and the Working Day*. Westport, CT: Greenwood Press, 1989.

Roosevelt, Eleanor and Lorena Hickok, *Ladies of Courage*. New York: E. P. Putnam, 1954.

Rosenburg, Rosalind, *Divided Lives: American Women in the Twentieth Century*. New York: Hill and Wang, 1992.

Rosenman, Samuel I., ed., *The Public Papers and Addresses of Franklin D. Roosevelt*, 13 vols. New York: Macmillan, 1938–1950.

Ross, Irwin, *The Loneliest Campaign: The Truman Victory in 1948*. New York: New American Library, 1968.

Salter, Joseph, *Boss Rule*. New York: McGraw-Hill, 1935.

Salter, Joseph, ed., *Public Men In and Out of Office*. Chapel Hill, NC: University of North Carolina Press, 1946.

Schlesinger, Arthur M., Jr., *The Age of Roosevelt*, 3 vols. Boston, MA: Houghton Mifflin Company, 1957–1960.

Schwarz, Jordan A., *The Interregnum of Despair: Hoover, Congress, and the Depression*. Urbana, IL: University of Illinois Press, 1970.

Steinberg, Alfred, *The Bosses*. New York: Macmillan Publishing Company, 1972.

Steiner, Gilbert Y., *The Congressional Committee: Seventieth to Eightieth Congresses*. Urbana, IL: University of Illinois Press, 1951.

Stelhorn, Paul A. and Michael J. Belkner, eds., *The Governors of New Jersey, 1664–1974*. Trenton: NJ: New Jersey Historical Commission, 1982.

Tobin, Kathleen A., *The American Religious Debate over Birth Control, 1907–1937*. Jefferson, NC: McFarland & Company, 2001.

Troy, Leo, *Organized Labor in New Jersey*. Princeton, NJ: Van Nostrand, 1965.

Tygiel, Jules, *Baseball's Great Experiment: Jackie Robinson and His Legacy*. New York: Oxford University Press, 2000.

Vanderbilt, Arthur T. II, *Changing Law: A Biography of Arthur T. Vanderbilt*. New Brunswick, NJ: Rutgers University Press, 1976.

Vernon, Leonard F., *Images of America: Jersey City Medical Center*. Portsmouth, NH: Arcadia Publishing, 2004.

Young, Roland A., *Congressional Politics in the Second World War*. New York: Columbia University Press, 1956.

ARTICLES

Alexander, Jack, "King Hanky-Panky of Jersey City," *The Saturday Evening Post* 26 (October 1940), pp. 9–11, 119, 121–24.

Altman, O. R., "Second and Third Sessions of the Seventy-fifth Congress, 1937–38," *American Political Science Review* 32 (December 1938), pp. 1099–1123.

Anthony, Susan Brownwell, 2nd, "Woman's Next Step: Interview," *New York Times Magazine* (January 12, 1941), pp. 11ff.

"Aunt Mary's Applecart," *Time* 31 (May 16, 1938), pp. 14–15.

Bamberger, "A Congresswoman from New Jersey," *The Charm* (March 1926), pp. 27–28.

Black, Ruby A., "Women in Two Big Labor Posts," *Independent Woman* 16 (July 1937), pp. 200ff.

Borsky, Frank, "Part of an Era Will Fall with Roosevelt Stadium," *New York Times*, July 1, 1984.

Bruner, Jerome S., and Sheldon J. Korchin, "The Boss and the Vote," *Public Opinion Quarterly* 10 (Spring 1946), pp. 1–23.

Camp, Helen C., "Mary Teresa Hopkins Norton," *American National Biography*, Vol. 16 (New York: Oxford University Press, 1999), pp. 529–30.

Chambers, John Whiteclay, II, "Mary Teresa Hopkins Norton," *Dictionary of American Biography*, Supp. Six, 1956–1960 (New York: Charles Scribner's Sons, 1980), pp. 479–81.

Choen, Robert, "Jersey City's 'Fighting Mary' Reclaims Place of Honor," *Newark Star-Ledger*, March 19, 2004.

"A Congress to Win the War," *New Republic* 106 (May 18, 1942), pp. 700–3.

"Congresswoman Who Learned from a Master," *Newsweek* 19 (June 26, 1937), pp. 17–18.

Cowan, Ruth, "Snappy Title Needed for Mrs. Norton's Life," *Jersey Journal*, January 14, 1952, p. 3.

Crawford, Kenneth G., "Assault on the NLRB," *Nation* 149 (December 30, 1939), pp. 726–27.

Davies, John O., "Frank Hague: Last of the Bosses," *Newark Evening News* and *Newark Sunday News*, July 17–September 2, 1949.

Davis, Maxine, "Five Democratic Women," *Ladies Home Journal* 50 (May 1933), pp. 22, 117.

Denlinger, Sutherland, "Boss Hague," *Forum* 99 (March 1938), pp. 131–37.

Douglas, Paul, and Joseph Hackman, "The Fair Labor Standards Act of 1938 I," *Political Science Quarterly* 53 (December 1938), pp. 491–515.

Douglas, Paul, and Joseph Hackman, "The Fair Labor Standards Act of 1938 II," *Political Science Quarterly* 54 (March 1939), pp. 29–55.

Feyerherm, Miriam, "Alice Paul: New Jersey's Quintessential Suffragist," *New Jersey History* 111 (1993), pp. 18–39.

Fleming, Thomas, "I Am the Law," *American Heritage* XX (June 1969), pp. 32–48.

Forsythe, J. S., "Legislative History of the Fair Labor Standards Act," *Law and Contemporary Problems* 6 (1939), pp. 464–90.

Foster, Mark S., "Frank Hague of Jersey City: 'The Boss' as Reformer," *New Jersey History* 86 (Summer 1968), pp. 106–17.

Gayle, Margot, "Battling Mary Retires," *Independent Woman* 29 (July 1950), pp. 198–200.

Gilfond, Duff, "Gentlewoman of the House," *American Mercury* 18 (October 1929), pp. 151–60.

"Jackie Robinson Made History Here First," *Jersey Journal*, April 13, 2007.

Karnoutsos, Carmela Ascolese, "Mary Teresa Norton, 1875–1959," in Joan N. Burstyn, ed., *Past and Promise: Lives of New Jersey Women*. (Syracuse, NY: Syracuse University Press, 1997), pp. 368–70.

Kempfer, Katherine and Dorothea K. Blender, "Our Congresswomen in Action," *Women's Lawyers Journal* 33 (Summer 1947), p. 204.

Keyes, Frances Parkinson, "Truly Democratic," *The Delineator* 122 (March 1933), pp. 12ff.

"Labor: Absent Without Leave," *Time* 61 (January 11, 1943).

Lewis, Dorothy M., "The Listening Post/More Federal Aid for Mothers and Children," *Educational Leadership* 4 (December 1946), p. 203.

Longworth, Alice Roosevelt, "What Are the Women Up To?" *Ladies Home Journal* 51 (March 1934), pp. 9ff.

Lovero, Joan, "New Jersey City's Mary Norton Blazed a Path for Women in Washington," *Hudson County Magazine* (Spring 1991), p. 28.

Lynch, Denis Tilden, "Her Honor, the Mayor of Washington," *Literary Digest* 119 (March 30, 1935), p. 24.

Martin, Antoinette Martin, "A New Lease on Life for Jersey City Complex," *New York Times*, February 27, 2005.

"Mary T. Norton," *Current Biography* 5 (1944), pp. 500–503.

"Mary T. Norton," *Ladies Home Journal* 4 (May 1933), p. 22.

"Mary Teresa Norton," *U.S. News* 9 (May 10, 1940), p. 37.

Meagher, Helen, "Notes of Interview with Mary T. Norton," *Woman's Voice* (March 26, 1931), 5 pp.

Mitchell, Gary, "Women Standing for Women: The Early Political Career of Mary T. Norton," *New Jersey History* 96 (Spring-Summer 1979), pp. 27–42.

"National Affairs: Roast Chicken," *Time* 26 (August 23. 1937).

Newsweek 15 (June 17, 1940), pp. 67–68.

Porter, Amy, "Ladies of Congress," *Collier's* 112 (August 28, 1943), pp. 22–23.

Rees, Maureen, "Mary Norton: A 'Grand Girl,'" *The Journal of the Rutgers University Libraries* 47 (December 1985), pp. 59–75.

Richter, Irving, "Four Years of the Fair Labor Standards Act of 1938," *Journal of Political Economy* 51 (1943), pp. 95–111.

Shannon, J. B., "Presidential Politics in the South," in Taylor Cole and John H. Hallowell, eds., *The Southern Political Scene, 1938–1948*. Gainesville, FL: University of Florida Press, 1948.

Smith, E. E., "Frank Hague: Mayor-Boss of Jersey City," *National Municipal Review* 17 (September 1928), pp. 514–21.

Strauss, Sylvia, "The Passage of Woman Suffrage in New Jersey, 1911–1920," *New Jersey History* 111 (1993), pp. 18–39.

Time 35 (March 25, 1940), pp. 21–22.

Tomlinson, Barbara, "Making Her Way: The Career of Congresswoman Florence E. Dwyer," *New Jersey History* 112 (1994), pp. 40–77.

U.S. News 30 (March 30, 1951), p. 44

Wittels, David, "The Hague Machine," *New York Post*, January 17–February 14, 1938; May 6–May 17, 1938.

"Women in Congress," *National Education Association Journal* 38 (April 1949), p. 283. WEB Publications

INTERNET PUBLICATIONS

"Alfred Sieminski," http://www.politikernj.com

The American Presidency Project, Franklin D. Roosevelt, Radio Address. Foreign Policy Association, New York City, October 21, 1944, http://www.presidency.ucsb.edu

The American Presidency Project, Harry S. Truman, "Special Message to the Congress Presenting a 21-Point Program for the Reconversion Period," September 6, 1945, http://www.presidency.ucsb.edu

Congressional Research Service, *Women in the United States Congress: 1917–2011*, March 20, 2011, http://www.crs.gov

DeLaurio, Rosa L., Press Release, June 25, 2008, http://www.delaurio.house.gov

Featured House Publications, *Women in Congress, 1917–2006*, 108th Cong., 1st sess., H. Doc. 108–223, http://www.gpo.gov

Karnoutsos, Carmela, "Frank Hague, 1876–1956," *Jersey City Past and Present Home Page*, New Jersey State Historical Commission, http://www.njcu.edu

Karnoutsos, Carmela, "Margaret Hague Maternity Hospital," *Jersey City Past and Present Home Page*, New Jersey State Historical Commission, http://www.njcu.edu

Karnoutsos, Carmela, "Mary Teresa Norton, 1875–1959," *Jersey City Past and Present Home Page*, New Jersey State Historical Commission, http://www.njcu.edu

Karnoutsos, Carmela, "Medical Center Complex," *Jersey City Past and Present Home Page*, New Jersey State Historical Commission, http://www.njcu.edu

Karnoutsos, Carmela, "Roosevelt Stadium," *Jersey City Past and Present Home Page*, New Jersey State Historical Commission, http://www.ncu.edu

Kutlin, Lisa, "Congresswoman Mary T. Norton: Matriarch of the Living Wage," Georgetown Law Library, Gender and Legal History MSS, 2004, http://www.11.georgetown.edu "Mary T. Norton, 1875–1959," http://womenincongress.house.gov

McGrory, Mary, "They'll Miss the Back of Mary's Hand," *Washington Star*, March 1951.

Nancy Pelosi, Press Release, "Pelosi Remarks on Portrait Unveiling of Former Congresswoman Mary T. Norton," March 18, 2004, http://pelosi.house.gov

Office of the Clerk, U.S. House of Representatives, "The Fair Labor Standards Act," http://www.artandhistory.house.gov

"Our Campaigns, "NJ – District 13 – History," http://www.ourcampaigns.com

Priest, Ivy Baker, and Eliza Jane Pratt, "Women Elected to Public Offices," http://www.maxizip.com

"Troubled passage: the labor movement and the Fair Labor Standards Act," http://www.thefreelibrary.com

Wiltanger, Christine, "Remember the Ladies," The Official Jersey City Web Site, http://www.cityofjerseycity.com

"Women Pioneers on Capitol Hill, 1917–1934," http://womenincongress.house.gov

Women's History Museum, "Women Wielding Power: Pioneer Female State Legislators: New Jersey," http://www.nwhm.org

WEB SITES

www.artandhistory.house.gov
www.cityofjerseycity.com
www.crs.gov
www.delauro.house.gov
www.thefreelibrary.com
www.govtrack.us/congress/vote
www.gpo.gov
www.house.gov
www.maxizip.com
www.njcu.edu
www.nwhm.org
www.ourcampaigns.com
www.pelosi.house.gov
www.politickernj.com
www.presidency.ucbs.edu
www.ll.georgetown.edu
www.time.com
www.womenincongress.house.gov

Index

Index

About the Author

David L. Porter is Louis Tuttle Shangle Professor of History at William Penn University, where he has taught since 1977. He has a B.A. degree in history from Franklin College of Indiana, an M.A. in history from Ohio University, and a Ph.D in history from Pennsylvania State University. Porter has authored or edited numerous books and articles on the U.S. Congress and sport history and specializes in U.S. biography. His books include *The Seventy-sixth Congress and World War II, 1939–1940* (1979), *Congress and the Waning of the New Deal* (1980), the *Biographical Dictionary of American Sports* series (10 volumes, 1987–2005), *African American Sports Greats* (1995), *The San Diego Padres Encyclopedia* (2002), *Latino and African American Athletes Today: A Biographical Dictionary* (2004), *Michael Jordan: A Biography* (2007), and *Their Greatest Victory: Athletes Who Overcame Illness and Injury* (in press). Porter also writes a weekly sports column for the *Oskaloosa Herald*. He and his wife, Marilyn, live in Oskaloosa, Iowa, and have two grown children and three grandchildren.